THE ISRAELIS

The Israelis

PROFILE OF A PEOPLE

by RUTH BONDY

Translated from the Hebrew by Israel I. Taslitt

SABRA BOOKS
FUNK AND WAGNALLS
NEW YORK

SBN 87631–007
LIBRARY OF CONGRESS CATALOG CARD NUMBER 69–19436
PRINTED IN ISRAEL BY E. LEWIN-EPSTEIN LTD., BAT YAM
COPYRIGHT © 1969 AMERICAN-ISRAEL PUBLISHING CO., LTD.

Contents

Prologue

IT IS SHEER *chutzpah* to talk about *The Israelis* as if they all came off the same assembly line. A more accurate title for this book might have been *Some Traits, Qualities, Habits and Peculiarities Seemingly Characteristic of the Israelis of the Late Nineteensixties*, as seen through the eyes of one Israeli by choice, Jewish by birth, central European by background, female by gender, journalist by profession.

For no Israeli—not even the most objectively detached sociologist—is capable of writing a book about his countrymen without involving his own likes and prejudices; I have not even tried to do so. Mine is an unashamedly biased book, and only innate modesty has dissuaded me from calling it: *I, the Israeli—Plus All the Others*. The Israelis would emerge looking quite different if the writer were an expert on zoology, or a pious scholar, or a twenty-year-old with a mustache to match. So much for objectivity.

As for wall-to-wall coverage of the subject: the topics omitted in *The Israelis* would in themselves easily fill another volume. In this book there are chapters about Israelis of German and Rumanian origin, about old-timers from Russia and newcomers from the United States—but what about all the others: Bulgarian Jews, Kurdistans, Jews from Argentina? Well, there is a superabundance of them: the Israeli individual, so-called, is a composite of 70 communities, and the reader will be thankful I did not exhaust the subject. In this, I was guided by the basic principle of the modern museum curator: no walls crammed from floor to ceiling; just a few selected paintings with ample breathing space on all sides. Like snapshots from the family album, the topics I did select tend to capture the mood of a people at a precise moment, and to record that moment before it fades into history.

7

Writing about the Israeli way of life is like scribbling in the wet sand of Herzliya Beach: no sooner did you etch "I LOVE YOU" and circumscribe it with a perfect heart and up comes a huge wave—and the sand becomes as pristine as ever. Today's venturesome forecasts are tomorrow's facts-taken-for-granted; wishful thinking becomes reality, reality moves on to confrontation. In these times, ways of life tend to change quickly, everywhere, but here in Israel the pace far outstrips the writing. And since the chapters in this book were written over a period of more than two years, with a war thrown in for good measure, things have moved on quite a bit from the day that the typewriter pounded out the last lines. But such is the Israeli preoccupation of chasing Time.

Life in Israel may seem from a distance to be one unremitting armed struggle. But international news, with its thirst for the dramatic, is misleading: for most of the people, most of the time, life as lived in Israel is just living: crowding into buses, seeking extra income, battling red tape, loafing in the sun, yelling at the children. It is only our awareness that all these, and everything else, *cannot* be taken for granted, that they are a gift which could disappear at any time—this is what sets life in Israel apart from the way of life in any Western-oriented or westernized-Oriental country.

My love affair with Israel is now in its twentieth year. It is no longer a naive infatuation but a sense of common fate, of lifelong partnership, with all the tolerance that such relationship demands. We who became Israelis after having been something else never cease appreciating the privilege of having a home, a country, a state, of living in this particular area and at this specific juncture of history, a history to which the Israelis relate first and foremost as Jews, obsessed with the quest for survival as the key to continuity. For when all is said and done, this is our sole reason for being here—to make sure that the Jewish people lives on. It may sound presumptuous, but we simply cannot imagine the world without us.

R.B.

Homo Judaeus

An Immigrant: Once and Always

AN IMMIGRANT, whether a recent arrival or of older vintage, remains an immigrant. Somehow his true identity tends to reveal itself, even after a decade or two in the country.

The meaning of the term itself varies quite a bit: to the Sick Insurance Fund you are an immigrant for 90 days (thereafter your privileges cease); to the Jewish Agency—one year; to Customs—three years; to your children—all your life. The very fact that you have ties with a remote locality called "diaspora," peopled by Jews in long coats and fur-trimmed hats, addicted to *gefilte fish* and *cholent* and pursued by the Czar's minions with whip in hand—this in itself reduces the worth of your paternity. It makes no difference whether this particular diaspora of yours consisted of the gilded spires of Prague's churches or the band in the Municipal Gardens playing "The Blue Danube" or a kayak gliding down the mountain stream between forests of spruce. Children of foreign-born parents suffer this stigma in silence, as being something they have to live with. At times, in the afterglow of a birthday party or the thrill of a Chanukah gift, they are ready to forgive them. If only the parents were proficient in the Bible, or knew more about the writings of Feierberg or Frishman or the other great figures of Hebrew literature, and would not stand suddenly revealed in their shortcomings, in front of schoolmates or neighbors, in a ridiculous accent, an error in grammar, an alien expression, an irritating foreign phrase of endearment.

There are parents who do get to be like Israelis. Their Hebrew is impeccable; there is hardly any trace of an accent; their dress is strictly Israeli. But they fail the supreme test: the Pumpkin Seed. They take a seed, split its outer coating with a finger nail,

11

extract the seed with two fingers of the right hand and pop it into their mouth, as though it were a chocolate drop. Seed-splitting is not taught at any *ulpan;* whosoever didn't get the knack, in his formative years, of separating seed from shell, prying out the former with his tongue and spitting out the latter with the same motion, without using his fingers, is beyond the help of the Ministry of Absorption.

Fluency in Hebrew does not annul the immigrant classification. We have old-timers, fifty years in this land, who still read a book only if it is in Russian. There are new immigrants, on the other hand, who know Hebrew from the days of their youth in Munkatch or Baranowicz, and are familiar with idioms of which no native Israeli has ever heard. Nevertheless, an old-timer is an old-timer and an immigrant is an immigrant, and there is no margin for error. So long as you are not at home with profanity in Arabic and do not know your way around curses in Russian nor are familiar with the names of engine parts in English and cannot tell anecdotes in Yiddish, you simply are not acquainted with Israeli Hebrew.

In the first glow of his sojourn, the new immigrant may decide that he would fare better speaking a miserably stuttering Hebrew rather than his mother tongue, as a sign to the local citizens that he wants to be one of them. Too late does he realize that nothing can make him look more pathetic than this attempt to master the speech of the natives. If you continue speaking your native tongue (particularly if it happens to be one used by the cultured set— English, French or German—and not the second-class Rumanian or Polish) and insist that you be understood, then you put the others on the defensive, but the moment you begin to apologize ("not know Hebrew good, but wants to learning"), you are through; your prestige plummets. You are a pigmy, forcing others to speak to you as to a witless child.

It is not the Hebrew language that converts the immigrant into an old-timer. Bathsheba de Rothschild can go on speaking English as long as she wants to and no one will regard her as an immigrant. Dr. George Wise, President of Tel Aviv University, never was regarded as an immigrant nor will he ever be; everybody knows he is a millionaire and can get along without the State of Israel. A real immigrant is one for whom there are no two ways about it.

One hears that Israel must have immigrants, but inasmuch as it cannot talk, let the Israelis do the talking. And this is clear: we are so taken up with things that we wouldn't miss them. They may be just the thing for new settlements and for development areas, far from the social mainstream, but they are an awful bother as soon as they enter our daily lives as relatives, friends, relatives of friends or friends of relatives. It's all right to invite them once, on some Sabbath afternoon, for coffee; this is still bearable. We may even offer them some practical advice, assure them that now they are better off, give them a few addresses to look up, but we draw the line when we feel that we are expected to bear the responsibility for their coming. Did we beg them to come? They must have had their own good reasons. What's more, they have their own institutions to worry about them: the Jewish Agency, Malben, Youth Aliya, the Housing Ministry, the Absorption Ministry, where people are being paid salaries to do it. Immigration today is a vocation, like textiles or philately: it is certainly not for the average Israeli to worry about.

The relationship between the old-timer and the newcomer, if any, is one of envy. The old-timer is envious as he recalls how many of his best years went by before he could own all those things that immigrants now get as a matter of policy: a home, a job, furniture, schooling. The immigrant is envious of the old-timer's contentment, self-assurance and air of superiority. And nothing will bring them closer to each other except the advent of a still more recent newcomer, one with even more privileges. That's our national merry-go-round: the community which had been existing on dole looked askance at the *Bilu* pioneers of eight decades ago; the *Bilu* people did not go out of their way to aid the Second Aliya group; the Second Aliya looked down its collective nose at the Third, and the latter derided the Grabski immigration from Poland, which in turn sneered at the refugees from Germany, who were not greatly enthused about the survivors of the concentration camps, who in turn had nothing good to say about the Moroccans, who jeered at the Rumanians, who cannot get together with the South Americans. All the world loves a lover, but no one loves an immigrant.

The situation reminds one of those army sergeants who make the lives of privates as miserable as their own had been, on the theory that, in the end, no one gets hurt. We, immigrants of yore, do not approve of this pampering of new arrivals, particularly those who come from "affluent" countries, as the Jewish Agency calls them. How can we be expected to sympathize with the immigrants when they complain that there is no high school in Dimona or that it's too far from the Jessie Cohen Project to their place of employment in Ramat Gan or that the import duty on their car is too high, when we can still remember the tents and the transit camps and joblessness and abandoned Arab huts without water and electricity, plus the Jewish Agency stipend of all of two Pounds. But the suffering of those days cannot be empathized. An immigrant from Argentina will lose nothing of his irritation, as he queues up at the bus stop, if we were to tell him that *we* didn't even have the fare, and had to make the trip from Tel Aviv to Tel Litwinski on foot. The first years in this country are tough and difficult, now as ever, and each is inclined to bear his burden as though he were the first immigrant.

Today, fortunately, you can live in Haifa or Tel Aviv or Ramat Gan till you're one hundred and not run into any immigrants from the depressed countries, particularly if you don't travel by bus and are not serving in the army. At times, on the deck of a ship returning to Israel from foreign ports, or at the airport where you are seeing friends off, you catch a glimpse of them—laden with parcels, dressed in clothing too dark and too heavy, flustered, excited, suspicious, insecure, eager to start a conversation that may validate their decision to come to Israel, and suddenly they are swallowed up in the confusion and re-appear beyond your horizon, elsewhere on the map.

You may see them—but you're under no obligation to pay them any attention—as you stroll along the seafront on the Sabbath, or at a soccer game, at a memorial meeting arranged by the *landsmanschaft* or at a performance (in Yiddish) of "Lovely Like Luna." You identify them, especially the East Europeans, by their clothes: the men's trousers much too baggy, the jackets over-padded at the shoulders, thickly-knotted striped ties and hats set down squarely on the forehead. The women wear their eyebrows thin, use purplish lipstick, wear fur-trimmed winter coats and long strands of pearls. The air of the diaspora is even more marked on the holidays. The weekday work clothes, cheap and common to all, give way to the Sabbath best, in which they try to recapture the dreams of their youth, to look like Greta Garbo or Rita Hayworth, like the squire of the town or the governor of the province.

On the Sabbath, too, immigrants tend to be more conspicuous than on weekdays, when they are cloistered in their work locales, squeezed in among bus riders, invisible in the dark of the movie houses. The pressures keep their minds occupied. On the Sabbath, every Israeli is more vulnerable; it is then that he gives way to his foibles, his loneliness, or his closeness to the family. On weekdays a man is what the realities of life force him to be, but on the Sabbath he strives to be the person he would like to be, and this is much more difficult.

The first years you live in an illusion: as soon as you learn Hebrew and speak in the vernacular, dress like the rest of them and move into a nicely-furnished apartment in a good neighborhood, no one will detect the odor of the diaspora. In time you come to realize that you will always remain an outsider, to the very people you try to imitate. The tone of your laughter, a misspelled word, your pronunciation of a foreign name, the language you use in counting, or the expression on your face when someone asks, "Do you remember the siege of Yagur?" or remarks, "Well, you wouldn't know about MacMichael."

The process is affected by where you live and whom you are trying to imitate. In Dimona you can get to be an old-timer much faster than in Gedera, in Kibbutz Gonen much faster than in Tel Yosef, in the Foreign Ministry service much faster than in the Ministry of Education, among charwomen much faster than among actresses. Every newcomer yearns to be mistaken for an old-timer; the old-timer likes to live like the Establishment, and the latter tries to be taken for the international elite. In one direction progress is from the diaspora to sovereignty, and in the other it's from the provincial to the cosmopolitan.

One area in which the product of the diaspora differs from the Israeli is the concept of Zionism. As long as the neo-immigrant gives voice to such Zionistic declarations as "I want to make myself useful to Israel's social order" or "I am happy to be on Israel's soil," and as long as his attitude toward the State of Israel is impregnated with emotion; as long as he is able to say "Zionism" and be serious about it; as long as he treasures the folder of documents and letters attesting to his fruitful activity on behalf of the Keren Hayesod, the Jewish National Fund or WIZO; as long as he goes around believing that someone will be thankful to him for all this—that's how long he will bear the imprint of neo-immigration. The Israeli views a long period of Zionist activity with a more jaundiced eye than he looks at assimilation: "If you've been such a devoted Zionist for so long, how come that you waited until now to make your *aliya?*"

The postman can tell at a glance who belongs to the immigrant category and who is a true native. A flow of mail from abroad, air mail envelopes emblazoned with large stamps of athletes or animals, Hebrew words in Latin script, parcels of newspapers wrapped in heavy brown paper—all these are proof that the recipient still has some roots abroad: love, sentiment, memories. An Israeli doesn't correspond with many people abroad; some chance non-Jewish acquaintance, perhaps, or a colleague in the profession.

You are still an immigrant if you look to the absorption agencies for self-betterment, if the Jewish Agency is still playing some role in your life, if you still make demands on public institutions, if you still depend on a letter of recommendation to get you anywhere, if you still think a promise is a commitment, if you still try to get things through pull. But when people come to you for favors, then you are indeed headed in the right direction, toward the wonderful world of the old-timer.

And there are other dead give-aways: if you allow sentiment to draw you to Polish films or to performances by a visiting Rumanian troupe; if you hum along with a Lehar melody on the radio or when Richard Tauber sings; if you attend "La Boheme" at the Israel Opera, or if you take part in a gathering of your former townspeople.

The diaspora is admissible in one area only: food. More than that, it is desirable. You must be careful to have an Israeli home: formica and teakwood all over (the family album, which inevitably reveals your immigration calendar, should be locked in a bedroom drawer). But no old-timer will voice a syllable of criticism if you serve him fish Sephardi style, apricot popovers, *kuskus* or *kolbiak* or any other exotic dish which may not be particularly Israeli.

You may even go so far as to say: "This is how we cooked back home," but don't belabor the subject. His memories about little Tel Aviv and the expulsion from Jaffa during the reign of the Turks or trips to Jericho and Baal-Bek are of historical value and significance, whereas your memories about the King of Yugoslavia or early years spent in the Carpathians, a snowbound hamlet or gathering mushrooms in a birch forest, these are simply personal recollections which you'd do well to keep to yourself and your townspeople. Let your motto be: "In thy tent, an immigrant be; when thou goest forth, an Israeli."

At celebrations—Bar Mitzvah parties and weddings, birthdays and circumcision rites—a person's origins and his measure of progress become immediately apparent. Uncles and aunts, former neighbors, townspeople, the oldsters represent the background of the family. On the other hand, the ceremonials at the celebration, the party attire of the assembled, the banquet hall and the menu will tell you how far the family has progressed and what it is trying to achieve.

There was a time when the old-timers knew what was going on among the immigrants—thanks to the maid (her chief virtue was that she had presented her mistress with the patriotic opportunity to employ an immigrant, give her advice, make her the butt of her memories and the recipient of her worn clothes). Today many maids have been in the country longer than their employers. Immigrant women do not automatically become housemaids, as in the good old days; the maid supply is now to be found among Hebrew-speaking old-timers, native-born, members of those strata of society (not necessarily Oriental) whom the gold-tipped wings of prosperity had not touched.

Economic circumstances are no longer a criterion. A home, a car, a TV set, a diamond ring, furs, a trip abroad—the trademarks of the consumer class—no longer denote the degree of a person's rootedness in the land. An immigrant can manage to achieve all these things in a short span of time, yet be unsuccessful in shaking off the vestige of the diaspora. On the contrary, the better his circumstances the more likely he is to make pilgrimages to Vienna or Bucharest.

And so it is that a person can live in this country twenty or thirty years and not become synonymous with it. Then, as he

17

departs from this world, the obituary notice will indicate where
life began for him:

> We announce, with deep sorrow, the passing
> of our dearly beloved
> **DOV (BRONISLAW) RAVIV-ROTBLUM**
> born in Cracow

and only then, when everything is truly said and done, all his
roots are in the soil of Israel.

Our Glorious Forerunners

TODAY, WHEN the last of the early pioneers, like gnarled olive trees, are casting their shadows on the growth around them, everything we ever held against them—the stubborn, the zealous, the forever right—is gone, and in its stead there is admiration and forgiveness and genuine nostalgia for what is vanishing before our very eyes. Of this we are certain: today there are no longer any models being cast in their mold. The selectivity of time and circumstance has distorted the attitude toward the pioneers on the part of the younger generation—the newcomers, the young and the green, who remember neither the Turks nor the British when they ruled this land. Those whom we see today and saw ten years ago, who survived the struggles against the world and among themselves, are truly the strong, the cedars, hewn out of rock; they remained steadfast in this attritional land and didn't run back to Mother Russia, nor did they head west, to the East Side and East End, and they didn't perish here, in the flower of their youth, but survived the ravages of hunger, poverty, malaria, the Arabs, despair. All the others no longer bear witness.

The structure of Israel's political parties, especially that of the labor parties (which have been ruling the state in sundry coalitional combines, from the day of its founding), is a direct continuation of the stormy disputations and bitter struggles over ideology, of merger and cleavage and cleavage and merger, that go back all the way to the early immigrations. Today only experts in the field are familiar with the evolutionary processes: *Poale Zion* Right and *Poale Zion* Left, *Hapoel Hatzair* and *Hashomer Hatzair*, the Labor Battalion and Labor Unity, the Eretz-Yisrael Workers Party and the United Workers Party, the United Kibbutz and the Kvutzot Association, and only those endowed with elephantine memories still bear rancor toward who said what, in the heat of debate, forty years ago. For better or for worse, the present generation has been blessed with neither the devastating zeal nor the granite stubbornness, with neither the eternal memory nor the capacity to nurse a grudge; today's models are simply not molded of the same material—it may be more flashy now, but it doesn't hold up as well.

The attitude toward the labor Mayflowerites of the Land of Israel, who largely determined the image of the country from the very outset, was always ambivalent. We knew that they indeed merited all kinds of admiration for their staunch faith in this barren, primitive land, yet everything within us rose up against this imperative of having to be grateful, having to listen, for the thousandth time, to stories prefaced by and predicated on "what-do-you-young-pups-know," of having to be ever-conscious of their infallible moral superiority. Actually there were thousands of these grandmas, each proud to have been a link in the generations; thousands of the old and weary who passed away in make-shift shacks or in small homes with colored floor tiles and an icebox and a kerosene stove—people whose names were hardly known beyond their doorstep, their *moshav* or *kibbutz*. But they were not the ones who set the image of the Second Aliya, as it was emblazoned for later generations. This was done by that handful of active workers in the ranks of the labor movement and institutions whose impress on the land is felt to this day, six decades after they first set foot on its shores.

Today one can hardly identify the demarcation lines between the Second Aliya (1904–1914) and the Third (1919–1923), lines which were so tangible after World War One. In our conception, the two are now merged into one stream of young women in long pleated skirts and broad-brimmed hats of straw, of young men in Russian shirts and visored caps; of valiant fighters for the rights of the working woman, with the pince-nez set belligerently on their dainty, erudite noses; of guardsmen with fierce mustaches and fur hats and muskets, looking into the camera with dead earnestness as they were being immortalized, in the worn photographs constantly repeated in commemorative albums. The distant, almost legendary images stare at you through the veil of time, and you find it extremely difficult to bridge the time span between those likenesses and the same persons as you know them now, in their advanced years, Cabinet ministers and Members of the Knesset and leaders of their parties, honored and eminent and bearing the burdens of responsibility as though they were inescapable. The exterior likeness may still be there—the unruly mane or the broad forehead, the round face or the bun hairdo—but the strands don't tie together. Today they are the dignitaries of the community, the custodians of ideals and integrity, the Israel Establishment, so concerned over the growing estrangement of the younger generation from sanctified principles. And there, beyond the reaches of time, they are the rebels of the beginning of the century, who left comfortable homes and well-to-do parents and the university, to live in poverty and dirt; they were the young men who shrank from the responsibility of building families, and the young women who secured husbands without marriage rites. On the other hand, even though their hair grew long and their beards were unkempt, the similarity between those pioneers and the beatniks or the hippies or the rebellious students of the 1960's is external and circumstantial only. The men of the pioneer immigrations (most of them, at any rate; some were simply swept up by the current) were driven by a religious zeal—anti-religious though it was by the accepted standards of Judaism—by fervent belief in their mission on behalf of future generations, of the future of the Jewish people, of the toilers of the world.

There is a good bit of irony in the fact that the Soviet Union will not have anything to do with Israel, that in the eyes of the Soviet Communists we are imperialists and capitalists and decadent bourgeoisie, whereas, in reality, loyalty to the ideals of international socialism and to its evolution in the Soviet Union was deeper and lasted longer here than in any other country. Not only was the entire thinking of the Second and Third Aliyas influenced by the Russian revolutionary movement; not only did many of the architects of Israel's society grow up in the lap of Russian culture and loved the Russian tongue no less than the language of the Patriarchs (even more, in moments of weakness); not only was Hebrew with a Russian accent considered to be the fashionable rendition of the tongue; not only was it here that the voluntarily collective way of life came to pass, "each according to his ability, each according to his needs." There also seemed to be

21

some kind of drive to prove to the Russians, whose attitude toward its Jews is deplorable at best, how good are thy tents, O Jacob, and thy dwelling places, O Labor Israel.

The close ties with the United States developed in far more circuitous fashion, via American Jewry, which is largely the same East European Jewry that one finds in Israel, except that it bears the "molded in the USA" label; and via the attachment of American society to the Bible; via the concept of the consumer society, via the Pattons and the Skyhawks, economic considerations, fund-raising campaigns and loans. But Russia could have gained the same affection and at less cost, in exchange for a measure of appreciation. Today, however, the composition of Israeli society is different; a new generation has arisen that knoweth not Ivan Alexeyevich Bunin, and its eyes are naturally turned to the West, to the U.S. For the older generation, unrequited love has stilled the former longings, but something of the affinity with things Russian still hovers in the atmosphere, like distant echoes of the singing of "Polyushka"; they still read Russian and cling to names such as Masha and Sasha and Yasha and Abrasha; a few actors still perform in the style of Stanislavsky, third-hand.

Of the pioneer immigrants who landed here between 1904 and 1923, only 70,000 stayed put (the others fled as quickly as they could make it), a small number when compared with the million, three hundred thousand who came later, yet their impact on what has unfolded here is far greater than that of any other single group, because they labored with an eye to the future, for the masses who would follow them; and consequently their number in the higher echelons of public office has been totally out of proportion. True, every Cabinet has had, ever since the inception of the state, two or three ministers from the Oriental communities, if only to be fair (these were in the less important ministries: Posts, Police, Religious Affairs), but their choice was dictated by the immigrants from Pinsk, Minsk, Plonsk or Bobroisk. The ones who make the vital decisions come from Russia and its environs, Poland, Lithuania, Galicia (Golda Meir came from Milwaukee, but she belongs on the roster of former Russians). Israel's first three Presidents (Dr. Chaim Weizmann, Yitzhak Ben-Zvi, Zalman Shazar), the first three Prime Ministers (David Ben-Gurion, Moshe Sharett, Levi Eshkol), the chairmen of the Knesset, the secretaries of the Histadrut, the Ministers of Finance, of Education, or Foreign Affairs (except Abba Eban, who, from a certain standpoint, has not as yet been taken into the family circle, despite the love that American Jewry has for him), all of them respond to the Slavic sound of their birthplaces. An outside observer may take this as a phenomenon of community discrimination, in that all these posts are in the hands of Ashkenazis, but this is an optical illusion. This is not a matter of preference for certain ethnic groupings—Ashkenazic Hungary and Yugoslavia, Austria and Holland, are also not part of the inner circle —but for East European background. Things change with the years, of course; age and death put in their claim, but when all is said and done, the pioneers in the visored caps have been at the helm of the Jewish ship of state, before and after the advent of Israel, longer than any ruling group in any other country, with the exception, perhaps, of Emperior Haile Selassie of Ethiopia or President Salazar of Portugal, but, unlike them, not through force of arms but force of habit.

The rebellion against trusteeship by the leaders is apparently a matter of generations. But as the younger generation (now in its fifties, after all these years of waiting) draws nearer to the major seats of power, the rebellion seems to center on the difference in what is recollected rather than on age. On one side is the veteran who recalls the long struggle for the rights of labor, for the employment of Jewish workers, for an eight-hour working day, sick benefits and the right to organize, who still remembers the miracle of a tomato grown by Jews and the thrills at the sight of the label, "Made in Eretz-Israel." On the other side is the individual who found everything prepared for him, the native or the immigrant, who is repelled by the sight of the dust that has collected on the magnificent structure of the Labor Movement, who scorns the petrified relics of adherence to the exterior symbols of the labor past (red flags at Independence Day celebrations, the May Day Parade, the singing of the *Internationale* at Labor Party conventions), who derides the strains of "O nation of slaves and hunger-ridden" when the singers arrive in chauffered official cars, and detects the false note in the speeches extolling manual labor, delivered by officials who have done nothing of the sort for the past thirty years.

23

The old-timers, convinced that they were destined for leadership by virtue of their adherence to the principles of pioneering *aliya* and inspired by the memories of the struggle against the British Mandate and of the necessarily secret underground activities, tend to relate to information media, especially the radio and the press, as though it were an alternative to instructive stories for youngsters. Criticism is fine—but only if it is positive! Satire is commendable—but it must be constructive! Truth? By all means—but it should be favorable! Coloration is not important as long as it is rosy. "Why do you newspapermen always dig up the wrong things, the shortcomings, the scandals, instead of devoting your talents to describing the fine and the beautiful?" ask the educators, on their way to the newsstand to buy the horrible trash—the yellow, dirty, despicable newspapers—to learn what is really going on. Perhaps this is a hangover from the days of the Czar and the early annals of socialism, when a free press (as free as can be) was regarded as a luxury which a young society locked in struggle can well forgo. The public should be informed—but not too much, and at the proper time, as determined by the educators, like when someone absolutely irresponsible lifts the corner of the rug, and the layer of dust is revealed.

In a way, the heroes of the Bible are closer to the young people in Israel, even the secular among them, than are the heroes of the past sixty years; they had been living, ever since childhood, with Gideon and Samson and David and Jonathan, who are a legacy rather than a topic for rational evaluation, and who are primarily human beings, with shortcomings and frailties and foibles, sinners and bedevilled—not the idols and the saints depicted in the biographical writings, in Hebrew, of contemporary figures. If the Bible were authored today, the Government spokesmen would not allow it to state what it does state; Jacob wouldn't have obtained the birthright by adroit dealing, and Moses would not have flown into the rage that caused him to smash the Ten Commandments, and David would have harbored no illicit intentions toward Bathsheba, the wife of his retainer. Not in print, anyway. Political considerations, public relations and concern for the proper historical image would have called for corrections, here and there.

The stalwarts of the early immigrations—A.D. Gordon and the

poetess Rahel, Beri Katzenson and Mania Shochet—are handed down from generation to generation, from the old-timers to the newcomers, from the old to the young, from close friends to distant acquaintances like flat cutouts, bi-dimensional. Their stories deal with internal struggles over ideology, with the fight for survival, with events and places, but not with people. The young generation shies away from perfection in people; it prefers its heroes to be human, the men to chase women and the women to gnaw at their fingernails. The outstanding figures of the pioneer *aliyas* are yet to be enshrined in modern biography, which would include a dose of ideology but would also contain a pinch of gossip and a vein of piquant data, a few love affairs, a few tight spots, a touch of melancholia and some intrigue.

Take Yosef Trumpeldor who "in the Galilee, at Tel-Hai, fell." He was a hero. He strove for freedom, and as he breathed his last he said: "Tis good to die for our land." I tend to be wary when it comes to stories about individuals who, at the mortal moment, possessed sufficient fortitude, especially when they were in the throes of physical agony, to formulate an announcement for posterity. I therefore hoped, secretly, for a substantiation of the persistent rumor which has it that the patriotic utterance was followed by the juiciest of Russian oaths. Yet today, almost half a century after Trumpeldor's death, all that the old-timers are willing to admit is that he did say something akin to "*Nu,* that's the way it goes," just before he expired.

People who come to Israel without having drunk deeply from the fronts of socialism cannot overcome being jarred by the word *chaver* (comrade). This is true especially when the reference is to the great and the esteemed. One can overlook it as long as *chaver* is followed with the family name. But when the combination applies to the personal name, *Chavera* Golda or *Chaver* Pinhas, the sound carries an artificial familiarity based on nothing more than habit and the membership card of the Labor Federation. Still, the socialist content of the word *chaver* is not anywhere as formidable as of "comrade." Today, a *chaver* in Israel may be anyone whom the word "Mister" does not suit—a kibbutz member or a sanitation worker, a *moshavnik* or a youngster, something akin to the Spanish *hombre*. After all, all Israelites are *chaverim,* but not all non-Israelites are comrades.

Who's A Rumanian?

A MAN DOESN'T choose his birthplace, but he may be hounded by it all of his living days—or be credited with it, as the case may be. A birthplace is like a label attached to an individual without much of an idea of what's inside; it provides a quick and ready method of classifying him. Prejudices attend our thinking about countries, regions, cities and communities, and their inhabitants are subjected to them, as the snail is subjected to the home that it carries around, until their final day (which includes the obituary on the following day). And there is no people like the Jews, in this respect; their prejudices apply to entire continents as well as to limited localities.

Like the wooden Russian dolls, each of which contains within itself a half-dozen other dolls of various sizes, each Diaspora presents a general image of its peculiar characteristics—the glib, hand-kissing, double-meaning Pole; the stiff, pedantic and punctilious German, and so on in the roster of prejudice. These images have sub-images, reflecting localities within the regions— the Galician sharper, the Lodz storekeeper, the Chelm simpleton.

In the days of the ghetto, a locality had a different connotation for the Jews from what it meant to the Gentiles (what does Belz or Kotzk mean to the Poles?). Today, however, the status of a locality, as far as the Jew is concerned, depends to a large extent on the status that the locality has in the eyes of the world in general. The Czechs of the First Republic enjoyed a universal good name because of Masaryk, Capek, guns and beer; accordingly, newcomers to Palestine from Czechoslovakia were given a cordial welcome. I never knew, until I came to Israel, that Prague is such a distinguished birthplace. You only had to mention that magic name and people would nod sagely and say something nice about

Prague the Golden (that was before Jerusalem the Golden was discovered); about the Golem, Kafka and *horke parky* (hot dogs in mustard). True, during the Slansky trial, I lowered my voice whenever I revealed the place of my birth, but still I had no reason to feel apologetic. We were still basking in the glow of Schweik, Dvorak and the arms which the Czechs made available to Israel at the inception of its War of Independence.

After the Six-Day War it no longer felt comfortable to be Czech-born. Those who at one time (for strategic reasons) shifted their Carpatho-Russian birthplace to the Bohemian territory quickly retreated to their original locality. After the murder of Charles Jordan in Prague, the number of Israelis claiming Czech derivation dropped by fifty percent, according to conservative estimates, but the liberalization of the regime in the spring of 1968 and the attitude of the Czech people toward the Russian invasion restored to Prague the Birthplace its halo of yore.

In human society, the status of a locality is like that of the individual; it is subject to constant change. At times the drop in status is a long process of many years; the prestige of the locality may rise very gradually, without anyone being conscious of it. At times a political episode may, in an instant, wreck a locality for generations: now no one is born in Munich, Nuremberg, Little Rock or Dallas, if he can help it.

Now the shining hour has come here for the Rumanians. During our first two decades, being a Rumanian expatriate meant having the cards stacked against you; as though accused of maintaining contact with a foreign agent, you had to prove your innocence before being given clearance. Some of these Rumanians tried to circumvent the calamity by dividing Rumania into its provinces. They suddenly ceased being Rumanians and became former Transylvanians, Bucovinians, Bessarabians or Moldavians, without mentioning the wayward family name. Others, regarding the query as to their birthplace in the dim light of a challenge to their veracity, would very vigorously reply: "Rumania!" and wait for the reaction of the other party. For twenty years they replied "I am from Rumania" in the same manner that a Jew abroad replied "I am a Jew," with overdone pride, or hestitatingly, or expectantly, or with a hint of "so-what-if-I-do-come-from-Rumania"—but always on guard.

Among the former Rumanians themselves one can distinguish at least two dozen categories, ranks and levels—Tchernovitz by itself, Jassi, Closz, Bucharest, every city with its own virtues and faults, but to the outside world they are all fodder for anecdotes about rogues and sharpies. Once, when the mood was upon me, I tried to list the people who had cheated me, in the course of my years in Israel. I noted down Czechs and Hungarians and Russians and *sabras,* all of them supposed symbols of honesty and integrity, but by chance not a single Rumanian. Yet, the minute that Mr. Yanovici of the dry goods store should ask, for a pair of nylon stockings, a price of twenty agorot above the national average, I would say to myself: "Aha! A Rumanian!" In a way, we are undergoing in Israel today, in our attitude toward a specific group or toward newcomers from one country or another, the same psychological processes which prompt the well-intentioned liberal Gentiles to say "You really aren't like other Jews" and regard it as complimentary.

People are generally pleased whenever they come upon someone who personifies the prototypes which they envisage—when they finally do meet the Englishman who is really tall and thin and wears a derby and smokes a pipe and is traditionally reticent, or the gesturing Italian with flashing eyes and vaselined hair who says *porce Madonna* most graciously. They substantiate the veracity of a man's prejudices. An Israeli would therefore be highly gratified to come upon a Rumanian who would "do" him in true Levantine fashion, because this proves that the world's right and prejudices are right, as right as can be.

But today, now that Georgi Maurer is a welcome guest at every capitalistic table, and Rumania is not demanding that we withdraw unconditionally from the territories we control but is buying our cotton and is standing up to Soviet pressure, the ill-wishers no longer smile knowingly when the word "Rumanian" is mentioned. Today you say, "I'm a Rumanian," and people will respond with "hats off to Rumania" or "there's nothing wrong with Rumanians" or "Bucharest is a beautiful city" or "I, too, am crazy about white roe," and everyone will suddenly remember that a dozen of his best friends are from Rumania.

If you wonder how it came about that an entire Diaspora community of Jews enjoyed such a reputation here—seeing that the Rumanians founded Rosh Pina and Zichron Yaacov and produced Reuven Rubin and Marcel Yanco, Prof. Ashkenazi and Dr. Sheba and other personalities' of Rumanian origin, plus *ciorba* and *mititei* and other Rumanian delicacies—you must go back to Rumanian Rumania, the most corrupt of all the Balkan countries, and to its reactionary feudal system. The western countries were suspicious of this Rumanian regime which, during the hundred years of its existence, was able to produce twist-and-turn diplomats of the calibre ordinarily reserved for the Great Powers. There was also a good deal of enmity toward Rumania on the part of the neighboring peoples whose territories had been annexed—Russian Bessarabia and Hungarian Transylvania. In the Jewish sphere, the Jews of Russia and Poland always considered themselves to be intellectually superior to their Rumanian brethren. The alleged Rumanian intellectual inferiority, plus the fact that the bribery-infested patterns of life in Rumania gave little opportunity to people to be honest, provided the fertile soil for the sprouting of all those anecdotes about the Rumanians.

Rumanian Jews did not become Rumanians until their arrival in Israel; as long as they were in Rumania, they were regarded as Jews, period. In 1914, only two thousand of Rumania's quarter of a million Jews had full rights of citizenship. Even after the Treaty of Paris, which gave Rumania new territories and another half-million Jews, most of them remained third-class citizens. Fate decided, ironically, that the first top-ranking person in Rumania's new ruling hierarchy should be a Jewess, the late Ana Pauker, and she did not last very long.

In anti-Semitism, as in all of life, everything is relative. There were pogroms in Jassi and Bucharest, camps in Transnistria, death trains, Antonescu and the Iron Guard, but, in view of the fact that half of Rumania's pre-World War Two Jews remained alive, one must conclude that the Rumanians were relatively decent—even fair, considering the overall dimensions of the Holocaust. The same may be said of the Communist regime. Yes, there was Ana Pauker; Zionists were imprisoned and immigration to Israel was prohibited, but, in comparison with the other "people's republics," the Rumanians were very decent; they did allow 300,000 of their Jews to leave for Israel.

In this country, anyone with political ambitions must have a vehicle to take him to the top (like Elijah's fiery chariot)—religion, the farm, the working woman. I find it surprising that only two high echelon politicians, jockeying for political power, rode the Rumanian nag to victory. This is far out of proportion to the number of former Rumanians in the Israeli populace. There are nearly 350,000 of them (including 50,000 old-timers) and, if my fingers serve me correctly, it would appear that every seventh Israeli is a Rumanian. The number of former Rumanians in the Knesset should therefore be around 17, plus at least two Cabinet ministers. There's something rotten in the Israeli social structure if even Rumanians are subject to discrimination. Perhaps what the Rumanian Israelis need is a leader from the outside, as was Napoleon for the French, Lawrence for the Arabs, and (German) King Carol for Rumania—a leader who would fight their battles, with the aid of a competent public relations director.

If we assume that the societal integration of the ingathered can be helped along, like love, via the stomach, it may be said that the first Rumanian assault on behalf of integration was made from the ramparts of small restaurants, scattered all over the country, with *gratar Romanesc* and fish in spicy sauce and fish roe with chopped onions and juicy *mititei* and sourish *ciorba* and spiced salami and translucent *zuica;* all this while the proprietress personally sees to it that all her customers eat heartily to the very last morsel, while her husband is engaged in a conversation, in Rumanian studded with Hebrew terms with *domenolu* Lupu and *domenolu* Bercovici (counting the number of Hebrew words you use, which cannot be translated into the mother tongue, is one way to measure the span of your sojourn in Israel).

Vis-a-vis the other European expatriates in Israel, the Rumanians have one tremendous advantage over, let us say, their Hungarian neighbors; their tongue is clearly human-sounding. A conversation in Hungarian, wafted somewhere above your head, tends to raise your blood pressure, cause a buzzing in the ears, a headache and the definite feeling that you are being sold down the river, together with your grandmother. On the other hand, there is pleasure in listening to Rumanian. You catch a word here, a word there: *la revedere, bune seara, lumine, ascoulla, nopte buna.* It is only when you hear Rumanian that you realize the extent of your own erudition: a bit of Latin from your school days, a little Italian from the movies, some French from song hits, and behold, Rumanian holds no secrets, as witness: *"complimenida a casa domenolu Greenberg."*

If I am ever asked, by one of the numerous polls now in vogue here (chiefly to determine the popularity of our Prime Minister), as to what image does the word "Rumanian" conjure up for me, I shall list the seller of the Government lottery tickets, sitting with his scissors in his dimly-lit booth on a rainy evening; the proprietress of the small dress shop, her nail polish peeling and her hair in sore need of a dye-job around the roots; a soprano in a glittering gown and pink decolletage, heaving forth Strauss arias; the building custodian in his long winter overcoat, and in one of his pockets a Keren Hayesod certificate, thirty years old, attesting to his meritorious services, which he once thought would open for him the gates to the goodly life; a *moshav* farmer, with peaked cap and silver teeth, driving his dray along the road and calling out to his mare: *"Dee-ee-ee, clodula, heida!"* In my Rumanian gallery I see artists with graying hair and attorneys with pearl stickpins, seamen and waiters, but not a single tractor operator or an Armored Corps officer or a *kibbutz* man or a physicist, not because such do not exist. but simply because the computer in the brain does not come up with any. These have already been transferred to the category of "Israelis."

Yeckis and the Land of Israel

ALL THOSE anecdotes, the snide remarks, the fun-poking, all have already been forgotten, in the maelstrom of the immigration which followed the coming of the German expatriates. Today the title *Yecki* denotes characteristics rather than the land of origin. "He's such a Yecki" means that he is pedantic, or meticulous, or more methodical than the average Israeli; the exact geographic origin is not the point at all, although it would be far-fetched to apply the term to a Yemenite or, in particular, to a Moroccan. Not yet, anyway. Insofar as the former Germans are concerned, however, the term has retained a distinctly negative connotation only when followed by a certain monosyllabic epithet which denotes the ill-concealed contempt for the dyed-in-the-wool Yecki on the part of the former East Europeans or Levantines (the difference in their mentalities is narrower than either group would care to admit), contempt for an individual who sticks to his convictions as a matter of principle.

The appellation *Yecki* did not originate in Israel. It became associated with German Jews long before the doctors turned cab drivers and actuaries took to poultry breeding. Some say that the term is derived from the German *Jacke,* a short jacket, by which German Jews could be distinguished from the long-cloaked East Europeans. Another opinion ascribes the term to *gecke,* in German a conceited braggart.

The Yeckis, as a race, are doomed to extinction. In another ten, twenty, thirty years no trace of them will remain, except for the second and third generations whose Yeckiness will have become adulterated in the admixture of a thousand Bad Habits Israeli Style, a pale replica of the genuine original prototype, untarnished by the Israeli influence. Already today, Yecki is heard mostly in combination: "an old Yecki," since a young Yecki is either not much of a Yecki or he isn't that young. Of the 70,000 who arrived in the Jewish Homeland before the outbreak of the Second World War, there are today some 50,000, of whom only about half are genuine Yeckis, that is, individuals who grew up in Germany, were brought up in its society, and came with families, occupations and professions—all the doctors and lawyers and professors and scientists and manufacturers and merchants, thrown into the Land of Israel during the 1930's like aquarium fish into the open sea.

As soon as the old-timers in Jewish Palestine began understanding the Yeckis and even showing them a slight glimmer of affection (without overdoing it, of course, since a birth defect cannot be entirely overlooked), it became clear that the Yecki fangs had been pulled and replaced with artificial teeth; they no longer presented a threat to the breezy Mediterranean way of life. The fact that, in Israel's present society, one can say "I'm a Yecki, you know" with a note of pride in his voice (because he had returned a book as promised or kept to the appointed hour on the dot), is a sure sign that Israeli prejudices are not what they used to be.

The influence of the German immigration was usually felt in a secondary stage, permeating from below upwards, rather than in reverse. The German expatriates revised the courses in medicine and jurisprudence and affected the formats of secondary schooling and higher education. They wielded a far-reaching effect on banking and poultry raising, on music and the upbringing of pedigreed canines. They founded nature-lovers societies and introduced the community to clean delicatessen stores and coffee shops with apple cake, and contributed to concepts of social service and burgeois vacationing, but their direct influence on political matters was in no proportion to their numerical strength in the community. Only a few Yeckis succeeded in being accepted into the exclusive and authoritative family circle of Minsk, Pinsk, Homel, Poltava or their immediate environs. Perhaps this was because, prior to Hitler's rise to power, only a few German Jews were involved in Zionist parties or factions, and most of these were not especially active or interested in politics in general once they were here. It may also be that navigating in the political waters of the Land of Israel called for the distinctive stamina granted only to the veterans of the Second (1904–1914) and Third (1919–1923) Immigrations.

Today, three decades after the arrival of the mainstream, the pain has subsided, but in retrospect it appears that no immigration suffered so much mental anguish, in its first years here, than the Fifth *Aliya,* as the German immigration is called. And it suffered in both worlds at the same time, the world that collapsed about them and the world they came to build. Many among Germany's Jews had regarded themselves as full citizens of the Reich in every respect, rooted in German culture and tradition. Their banishment from the Garden of Eden by the landlord, as though they had been but temporary tenants permitted to stay on sufferance, caused them emotional shock from which some never recovered, one without parallel among those who came from other countries. Most of the emigres from Eastern Europe had few illusions about the good will of their native countries toward their Jews, and these they could still maintain because their countries had not acted on their own but had to take orders from the Third Reich.

One of the basic aspects of life in Germany and central European countries was the faith in the validity of law and the readiness to act within its limitations without questioning it unduly, as opposed to the approach of the Jews in Eastern Europe, who never regarded the idiosyncrasies of Czarist legislation seriously; they accepted law as something which was enacted not to be observed to the last iota but rather to provide escape valves for the evil decrees which it legislated. This hard-facts approach obviously provided for a more practical preparation for life in the Land of Israel than attendance at Heidelberg or Goettingen universities. The paucity of understanding between the Yeckis and the former Eastern Europeans stemmed from the clash between the two philosophies of living: on the one hand, adherence to a world as it should be, and, on the other, the conviction that life is nothing but a series of compromises.

In a certain way, some of the German expatriates found more in common with British officialdom, which also subscribed to the validity of the legislated word, than with Palestinian Jewry, which looked upon their arrival with a jaundiced eye, to put it mildly— much in the same manner that the old-time German Jews once viewed the Polish Jews who invaded their localities and whom they labelled with the loving term of *Ostjuden* (Eastern Jews, if you pardon the expression).

The first dozen years of the Fifth *Aliya*, from the beginning of 1933 to the outbreak of the Second World War, produced a stack of anecdotes which portrayed Yeckis as being stultified or slow to grasp things or devoid of common sense or ridiculously polite or with an atrocious accent (as differing from the Russian accent, which is really not an accent at all but a phenomenon of nature). One of the final anecdotes, before Israeli humor turned in other directions, was the nutshell question: "If the British leave, without lifting the curfew, how will the Yecki know when it would be permissible to leave the house?"

At the root of the negative attitude toward the Yeckis lay the fact that their approach was essentially the proper one, i.e., that promise must be followed by performance; that appointments should be kept, and at the hour set; that payment should be made in accordance with commitment; that people should be allowed to rest between two and four in the afternoon; that a man should be no better than his word; that food must not necessarily claim kinship with dirt. The Yeckis were right in the same fashion that a law-observing car driver is right; he can be in the right a thousand times, but should he not yield to a Mack truck on the highway, he'll be the one to be bashed in. It is for this reason that, to this day, Government comptrollers are recruited from among the Yeckis; on the one hand, it's good to know that the post is in the hands of someone not easily given to compromise, but, should political exigency demand it, his conclusions could easily be overridden. He is right, but no match for the Mack truck.

For years, classical works and chamber music, especially the latter, were considered to be the exclusive domain of the Yeckis. Today we have already forgotten that Paul Ben-Haim's name was once Frankburger and that Joseph Tal was once Gruenthal, not to mention Haubenstock-Haramati, Erich Walter Sternberg, Karl Salomon and so on. As recently as six or seven years ago, when we still had the *Kol Yisrael* musical quiz in its original format, the names of the knowledgeable ones that stuck in the memories of the listeners were like a paean to the Yecki parents of Walter and Ernst, Otto and Peter. (The boycott, still in existence here, of the works of Wagner and Richard Strauss clearly illustrates the fact, however, that while the Yeckis may have had the say in music, the tone was nevertheless set by the *Ostjuden*).

The impact of the German immigration on the Hebrew language is discernible, curiously enough, only in the field of gastronomy. Metwurst, Jagdwurst, Theewurst, Knackwurst, Schinkenwurst and Leberwurst are part of the acceptable Hebrew vocabulary in every non-kosher meat market. Streusel, Strudel, Schnecken, Kranzkuchen, Bienenstich and Pumpernickel are now baked and eaten by people who had never heard of Goethe. The only German word adopted by the Hebrew language, other than those relating to gluttony and pedigreed canines and without having first been Yiddishized, is—as far as I know—"Schwung," i.e., momentum, used wherever the pace is beyond Dispatch Israeli Style.

Today, now that the Ambassador of the West German Federal Republic is a welcome guest at all cultural events, and German tourist are visiting Israel in their thousands, and every pert *sabra* can identify a Volkswagen or a Mercedes, it is difficult to believe that there once was a time when author Arnold Zweig was not allowed to lecture in German, in Israel. The German language (which, like any other language, is in my opinion but a neutral medium for the spirit which inhabits it) was banned, with the entire culture to which it gave expression. Russian expatriates never had to renounce their affection for Tolstoy, Pushkin or Dostoyevsky, although the latter was not known for his love toward Jews, and they never felt, therefore, what it means to be stripped of your illusions, as well as of the privilege of longing.

Lecture series given in German for central Europeans have considerably dwindled in number. The organ of their Association has been coming out in a Hebrew edition, as well, for the past ten years. One German-language newspaper folded four years ago, and while the other is still publishing, the glad tidings and sad notices it carries indicate a change in the composition of its readers: fewer and fewer Yeckis and more Balkans, for whom German is a second language. And the German being spoken by the elderly Yeckis is no longer the German they brought with them, thirty years ago and more; it is as punctuated with Hebrew words as salami is with fat globules.

Of the Yecki business firms only the signs remain and, in some cases, the German-sounding name. But this can be misleading, as was the case in the episode of the Feuchtwanger Bank irregularities. The general public, unfamiliar with the intricacies of stock manipulation and behind-the-scenes ownership, was misled by its assumption that Feuchtwanger was a Yecki bank and therefore denoted staunchness and integrity. The coffee houses, for many years the domain of former central Europeans—Kripps & Rubin, Pilz & Frack, Herlinger and "Atara"—either went out of existence or changed hands or lost their atmosphere. The solid wooden tables were replaced with folding formica objects, the discreet men waiters gave way before waitresses always on the run, and the pleasant greeting *womit kann ich Ihnen dienen?* was pushed out by "what'll you have?"

In Naharia-*dorf,* which once needed only a forest of fir to become a *Bad,* there remain only a few Yeckis, among its population of 20,000; and yet, despite the *schwarma* (lamb on rotating spit) counters, the Rumanian coachmen and the discotheques, there is still something of the Yecki spirit hovering over the town: grown-up women pedaling bicycles, the promenade trail along Gaaton Brook, the relative cleanliness of the streets, a monument to the dreams of the once-Germans of pastoral life in the Promised Land, of the tiller of the soil with an academic degree.

Not all the Yeckis who came here with capital funds became alchemists, that is, versed in the unfortunate art of converting gold into sand. But they had their business acumen. After all, quite a few Yeckis, including some of the most steeped in German culture, kept in the deep recesses of their desks a birth certificate (theirs or their fathers') issued in some locality east of the Oder-Neisse. They were able to adapt themselves, amazingly well, to the demands of local commerce, and the fact that one Yecki, at least, became a millionnaire in this country points to a basically fine grasp of Levantine finance.

A significant turning point in the life of the former Germans in Israel came, mentally and materially, with the German reparations payments. These payments were like penicillin salve on the wounds inflicted by Nazi rule. They restored some of the faith that there is a bit of justice in the world, after all. They made it possible for the Yeckis to go back to patterns long forgotten and

37

to comforts which, at one time, were taken for granted: to live in a spacious apartment, to ride in a private car, to vacation every year in Switzerland, to spend the holidays at the Dagon Hotel in Ashkelon, to give up the job of cabbying or of running a tobacconist's, to attend a concert with a handbag of real leather or in Bally shoes, to shop every Friday in a delicatessen, to employ a maid, to feel once again some of the self-assurance of those years, before deep darkness fell.

East and West

A JEW IS a Jew is a Jew until he sets foot in Israel and suddenly discovers that he cannot be just a Jew. He must be an Ashkenazi or a Sepharadi or one of the Orientals (North Africa-Middle East-India), classified and categorized with respect to religion, statistics, social sciences, medical care and discrimination. An Ashkenazi is of European origin, perhaps Yiddish-speaking and praying in accordance with the Ashkenazi rite; but—he could have been born in South Africa, he could be ignorant of Yiddish, and never pray—and still be an Ashkenazi by virtue of the fact than an Ashkenazi is anyone who is not a Sepharadi. But who is a Sepharadi? This is an intricate matter. Technically he is a descendant of the Spanish Jews who fled from the Inquisition in 1492 to various Mediterranean countries, taking with them their worship customs and the language of the locality, which in time developed into Ladino. In Israel the term "Sepharadi" is much broader, or narrower, as circumstances may demand. On the one hand, an Italian Jew who is a professor of physics may be a Sepharadi from the viewpoint of religious rite, but he is nevertheless not regarded as a Sepharadi socially, and an Ashkenazi mother would not object, despite her prejudices, to having him for a son-in-law, as "one of ours." On the other hand, the broad concept may encompass anyone who is not an Ashkenazi, that is, any Jew from Asia and North Africa, who is also called a "Frank," with equal lack of logic, since his forebears never saw Franconia, whence the name originated, and which in time became a term of scorn.

In the old Jewish community of Palestine, the distinction between Sepharadi and Ashkenazi lay in ritual, culture and language. The twenty thousand Sepharadi Jews in the country before

World War One were the leaders of Jewish society. They were the dynasts, the dignified merchants who had learned, over the generations, how to live in palm-greased peace with both the Arabs and the Turkish rulers. They regarded, with justified suspicion, the Ashkenazi barbarians who descended upon them from the north, without families and social graces, bearing dangerous ideas of political Zionism, a Jewish State, socialism, equality for women, and cohabitation between young men and virtuous Jewish daughters. The fifty years that followed more than vindicated their fears. The rampaging Ashkenazi turned the Land of Israel into a state of their own, structured in accordance with their ideas, their views and their culture. Furthermore, it was their declared intent to liberate the land from the Levant, where it belonged geographically, and annex it, in spirit, to western Europe. The word "Levantine" became, with all its hyphenates, a term synonymous with corruption, indolence, a sword-thin stratum of the affluent versus the exploited masses, a cesspool of noise and filth, the double-talk of promise and performance, haggling for its own sake, a weakness for perfumes and ostentation without refinement.

The large *aliya* of Jews from the Moslem countries did away with the old demarcation lines between Ashkenazi and Sepharadi. Jews from Yemen and Babylonia (Iraq) had settled in those countries long before there were any Jews in Spain. The new distinctions no longer entailed speech or ritual or culture but rather social status. Of course, only the ignorant "voos-voos" (as the Orientals scornfully call the Ashkenazi) are inclined to lump all the Orientals into one category, being unable and incompetent to sense the difference in rank and prestige between Iraqi and Kurd, Bokharan and Afghani, Moroccan and Tripolitanian, Bombay Jews and Beni Yisrael, Casablancans and the inhabitants of the Atlas Mountains—these being the distinctions which comprise the shades and nuances that allow a person to bask in the good feeling that there is someone of a less important pedigree than his own, someone upon whom he might look down. In this respect there is no difference between Ashkenazi and Sepharadi and Oriental; each has his own status rating.

No theme lends itself less to humorous treatment than the subject of the Oriental communities. The Ashkenazi are the butt of all the barbs, sarcasm, spoofing and criticism, all of the satire and ridicule; they are the ruling class, the old-timers—and the powerful and the impervious. The Orientals are not criticized for the same reason that liberals all over the world refrain from criticizing the Jews about them, even when they deserve it, lest they be accused of anti-Semitism. At times the Ashkenazi interpolate into their remarks about the Orientals (at least into those made in public) the equivalent of the delicate remark by the well-intentioned Gentile: "You don't look like a Jew." When they are made the objects of satire, because of their backwardness, the reference is well-camouflaged: actually they are more clever and astute than any Ashkenazi around, and under their rough exterior beats a heart of gold. If an Oriental type were to be the villain of the piece, as are the Ashkenazi misfits who populate our dramas, we could be guilty of attacking the weak, something which we might do in private conversation but never in the open.

It would appear that, just as there is a variety of Oriental communities there should also be Occidental communities, but such is not the case; in fact, the term "community" in itself denotes the Oriental. Members of these communities wear exotic raiment, follow outlandish customs, eat fiery food, play Oriental tunes, and wear ornaments and hand-embroidered items with which any Ashkenazi matron would be happy to adorn her person. These communities gradually merge with the mainstream, flowing westward, to the Age of Technology. On the other hand, there can be nothing outlandish about the customs, food and attire of the Occidentals (even though the latter are former Russians and Dutchmen and Americans and Austrians)—since everyone else is trying to imitate them.

When Israelis talk about the problems of the Orientals they don't have in mind the wealthy Iraqi expatriates who live in those Ramat Gan mansions, or the North African graduates of French universities, or the Bokharan rug dealers of Jerusalem, or the bankers, importers and businessmen from Egypt and Syria. The Orientals are the dwellers of the slums and the development towns, the unskilled laborers, the large familites without a fixed income, the welfare cases, "the other Israel," as they are called in the aggregate. Fully 80 per cent of the welfare clients are Orientals, and the gap between them and their own rich ex-country-

41

men is not smaller than the gap which separates them from the Ashkenazi.

At the inception of the state, when the cities of the Promised Land became inundated by hundreds of thousand from the lands of Islam—homeless, jobless, without income and without the slightest measure of security for the future—it was believed, by those in the know, that the problem would be solved within a single generation. The youngsters would be given a good start with eight years of free compulsory schooling, like the Ashkenazi kids; they would acquire a secondary or vocational education, like the Ashkenazi kids; they would enter the army and later be absorbed in civilian life, like the Ashkenazi—and "the other Israel" would vanish. And, indeed, the external factors *have* been in operation: the nine or even ten years of free schooling are theirs, plus scholarships, military service opportunities, courses— but the distinctions are disappearing very slowly, and the hopes are now pinned upon the *next* generation. The dichotomy begins with the cradle—and even before it. On one side are illiterate parents and six or seven children living in two or three little rooms; on the other are parents with high school diplomas, two or three children in as many rooms, with a library and records, a vocabulary, and a chance to ask, "Mama, what does it mean here?" or "Daddy, how do you spell this?" The opportunities are unequal from scratch, despite everything that the Ministry of Education is doing for students requiring special help, by way of additional instruction and tangible exemptions. Today, children of Oriental parents account for 60 per cent of the elementary school population but comprise only 27 per cent of the regular high school enrollment, 12 per cent of the student body on the university level, and only 6 per cent of the holders of academic degrees.

Among the Ashkenazi, the term "erudite" is applied to a well-learned individual. He is not required to be exceptionally clever or successful, and his being erudite does not guarantee him any privileged status, unless his erudition is fortified with intelligence, ambition and professional skills. Among the Orientals, on the other hand, as among the Arabs, being erudite in itself denotes a certain position. The Ashkenazi *intelligentsia,* the early pioneers, could afford to engage in physical labor without thereby casting a blemish on their erudition, which was taken for granted. But a high school graduate from among the Orientals who is forced to engage in manual labor views the fact as a gross insult to his person. Education has become a talisman, an "open sesame," the basis for equality and for climbing the social ladder to success. Later, when the high school diploma is in hand (a testimonial to the tremendous effort that it entailed), it first becomes evident that a high school education alone is insufficient, guaranteeing neither occupation nor status, and the bitterness and frustration go even deeper.

The principal and overriding importance of the Orientals, to Israel, lies in the very fact of their being here, in their masses, populating its soil—and taking root. They are the backbone of the *moshavim;* they are Kiryat Shmoneh and Beit Shemesh, Ofakim and Dimona; they are the development towns. They are in Israel to live, without having been reared in the Zionist movement. Their rate of *yerida* for points west is one-third of the Ashkenazi. They may have temporarily lowered the cultural levels of Israeli Jewry, but they have doubled the number of those who bear its burdens.

When Ben Gurion was Prime Minister, he once stated that he would like to see a Yemenite in the post of Chief-of-Staff, as incontrovertible proof of the integration of the ingathered. Actually, this proof of absolute equality will come when a Yemenite will be Chief-of-Staff and no one will stress the fact that he is a Yemenite, just as now no one makes much of the fact that the Chief-of-Staff is of Russian or Polish parentage. Achievement will not be marked by their being assured of two or three Cabinet posts—which they already hold—but by their receiving their due as a matter of course and not as a concession or a matter of expedience.

Whenever mention is made of the change for the better in the way of life of the former African or Asian immigrants, from what it was when they first arrived, the reference is usually to their having adopted and adapted themselves to western formats: they no longer wear pajamas in the streets nor spit out pumpkin seed shells from the balconies; they no longer play Arabic music full blast (only Israeli music at full blast), and they do not squat on the floor. They have furthermore learned to use contraceptives; they no longer bake *peetah* in the house but partake of delicate white Ashkenazi bread; they hold weddings and Bar Mitzvahs in the same rented halls as the Ashkenazi, consume a quarter of a chicken and trot to the music of a paid orchestra; they speak the jargon of politics and are embroiled in party hassles.

Since the Europeans among us have always looked down on Mediterranean culture, as being much inferior to theirs, they never tried to extract the good that is in it—the family attachment, the ability to relax, to live without an eye on the clock, the secret of how to enjoy life. Oriental patterns assimilated into the Israeli bloodstream have been accepted unconsciously, unintentionally, grudgingly, in compromise. As a result of this attitude of belittlement, the young people in the Oriental communities have turned against their past, in order to be more like the Ashkenazi.

Only toward the Yemenites is this attitude different. Yemenite songs are part of the popular repertoire, and Yemenite songstresses have climbed to stardom. Ashkenazi girls have gone in for Yemenite dances, Ashkenazi women adorn themselves in Yemenite embroidery, and use Yemenite condiments in their kitchens. Even though the Yemenites were centuries behind the times when they first came here; even though they were detached from world Jewry and their Hebrew is unlike the general vernacular—they do not even resemble other Jews—their integration in Israel came much more easily than it did for other Orientals. Why? Perhaps it is because of their intense religiosity, or their simplicity, or their *joie de vivre,* or their readiness to make do with little, or because they lacked the external veneer of "universal culture" with all its frustration, or perhaps they have retained pride in their past and have employed their unity as a means of self-defense. The fact remains that relations between Yemenite and Ashkenazi are not inhibited by the uneasiness and guardedness which is felt, all too often, in the relations between the ex-East Europeans and the ex-North Africans.

Ten Little Americans

For years, Israelis tended to regard the immigrant from the United States or Canada with deep suspicion—and rightly so. Anyone who exchanged America for Israel, of his own free will, coming neither as a consultant or as a tourist but as a settler, had to have something wrong with him. He had either been declared bankrupt or wanted to run away from family problems or hadn't made a go of anything he tried or was a hopeless case of something or just naturally a bit odd.

Immigrants from America, on the other hand, lulled by the innocence of their Zionism, expected to be welcomed by a people ready to shower them with gratitude for their outstanding contribution to the national rebirth. On arrival they discovered that they were looked upon as bereft of sanity. Which rational human being would come to a problem-ridden land suffering from unemployment, a housing shortage, an unstable currency, a depressed standard of living, and borders rife with daily "incidents"—when he could have remained in the tranquil environs of Oak Park or New Rochelle, and could have come to Israel as the honored guest of Zionist institutions? An immigrant from America, in those days, was obliged to prove his sanity twice: first to the community he was leaving, and again to the skeptical denizens of the Promised Land.

With the Six Day War, a dramatic change occurred in the attitude of the Israelis toward *aliya* from the United States—they discovered its existence. The echoes of war had hardly died away, when the dwellers in Zion suddenly beheld visions of the Exodus from Brooklyn—ten thousand, a hundred thousand, a million. Now that the boundaries of the Land had widened and entire areas were crying for settlers (said the journalists, the Cabinet ministers, and sundry others charged with bearing the burdens of the State), surely the American Jews would begin coming in their multitudes, in order to become part of the building of the more or less unabridged Eretz Yisrael. Several prominent Israelis immediately packed their grips with the allowable forty-four pounds of air luggage and set out on an extended tour of the North American continent to bring the tidings of Exodus Number Three. True, they did not come back with an American *aliya* trailing them, but each returned with the distinct conviction that he had done his best. Since then, the number of American immigrants to Israel did spiral up to the dizzying annual figure of 3,000 souls, or one-half of one-tenth of one per cent of American Jewry.

The sad truth—which we in Israel refuse to accept, time after time, but which we, of all peoples, should realize from our very own experience—is that anti-Semitism achieves what love for Zion does not. Mass immigrations to Israel have been generated by political persecution and the fear of annihilation, by economic distress and similar upheavals, and not even these propellants were always successful in convincing Jews to detach themselves from their habitations, as witness the twilight years before the Holocaust. Ideals are not wholesale commodities; they are sold to individuals, not to masses. Twenty years ago we thought that American immigrant who complained about bureaucracy or of virulent anti-Semitism, but the expected catalysts—the Ku Klux Klan, the fascists and real pogroms—did not materialize; on the contrary, the position of Jews in American society became more entrenched. Even the open anti-Semitism of Black Power leaders does not augur a mass exodus of American Jews. We are perforce obliged to pursue the same tiring and time-consuming process of persuading the individual. Whereas heretofore the American immigrant who complained about bureaucracy or sanitation was met with an accusing finger, namely, "so-why-did-you-come-here?"—today the same finger is being pointed at every American student, consultant, visitor, or temporary guest (who came here out of innocent considerations of sentiment, Jewishness, or a thirst for adventure), now the accusation has a new twist: "So-why-don't-you-live-here?"

The Israeli authorities know quite well that Americans do not take kindly to bureaucracy, inefficiency and excessive taxation. The logical thing to do, then, is to exempt them from taxes and spare them the irritations of bureaucracy; once they are drawn hither, they can be lumped together with the other Israelis, who also loathe bureaucracy, inefficiency and high taxes—but cannot escape them. At the same time, we all realize that the Americans are accustomed to quite other standards of living. We should not take it for granted that an American immigrant with a wife and two children would be able to do with the average Israeli dwelling of two and a half rooms (kitchen excluded) plus an enclosed porch. He must have more breathing space, while we, the lucky ones, have already had the opportunity to get used to congestion. We do not begrudge the immigrants anything; we have so yearned for them in editorials and letters to the editor, that it is no more than right that they should be given their due, as legislated—but quietly. We Asians are allergic to envy.

The image of the potential immigrant from the United States has already undergone several mutations. There was a time when all of them tended to be elderly and Yiddish-speaking and on the loud side. In due course we also assumed that all Americans are millionaires. Currently our impression is that they are all academicians. (There's a persistent rumor being bruited about here, to the effect that, at the corner of 82nd Street and Riverside Drive, New York, someone met two Jews who admitted to never having gone to college, but he refuses to swear to it). A far-sighted Israeli father, figuring how many academicians could possibly be absorbed by a country of three, four, or even five million inhabitants, would do well for his son's future by denying him an academic education; in due course, the young man would command his own price. I can already see the bold-type ads in the Help Wanted columns: GOVERNMENT MINISTRY REQUIRES EXPERT TEA-CART MANAGER. COLLEGE GRADUATES NEED NOT APPLY. It is just like in the good old days of mass immigration from Germany, when one good crabgrass puller was worth three Ph.D.'s, *summa cum laude*.

The story of U.S. *aliya* to Israel is a Jewish version of the well-known recitation of "Ten Little Indians." One immigrant became ill, went back, leaving nine. Another couldn't find work, and eight were left. A third couldn't stand the climate, leaving seven.

47

The fourth couldn't find a wife, and there were only six. The fifth grew disillusioned, leaving five, and so on, up to the last one, who was stubborn by nature and decided to stick it out. In the early days of the State, the ratio of Americans (mostly volunteers for army service in the War of Independence) who went back was nine to ten; now, following the emotional revival brought on by the Six Day War and thanks to better absorption schemes, the ratio has dropped to six or seven out of every ten immigrants. The ratio for the other residents is about one to ten, but one cannot compare West and East, neither Eastern Europe nor the lands of the Levant, whose refugees, having nowhere else to go, had to hang on and integrate successfully, unless they perished in the process. The rulers of Morocco and Iraq, Poland and Hungary, did more to cause their former residents to take root here than did the Jewish Agency and the Israel Government combined. They were the ones who liberated their Jews from Hamlet's dilemma: to remain in Israel or to go back. Most Americans who come here classify themselves as temporary residents rather than immigrants, so as not to burn all their bridges behind them—and we can readily understand the motive. On the other hand, if Israel does exist and if its citizens are ready to fight for it—once, twice, thrice (and a fourth time, if need be), it is because they have nowhere to go back to; all the bridges have been irrevocably burned.

Aliya from the United States sprouted even before Herzl discovered his people. Around the middle of the nineteenth century, an American proselyte by the name of Michael Boaz Israel (only a convert to Judaism would take unto himself so Jewish a name) attempted to establish an agricultural colony, "God's Vineyard," near the approaches to Jerusalem and to settle there two hundred Americans—Christians and Jews. He did not get to eat of the fruits of the Holy Land; the latter consumed him first. In the 1880's the experiment was repeated by an American Jew of Polish parentage, Simon Berman. His plan was to set up a cooperative farm near the Mikveh Israel Agricultural School and later in Tiberias, under the auspices of the Holy Land Settlement Society, but this also came to naught.

The number of North Americans currently residing in Israel is said to be some 23,000 (of whom 5,000 came prior to the establishment of the State), amounting to about one percent of the population. Despite their modest proportion, North American Jews may pride themselves on having made several important contributions to Israel's growth and development, as immigrants and as non-immigrants: they gave us Dov Joseph, former Cabinet Minister who introduced us to the late lamented austerity; Sam Hamburger, who introduced cotton-ginning to Israel; Col. David (Mickey) Marcus, who brought his West Point know-how to aid Israel's cause in 1948, and Eliezer Yaffe, a founder of Nahalal (the story of his *aliya* follows the familiar pattern: his American *Hechalutz* group had several dozen members; twelve joined the Young Farmer group for settlement in Eretz-Yisrael: five came here and joined Kvutzat Kinneret, one was killed, another went back, three remained).

The first bathtub in the coastal area, say some, was brought from America, in 1927, by Sam Friedlander, a founder of Avihail, the settlement established by the Jewish Legion veterans of World War One. Scattered throughout the land are several *kibbutzim* and *moshavim* with nuclei of scores of Americans, but efforts to set up a purely American colony have so far been fruitless, and the nebulous plans regarding an American town in the Negev are not too promising. In the Israeli climate it is apparently more practical to dilute American bourbon with Israeli seltzer. In America the Jews, when in their own company, are too Jewish; in Israel, American Jews amongst themselves are too American.

It is rather difficult to measure the impact of American *aliya* on Israel, for the simple reason that it is not easy to separate the influence wielded by former Americans living here from the more general impact of the American way of life on the country. Russian customs, from borscht to open house, were introduced by the Russian Jews in person, but Americana seeps in on its own, even without Jews, whether it is in the guise of hot dogs or Coca Cola, or tinted toilet paper, supermarkets, opinion polls or jazz. Americans did have direct impact on the Israel Air Force during its early years, when most of the pilots were volunteers from the United States and Canada; this influence is still present in the aeronautics industry. You will find Americans in electronics and a few promising young men in Government ministries. There are Americans in education and social work—and more recently in basketball—but the principal American influence is felt in the institutes of higher learning and research, in the Haifa Technion, the Hebrew University in Jerusalem, the universities of Tel Aviv and Bar-Ilan, the Weizmann Institute in Rehovot. Indeed, the American-accented Hebrew of the researchers, lecturers and consultants one hears on the radio is becoming as acceptable as the Russian was, once upon a time, among the actors.

The young American recently arrived in Israel is distinguished, in general, by a generous growth of beard and careless attire (in the *kibbutz* rating of diligence among the "foreign legion" volunteers the American student is on the bottom of the ladder, several rungs below the non-Jews from Switzerland, Germany, Denmark, Sweden, and Jews from Rumania and Czechoslovakia). If he is married, he tends to have more children than his colleagues. He shows less interest in politics, less ideological fieriness; he has a distaste for flowery speech and bears a pragmatic approach to life—very much like the young native-born, except that he adheres more strongly to tradition, longs for a small house with a well-kept lawn in the suburbs, and has a weakness for clean and spacious bathrooms. Unfortunately, the only public comfort stations in working order, other than those in the Israeli home itself, are to be found in facilities for American tourist, chiefly the major hotels; the tourist who wanders away too far from this base of operation is in constant danger. The Israelis, much as they appreciate clean rest rooms, have learned the art of self-restraint, from the days of the Mandate.

What apparently draws the American Jew to Israel, other than the desire to live as a Jew among Jews, is the fact that, here, the individual still counts for something—so far; social climbing is not yet an eroding exercise; there is still no violence in the cities; as yet, the tempo of life is not dizzying; retired people can live on their pensions more comfortably, so far; there's a seashore and more or less pure air, so far—in short, Israel has not as yet achieved the Age of Tomorrow, for better or for worse. What we call an industrial plant is, by American standards, a workshop; our "efficiency" is really a pattern for obviating work norms; industrial research is still in its diapers. This situation represents a challenge to the Americans, but they dare not comment upon it, lest the Israelis come back with a more formidable one: "Fine, come here in your masses and change things." And if you don't make changes, the place will change you.

Actually, what's so bad about a little disorder? What's wrong with leaving things to chance a bit? What evil can there be in a few airtight privileges? What's wrong with doing things the way they have been done for forty years? What's wrong with being a real Israeli?

Immigrants in Reverse

THERE'S NOTHING wrong with the word "immigrant." Half the globe is populated with the progeny of people who, for certain reasons (primarily economic), left their birthplace and settled elsewhere. But he who leaves Israel in order to make his home in another country is a *yored,* and no translation is capable of transmitting the repugnance, the final judgment, the dissociation and the disillusionment contained in the Hebrew designation of the individual who "defected," who ran away from the home front, who sold his soul for a mess of pottage, who crumpled when the chips were down, who preferred comfort to history.

The Israel Government, may it live long and be well, guides its citizens along so many paths of living, yet it offers no relief in the heat of this question: how are they, the citizens, to behave toward the phenomenon of *yerida?* Should they show understanding? Should they vehemently condemn it? If this were to happen in a country where everything goes by the book—we are thinking of the Hapsburg ideal—the matter would have long been established, to wit.: a *yored* is he who . . . and is to be treated in accordance with Section 57, Paragraph 14 of the temporary emergency legislation, in force until further notice. Israel, however, is still running riot with freedom of thought, almost, and everyone is free to relate to *yerida* as he sees fit. This unbridled freedom is irritating and of dubious virtue and should be halted; once and for all and forever, it should be determined who is to be called a *yored,* who should be treated with scorn and who with tolerance, who should be ostracized and who should be coddled; how much should an ex-Israeli have in his savings account before he can progress from a poor *yored* to a respectable Zionist; how wide an acclaim must an Israeli artist earn before he is forgiven his change of permanent residence and his Israeli origins noted with pride.

What is needed here is classification—each *yored* and his rating, each rating and its status. He who is a *yored* with conniving aforethought, openly, is more of a *yored* than he who remains abroad out of sheer inertia, innocently. A Wall Street broker deserves a different rating from the wretch who repairs zippers and cuffs in a Brooklyn dry cleaning establishment. *Yerida* should be worthwhile, otherwise one may as well live in Israel.

Only welfare cases, or unimaginative East European types, leave Israel with crates and emigration permits. People of vision go abroad with two medium-size valises; obviously, whatever one can get in Israel can certainly be acquired in America, and a later model to boot. They reside abroad two, three, four, five years, become expert in the interior decoration of Eskimo igloos or in de-kinking hair—occupations which, much to the regret of the people involved, are not in demand in Israel; how, then, could anyone insist that they return? Whoever wishes to be regarded as an Israeli residing, by pure chance, in Houston, rather than a *yored,* should take certain precautions:

a) he should not talk too much;

b) he should choose a calling which demands prolonged and indefinite sojourn abroad;

c) he should become outstanding and/or rich.

Even an absolute monarchy observes the happy custom of granting a reprieve to criminals at coronation time. Why should it be different in a coalition democracy? According to the official definition, a *yored* is one who left Israel for good, after the State had already been founded. Whoever left prior to that event cannot be counted, inasmuch as the Central Bureau of Statistics was not in existence. If all who left us since the days of the *Bilu* pioneers (that is, during the past eight decades) were here today, we would be nearing the fourth million in population. Refugees from the Russian Revolution (the full contribution of this upheaval to the growth of pioneer *aliya* is yet to be fully evaluated) came here, looked around, recoiled from what they saw and went on to New York, where, if they are still alive, they are residing in comfort to this day and are indubitably loyal supporters of the Zionist cause. The time has also come for removing from the list of *yordim* all who left Israel during its period of austerity, i.e., during the country's first decade. Why should we tag with the *yored* label the Australian citizen, of Hungarian parentage and the Mosaic faith, who went to Israel in 1949 because the Hungarians would not issue exit permits elsewhere and, finding neither the immigrant camps nor the shanty towns to his liking, kept going on to work for his brother in a knitwear factory in Melbourne? We should now resolve that, after ten years, a *yored* automatically loses his title to the name and may furthermore be invited to all functions tendered by Israeli delegations abroad and be held in equal esteem with those who hadn't even made the attempt to settle in Israel, thereby keeping their Zionist record unblemished.

For two thousand years the Jews wandered across the face of the earth, building homes although sure that, some day, they might have to abandon them, in an endless chain of the pale of settlement, ghetto, pogrom, expulsion, Frankfurt, Lemberg, Vienna, Bukovina, Spain, Turkey, Europe, America. When evil times descended upon them—conscription or nationalization, war or famine—they packed up and moved on. This wandering apparently penetrated into our very marrow, and even the potent air of the Land of Israel cannot dissipate it. One must have the solid character of the Gentile (or at the least his sedentary faculties) in order to dwell on the same plot of land, even as regimes come and go, and recessions billow up and peter out. Our difficulty is that we did not get a country of our own while the world was still wide open, with long stretches in between, so that grains of sand had time to develop into protective havens. Now the world is in motion, and the same *modus vivendi* holds for everyone—the same refrigerator, the same mattress of foam rubber, the same grey flannel suit and mini skirt, from Alaska to the Falkland Islands. A country which has no citizenry tempered by hardship and attached to the soil to begin with, will require generations to develop. The rich and the intellectual are more mobile.

Yerida is like any other human failing: the moment you get to know the *yordim* from up close, you cannot pass sentence. Resentment and aversion melt into sympathy and understanding. Happy are the preaching zealots, the staunch pillars of society, in whose eyes every *yored* stands condemned! They are the righteous because understanding is a luxury reserved for days of peace, for retired warriors. Each of us, in Israel, can come up with a good reason for living here and with an equally good reason for not living here—if residence in Israel is something that can be weighed rationally, as if the subject were the purchase of an apartment or the replacement of a car. In that case, the decision to leave becomes a matter of grammar, a switch from first person to third. You stop saying "we" and say "they". They did, they didn't, they promised, they didn't keep their promise.

People leave Israel because, actually, they expected too much of its inhabitants. It goes against their spiritual grain to witness here corruption, "pull," bureaucracy, Levantinism, social inequity, selfishness or crudeness. Most of these shortcomings exist in their new country as well, but there they aren't as sensitive. As a new American, the *yored* does not have to feel for the downtrodden Negro or to resent America's involvement in the Vietnam war; he is outside the mainstream of American life to begin with. He is impervious to envying the social status of the Cabot Lodges or the Du Pont estate in Palm Beach; he has no intention of competing with them. It's different in Israel. The land is so small, and everybody knows everybody else; Sapir's name was once upon a time Kozlowski, and Eshkol they knew from Degania. All of us (except the few Rivlins and Frumkins) are Israelis without local family trees, and all of us arrived with the same opportunities before us. The Brooklyn teacher who instructs the Community Center Adult Education class in Hebrew is not upset because the Whitneys have a penthouse on Fifth Avenue and the Warburgs sport a private chauffeur. But in Israel it is most depressing to learn that the fellow who was your classmate in high school or on the training farm, or your comrade in the Brigade and your neighbor in the housing project, has suddenly developed affluence and importance. There's no justice in the world generally, but in Israel this injustice stares you in the face.

If you spend any time at all in America you are bound to meet some *yordim*. Each of them will recite to you a long list of people, of much greater prominence, who left Israel and aren't even considering going back. Each of them will fish out a newspaper clipping about some depressing occurrence back in Israel. Each will trot out the hackneyed allegations about provincialism and nepotism, sales taxes on cars and seniority manipulation at places of employment. Under the impact of this barrage you feel yourself

55

being drawn into this whirlpool: perhaps you had been living with
your eyes shut; perhaps you are blind—all of Israel consists of
potential *yordim,* including Avraham Hartzfeld and S.Y. Agnon
and General Ezer Weizmann and Golda Meir . . . And then you
come back home, and the anemones are in bloom, and the *kibbutzim* are where they always were, and the taxi pullers-in are
shouting "Haifa-Haifa-Tel Aviv-Tel Aviv," and the Girl Scouts
sing as they trudge along, the kerosene dealer's bell peals in the
streets and the wash is on the line in the sunshine—and suddenly
you wonder what could have gotten into you, at the midtown
hotel in New York, among the widows and their dogs and the
traveling salesmen.

Yordim who have not made peace with themselves (and it takes
a long time to forget Israel, whether one thinks about it with
hatred or with longing) are like hasheesh smokers; they're just
trying it out, just to see whether it's good, like people say. They
go abroad to see the world, nothing more, to visit for a year or
two, then a bit longer—by a few months or years, a bit more money,
another set of dishes, more English for the children. And the
environment works like the waves of the sea, washing away one
grain after another, until everything is eroded. They stay on not
because they had decided to leave Israel for good but because
they don't know how to make up their minds to go back.

You meet the ex-Israelis in Toronto and in Miami, in Flushing
and San Juan, and since you are not given to nurturing prejudice
or being hidebound about things, you drink tea with them, go
with them to dinner in a Chinese restaurant, attend the theatre
with them and chat with them about Dayan and Topol—but you
discreetly stay away from one subject, even though it's on everyone's mind: what in hell are you doing here? You don't ask the
question because it would place you in the seat of judgment or in
the shoes of the prosecutor, or in the position of being right, or,
what is even worse, righteous. Instead, you swing the question to
yourself: am I really better than he? Haven't I remained in Israel
because I had grown weary, or because my profession would be
useless abroad, or because I have a good job with fringe benefits,
or because I am invited to all the premieres? Our generation has
received all those sanctimonious cliches all chewed up, like a
grey and petrified wad of chewing gum, without any taste, and

we therefore have difficulty in enunciating them: roots, homeland, the last chance for the Jewish people. We find it much easier to say: "I should leave Israel? I love sunshine. I couldn't go back to those long winters."

Plato's principle—that the chosen few can bring the ideal republic into being—is applicable to Israel as well. What we need is a nucleus of permanent Israelis for whom residence in Israel is an indispensable ingredient of existence, and who do not require the comfort of knowing that the *yordim*, wherever they are, do not enjoy life, either economically or socially. There was a time when we thought that anyone born in Israel would automatically belong to such a nucleus, but we were mistaken. A birth certificate is no substitute for sentiment or a sense of responsibility. If the world survives on the merits of thirty-six just men, as Jewish tradition teaches, then Israel can survive if it has a million souls who would never say that you can't exist in this land; and if not a million, then a hundred thousand, and if not a hundred then ten.

In the days when we sang "On to Zion with Flag and Banner," in our youth group abroad, and our counselor told us about the plywood factory in Afikim and the wine cellars of Rishon Le-Zion, the very thought of someone leaving Eretz Yisrael of his own free will was something that our young minds could not digest. When the rumor came that Harry Pick, Sonya Pick's brother, who had gone to Palestine on a pioneer's certificate (to the envy of us others), had not only dropped out from training and quit the *kibbutz* but had also gone off to America (where he was making a living, according to the rumor, playing an accordion in coffee shops), we thought that this was the lowest gutter to which anyone could sink. Harry's case became the symbol of the Fall, compared with which the affair of Adam and Eve in Eden was no more than a regrettable episode.

Now we are adults. We have read Freud and learned how to be tolerant, and the list of our friends and companions who left Israel is steadily growing: Feuerstein is a stamp dealer in New York; Old Man Rosenberg went back to Hamburg; Ilana stayed on in London, Miriam is teaching in Quebec. We exchange letters and give regards, and we have learned to live with *yerida* as one lives with rheumatism; it's unpleasant, but not fatal.

Viewed statistically, the situation is not so gloomy. Of those who immigrated to Israel, some 180,000 (about 12%) left the country since the founding of the state. Statistics, however, like primeval deities, numb our hope that fate is subject to change. This Christmas, asserts the American TV announcer on the eve of the holiday, 550 will perish in traffic accidents. It's all cut and dried, and there is no escaping this predestined death toll. And so it is much better to treat *yerida* as being an inevitable feature of *aliya* (as school dropouts are treated in various localities as part of school enrollment), especially now that immigration restrictions to the U.S. have been eased and employment there is plentiful and *aliya* on the other hand, does not necessarily leave burned bridges behind the immigrants from America. Much better this approach to *yerida* than to harp on the reasons and causes for it. Most of the *yordim,* if they do give the reason for having left Israel, cite one decisive incentive: health, the climate, the income tax, lack of livelihood, or claustrophobia, but the decision for *yerida* grows in a mixed soil. If we assume a personal guilt for the *yerida* of others (in accord with the tradition that all of Israel are responsible one for the other), then we would have to add it to our other responsibilities— for the ingathered, for the preservation of wildlife, fighting air pollution, developing the Negev— toward all of which we feel that we must make our personal contribution. For this reason, when we hear of someone about to commit *yerida,* our reaction is "dammit, let him be a *yored!*" Does this, too, have to be our concern? Our shoulders are already worn raw from bearing our common Israeli burdens.

Arrival and Departure

Stumbling After the Sun

HAD THE owner of that tent at the "Terebinths of Mamre" said to the three travelers waiting outside: "Sorry, gentlemen, but this isn't a hotel. You should have seen to lodging in advance," then Isaac would not have been born to Sarah after her change of life, and Jewish history would have gone off on another tangent, if at all. In those good old days, however, travelers from distant places had to depend on the hospitality of the local citizens. Anyone who wanted to see the world had to throw himself on the mercy of others, with the hope that man to man is not a wolf and that, in the hour of need (especially after night had fallen), someone would be there to fetch him some water, a loaf of bread and a mat, in return for a coin, a piece of fabric, or simply out of generosity. The traveler usually lodged with his peers: nobleman with nobleman, craftsman with craftsman, scholar with scholar, Jews with Jews. Of hotel or restaurant there was none, neither tourist motor-coaches nor travel agencies to lead the flock from one well to the next.

The Age of Technology has wrought a deep cleft between the tourist and the local populace. Today you can visit any country you desire and spend there days and weeks without exchanging a single word with any natives other than those engaged in tourism. The local population is represented by the waiters and chambermaids, the reception clerks and cab drivers, guides and the souvenir vendors, airline clerks and hotel hairdressers—people either engaged in serving the tourist or placed there to disengage him from his money, neatly and efficiently—an international legion with the same traits everywhere, set apart by slight details of one kind or another.

There is something pathetic and disheartening about the flocks of tourists in colorful pre-season dresses and Bermuda shorts, *tembel* hats of local make in various stages of disrepute, as they clamber aboard the tourist coaches, cameras dangling from their necks, then trip down at an historical site or near a genuine camel, make click-click and aboard again to a tourist restaurant for a meal advertised as international cuisine especially for tourists, and on to a souvenir shop (forcefully recommended by the guide), returning at eventide to the tourist hotel, whose impersonal tone rises with its rates. Tourists upon tourists, from dawn to dusk, secluded in an air-conditioned cage of wall-to-wall carpeting: you see them throughout Israel.

In the evening the ladies, tinted hair stiff with spray, crowned with a halo of more or less precious stones, plunging necklines revealing delicate shades of semi-roasted fowl, in cardigans with mink collars, or men in silk suits with a white handkerchief in the breast pocket, they sit back deep in the square lounge chairs of the de luxe hotel, waiting for the guide to take them on the night club circuit or for a distant relative living in the area, who will come dressed in his Sabbath best, with his wife, to render a report on the fate of the family and their perished townsmen. Or they simply lounge about, their tired feet stretched out under the low tables and wait for the advent of a decent hour to get up and go to sleep, without giving the impression that they are not enjoying themselves. Anyone who pays for a first-class flight and a stay at a de luxe hotel, plus a de luxe tour packed with exciting thrills *must* enjoy himself, else he has obviously made a poor investment —a serious indictment in a society which measures success in terms of money made and money spent.

And so the women laugh boisterously, call themselves "girls" even if their daughters are already themselves mothers, and the men tell spicy anecdotes—not too spicy, so as not to embarrass the "girls" when they are in male company, but enough to insinuate that sex still holds their interest. The captains of the tourist trade like the American tourist, and tourists are mostly Ameriican, at the Hilton and the Sheraton and the Dan Carmel and the King David, for he is known in the parlance of the trade as a "high-spending-habit tourist." He is more desirable than his counterpart who stays with relatives, goes on Egged bus tours, wears orthopedic shoes and carries a large straw receptacle embossed with "Capri" or "Majorca." The liberal spenders leave behind, on the average, some $350 per capita, while the poor edition can get away with less than $100, including the $20 spent on souvenirs.

Tourists are currently an export industry, like polished diamonds or artificial teeth. They have a monetary and economic value, added and marginal value; they provide foreign currency and employment. They no doubt have soul and sentiment, but the agencies involved haven't as yet made a study of the subject.

It is an irony of circumstance that the income from tourists in recent years should have been not much more than the expenditures incurred by Israelis traveling abroad. In a year or two we are hopeful of hitting an annual figure of 500,000 tourists, which will force us Israelis to yield some room along the beaches, at the picnic grounds, in the restaurants and museums. This will in turn make it mandatory that we go abroad and undergo the tourist coaches, the tourist hotels and tourist guides—eight countries "visited" in ten days. The objective of this arrangement may well be to attain a complete population exchange: three million tourists for three million outgoing Israelis. Invalids will be able to obtain a deferment of the exit decree upon presentation of a medical certificate.

Italy already has one tourist per 2.5 natives, but in contrast with the Israelis, the Italians stay put, tourist avalanche or no (except for a few Milanese industrial tycoons, princesses from Rome, and job-seekers all over Europe). What can one find in the great wide world that Italy doesn't have? Where is the sun brighter, the spaghetti fuller, the wine better, the girls prettier? If, in the course of centuries, so many people have been drawn to Italy from so many countries, it is obvious that there is none better. Nor do the Swiss intend to vacate their country to make room for the tourist inundation, and their one reason is clear and convincing: should they waste all that good money brought in by tourists on visiting all sorts of backward peoples, on strangers and foreigners, and undisciplined spendthrifts to boot? The average Israeli, on the other hand, if he is to reach the happy and obvious conclusion that there's no place like home, must perforce reach it via personal experience, namely, after having traveled and toured and investigated and suffered all the way home. There are

63

no better Zionists than those who come back from a peregrination abroad.

If tourists were to come to Israel merely to "follow the sun"—as do the Scandinavians in Eilat and the French at Gesher Haziv, in quest of a suntan, a dip in the sea, relaxation on the beach or a mild flirtation—they would get all this, more or less, without putting us on the spot. The trouble is that people come to Israel primarily for spiritual resuscitation, the romance of pioneering, Jewishness, the sacred atmosphere, ancestry, glory and all the other hard-to-get items, plus the magic of the East, tastefully spun.

Tourists love the primitive, minus its smells, particularly if they themselves dwell in private air-conditioned homes, set amidst well-tended gardens in a good neighborhood. They love a Bedouin encampment and a sheikh in living color, sporting a few wives, if possible (in this respect Sheikh Suleiman al-Huseil has done yeoman service for the tourist trade: he has it all—an encampment just off the main highway, a harem and the sense of humor to pose gracefully for the popping cameras). Tourists also appreciate the sight of supple Arab maidens at the well, of an Arab dignitary seated on a stool and counting his prayer beads, of an Oriental market with a muezzin's cry floating overhead—all photogenic objects which can readily be shown to friends back home. From a specific viewpoint, the Arabs are worth more to Israeli tourism than are the Jews, especially when they adhere to tradition. An Israeli Jew is similar in appearance to anyone else, unless he is from Meah She'arim, where a tourist can find an ascetic youth in shiny cloak and white stockings who is certainly worth almost as much as a Bedouin in a flowing burnoose or a Yemenite woman in embroidered pantaloons, now a very rare species. Tourists want to see progress, but it shouldn't be too ambitious; modern improvements have their place—in the bathroom, the garage, the hairdresser's—but not on tour. How can one dwell at length, back home, on a plant which turns out firefighting equipment, on a water conduit, a supermarket or a six-lane highway? But a market where sweaters are tried on in the open, and whole sheep are strung up in the doorway, and *peetas* are carried in flat baskets atop the head—that's something; truly and marvelously picturesque.

Many countries can dish out the picturesque, but Israel's *specialité de la maison* is Pioneering. The tourist may be taken aback by the sight of the cafe loungers on Dizengoff Street, but he will readily forgive the Israelis this letdown, as long as there are border *kibbutzim* and desert outpost settlements, immigrants digging into the rocky soil and vineyards flourishing among the boulders; in short, as long as there is incontrovertible proof that life in Israel is tough—at least some of it. Otherwise we would be in real trouble.

The very name "Holy Land" embodies an obligation. Even though direct contact with the Lord has been suffering from breaks in the line, here in Israel one wants to experience a bit of sanctity. A believing Catholic can probably feel this uplifting of the heart as he stands in a subterranean grotto before a marble altar on the very spot, according to the Moslem guide ("heer eez dee blaze"), where Angel Gabriel announced the forthcoming birth of Jesus to the Holy Virgin; half a dozen cameras flash in response, while behind the plywood partition workers with pneumatic drills are constructing a magnificent basilica overhead, and, at the entrance to the grotto, another group of tourists is waiting impatiently for the termination of the spiritual journey of those inside the grotto. A practicing Jew may similarly feel the Divine Presence hovering above him, as he stands in Elijah's Cave and beholds the walls, black with candle soot, and the cringing mendicants around the silk chair (reputedly from the Prophet's estate), and hears the rattling of the poor boxes and smells the lunches brought along by those who intend to hold a lengthy seance with the Prophet. The sites sanctified by Christianity are no more sacred than the Jewish holy places, but they are cleaner and more esthetic. King David, Meir Baal-Haness, Simeon Bar-Yochai and the others can be envious of their opposite numbers of the daughter faith, if cleanliness is a matter of interest to them at all.

The VIP tourists who come to pursue honor rather than follow the sun usually arrive for the Jewish festivals—Passover, the High Holy Days, or Chanukah, when they can relax among their own and combine pleasure with business: attend the dedication of a youth center bearing their name; witness the unveiling ceremony of a tractor they had contributed; hand out scholar-

65

ships commemorating the names of dearly beloved departed parents, or attend a meeting of the Board of Directors of the Friends of this or that institution. Only Israel is in the position to give the wealthy Jew, particularly the *nouveau riche,* who seeks an emotional outlet to his generosity, such prestige, status and honor. In London this Jew may be the owner of a lucrative string of betting spots, but no money in the world can eliminate his East End accent or open to him the doors of British high society. Here he comes to and into his own: an announcement in the press greets his arrival, children hand him flowers, the dignitaries of the community entertain him at dinner. Only in Israel can one approach the seats of the mighty—Ministers, heads of Government, Presidents—so easily and so inexpensively, relatively speaking.

Spring tourists (Passover and Independence Day) are mostly Jewish adults who can afford to take off three weeks and come to the Passover Seder graced with matza balls like Mama used to make, although what they really get is the commercial substitute cooked up by the hotels. These are the tourists propelled by sentiments of Jewishness, by the United Jewish Appeal, the Jewish National Fund et al.

Summer brings the young students, affectionately called "the foreign legion"—Swiss, Danes, Germans, Americans, French, English—Jews and non-Jews to whose ears have come the tidings that in Israel it is possible to get food and lodging and pocket money in return for work in the *kibbutzim.* As they toil and gambol, their fair skin assumes the hues of summer, from smoked-turkey-pink to borscht-and-sour-cream-purple, from the rust of tin to lobster red. They line the highways, thumbing rides, the fellows with long hair and tight pants and the girls in loosely woven blouses which reveal what makes drivers stop, free—at least here, under the southern sun—from convention and parental eyes.

Young Jews from families with religious orientation are different. They are more earnest and show interest in problems, statistics, integration, the religious crisis. They participate in symposia, summer seminars, Hebrew language courses. They keep a diary and send articles on Israel to the community paper back home.

There used to be a time when touring through a foreign country called for the expenditure of a certain amount of intellectual effort; it was incumbent on the tourist to visit museums, historical sites and examples of various styles of architecture. The age of TV and art reproductions has brought the treasure troves of the museums and art galleries into the living room and has absolved the weary tourist from the endless rows of sculptured heads of Rome's emperors, the cathedrals built in one style or another and all sorts of ruins of once-flourishing cities. Today one can admit publicly, without losing face, that the purpose of the impending foreign tour is to see how life is lived there, i.e., coffee shops, stores, restaurants, the theatre, landscapes.

The approach used by tourist guides has also changed, accordingly. Baedeker, father of the tribe, for a hundred years the bible of every traveling western European, regarded it as his sacred duty to visit every plausible spot, marking it with two stars (the Louvre, the Kremlin, Niagara Falls) or one star (peak of the Jungfrau). Baedeker was very basic, as befitted his German background, and filled with history and data. The tourists at times became so engrossed in the small print that they hardly had time to lift their eyes unto the statues. Baedeker published the first modern guide to Syria and Palestine in 1875; the maps were so accurate that General Allenby used them in his successful campaign to wrest those countries from the Turks, in the First World War. Down the centuries, visitors to the Holy Land used to publish amateur guidebooks for the pilgrims to follow, but the first Hebrew guides of this generation, especially those of Zeev Vilnai, remained true to the Baedeker tradition and have supplied the tourist with a broad cultural background and historical data rather than laundry prices.

And now a new generation of guides has arisen in the land. The valuable time (average stay, 14 days) of the tourist in Israel is no longer wasted on superfluous details and boring facts. Bazak (there couldn't possibly be a better name for it: "Lightning") devotes but six lines to Kibbutz Degania, including visiting hours at the Gordon Museum there (no charge) and the ancient synagogue at Beit Alpha (there is a charge). There are no bothersome dates or confusing names of monarchs. A peek into the guidebook, a click of the camera, a hop into the bus and off across Israel's countryside. On the other hand, Bazak furnishes the

67

tourist with the information he really needs: where the gas stations are, how the restaurants rate, touring maps and aphorisms by Harry the Tourist in the vein of, "Meah She'arim may look odd to you, but I couldn't help thinking that my sainted grandmother, may she rest in peace, would have been very much at home there."

It's not easy to be a tourist in Israel, almost like anywhere else, and perhaps even a bit tougher. We relate to the tourist with that haughtiness which every native bears toward the foreigner, who is detached from the realities of the place and is enthused about things which we take for granted, and particularly when he tries to communicate in the local tongue or otherwise demonstrate his friendliness. And if the tourist is hostile, critical or sits in judgment we feel a sort of animosity toward him. By what right and with whose permission? Let him settle here and we'll talk further.

You'd like it if everyone would love Israel and depart a sworn supporter of the state. You'd want him to enjoy every step he takes, that none should exploit him or address him discourteously, that he should not be served soggy French fries and a tough steak, that he should be shown to a clean bathroom and be given a map without grease spots on it, that the sun should shine brightly on him if that's what he is after, that he should experience Jewishness if he so desires and that he should be accorded honor if he has paid for it. We, the sober and the mature, are familiar with the facts of life. We may rant and criticize, quarrel and throw dishes—but the children must not know. Let them have fond memories of the ancestral home.

Your Obedient Servant, Sir!

BETWEEN US, Great Britain and the Land of Israel, it has been a long romance, in installments, interruptions, and alternating chapters of great expectations and rude awakening, of deep admiration and deadly hatred, and, as in every tale of unrequired love, a sediment remains which revives all emotions except indifference.

Now that we are blessed with maturity and have gained insight into the facts of life, we tend to have dark suspicion of the English as statesmen and much affection for them as Englishmen, natives of the Land of Marks & Spencer and Laurence Olivier. Our attitude toward the British suffers accordingly: on the one hand, we bear great love for charming London, the shops along Regent Street and the West End theatres, for the English language as spoken by Dame Peggy Ashcroft and the echoes of the St. Paul's Cathedral Choir, for polished furniture and country manors set in green, for superfluous and ancient relics of no intrinsic worth; on the other hand, we harbor distrust and animosity for that inscrutable institution called the Foreign Office and its long corridors, along which stalk senior servants carrying brief cases of black leather, for the British Intelligence which heartlessly dispatches spies into the cold, and for Labor's leaders who achieve the post of Foreign Secretary in the British power structure.

We know from experience that we can get along very well with the English Socialists—until they get into power. Perhaps it's because socialism tainted with oil is more enticing than socialism fragrant with orange blossoms, or because a Laborite from the working classes who attains a high post feels that he must prove, at all times and under all circumstances, that he is guarding Great Britain's interests more zealously than all those aristocrats, and therefore cannot allow himself any weaknesses, as does the upper crust, which mixes politics with ideals, naivete, mysticism and faith in the Messianic era. Perhaps we do better with Conservatives—and not only in Britain—because they can recognize an excellent fighting force when they see one.

There were times when we suspected every British Arabphile of being inclined toward homosexual aberrations and toward veneration of lithe sheikhs astride pedigreed steeds, who look so wonderful as they emerge from behind clouds of desert sand in scintillating technicolor. We are happy to note that the private life of several contemporary Arabphiles, with George Brown astride the list, forms conclusive refutation of our unworthy suspicions.

There is irony in the fact that, to this day, we are bound more to the British than to any other western nation, despite U.S. funds and on-and-off French arms and despite the bitter intermezzo of the final decade of the Mandate. Over the years, we have maintained ties through the Bible, as the guide for living and longing for the Promised Land, through Byron and Laurence Oliphant, through Balfour and Weizmann, Sarah Aaronson and Gallipoli, Wingate and Liddell Hart, Spitfires, the Jewish Legion and the Jewish Brigade.

By the time that Israel was only a few years old, all of the hatred from the period of the struggle against foreign rule had faded away, except in *Etzel* and *Lehy* circles, where memories were sharper. The old-timers fondly recalled Spinney's stores and Guinness beer, the Pound when it was a Pound Sterling and income tax was nominal. Time veered toward affection; forgotten were the blockade runners, the curfew and the search for arms. After all (so went the general thinking), any other occupying power—French, Dutch, Russian, Belgian—would have been infinitely worse. We kept the memory of the British presence alive through streets named for Allenby and King George, via the atmosphere in our courthouses, the figurehead post of District Officer, our resignation to the queueing up at the bus stop, the signs on the storefronts, the police stations, the pith helmets sported by building contractors, and the "Zalman" shorts, which somehow looked more elegant on the spanking-smart British officers. With the opening of the West Bank we have come across more memories of the British legacy, eroded but not erased by the passing years.

These are the days when an Indian yogi preaches the philosophy of life to the Beatles and other renowned Englishmen in search of spiritual revival (usually after they have already accumulated honors and material means), but for many generations the seekers for spiritual truth had their souls turned to the Holy Land. Here was the cynosure for generations of archaeologists who sought verification for the Holy Writ; fair-skinned gentlewomen with lofty ideas and stamina like steel who wished to bring Jews closer to Christianity; noblemen with a messianic spark in quest of faith or of life rooted in biblical values, with five o'clock tea and a bit more hygiene added.

The search for a new identification with the Middle East expanse led the British along two courses: the noble, proud, virile and hospitable Arab, and the depressed, suffering Jew with nothing to offer but his staunch faith in the good world to come. Lawrence of Arabia and Orde Wingate were but two sides of the same coin; there is great similarity between the two, in their zeal, courage and faith in their mission.

We are the fruit of British culture, in no smaller measure than the British are indebted to us for theirs. We tend to toy with dangerous "ifs," in national affairs as in private life, yet it is clear that, if it were not for the British, the State of Israel would not have come into being nor would it be what it is today; were it not for their attachment to the Bible, they would not have brought forth statesmen steeped in the belief that the restoration of the Jew to the Land of Israel was the first step to the Kingdom of Heaven. True, this faith was interwoven with considerations of strategy, politics and finance, but it is unthinkable that such astute statesmen as Joseph Chamberlain and Lloyd George would have otherwise been inclined to pay any attention to such a polit-ical nonentity as the Zionist Federation, or that Lord Balfour would have otherwise affixed his signature to a document so blatantly naive as the Declaration that bears his name (when you peruse the text of the Balfour Declaration, ". . . the establishment in Palestine of a national home for the Jewish people . . . nothing shall be done to prejudice the civil and religious rights of existing non-Jewish communities in Palestine," you are again amazed on how flimsy a sheet of paper we set out to build a state!) Were it

71

not for the British there would be no Jordan and no Hussein, no Mandate and no White Papers, no "Exodus 1947" and no Partition Scheme.

Israel arose not thanks to the British but because of British intransigence, of a stumbling policy, of that typical mixture of British politics: lofty ideals and materialistic goals. The label of "perfidious Albion" which we affix to Britain every time she disappoints us politically is quite erroneous, in that it connotes the perfidy to be in her political line. And yet there is no nation, other perhaps than the American, which has engaged in so much warfare, conquest or liberation out of higher motivation, to make good on moral obligations and formal promises, out of sense of responsibility for the future of the world or as missionaries to the nations—a motivation at times obscured (to satisfy the skeptics and the realists) by such material considerations as acquiring a military base, checking the advance of a hostile power, or establishing an outpost on the eastern fringe of the Empire. Later, as various moral obligations become burdensome and lofty goals become charred with disillusion and economic or strategic reasons dictate withdrawal, these considerations are camouflaged with swelling strains of granting independence, awarding the right of self-determination or caring for the welfare of the natives, and the cycle is done. Britain is no more perfidious than the other powers, except that the disappointments she creates always hurt more. You always expected more from her than from the others.

Compared with the Russians and the Poles at one end of the world or the Arabs and the Turks on the other—people with whom Jews had to deal for many generations—the English were angels, pure as gold and soft as down. They had no Beilis or Dreyfus trials, no Damascus libel and no Nuremberg Laws. What made them hated, by the people they ruled, was not primarily cruelty or exploitation or tyranny or corruption but arrogance, the relish for domination. If today we regard the British as being two-faced, it is not because we hate them more but because we once loved them more. A generation of Zionists courted Britain; in their eyes she was the fortress of justice and fairness—which, in comparison with Turkey, she was indeed. We fought in her ranks, learned her tongue, loved her literary greats. The younger crop of our leaders does not have the affinity for the English that Weizmann and Sharett had, but even among our native born the chief cultural attachment is to England.

Our disappointment in the English comes from a misunderstanding of the British character, plus the insult that while we have forgiven them the Mandate, they haven't forgiven us our independence. On the other hand, the attitude of the British toward the Jews in the Holy Land likewise emanates from a list of misunderstandings of the Jewish character. The depressed Jewish community in Palestine did not appreciate the effort of the Anglican clergy to lead it in the paths of truth; in the forefront of opposition to the Balfour Declaration were Englishmen of the Mosaic faith; the Jews did not stream to the Holy Land when they had the opportunity, as the English had thought they would, nor did they pour in their funds, in those early years, with the expected generosity (in this respect the British foresaw events by several decades; they were pre-Herzlian Zionists, and envisioned the millions of dollars long before the advent of the United Jewish Appeal). The Jews did not act the role of a persecuted people to be pitied, but stubbornly bit the hand that gave them the Jewish National Home; they made some of the Arab favorites of Great Britain look like impotent imbeciles, and they generally behaved with unbecoming arrogance, proclaiming loudly their mission on earth and their superiority over the nations, and indulged in absurd self-esteem and ridiculous illusions of grandeur, as though *they* were British.

We fully understand Hasnin Heykal, editor of *Al-Ahram* and Nasser's buddy, when he declares, via the British press, that the time has come for conversations between Egypt and Britain, as equals. That was what we wanted them to do: to repress their sense of superiority over the natives which remained with them even after the sun had set on the British Empire, and to give up the notion that the world exists for no reason other than to serve British interests, while the true reason, as we well know, is to have a world which would concern itself with Israel-Arab relations.

The Two Sons of Abraham

THE GOOD people of Tel Aviv and its suburban municipalities could have lived to be a hundred and twenty without a single thought about the Arabs as the sons of Adam (the parting of the ways came only with Father Abraham), were it not for the Six Day War. Not that we were indifferent, God forbid, to what went on in the country. But there's a basic difference between "the Arab problem" as a concept and the meaning of the two words when taken separately. We had experts to deal with this problem, as we have for industrial safety and the export of avocados. We had advisers and Orientalists to furnish expert opinion to Ministers and administrators of agencies which dealt with the Arabs; we gave them free rein and relied on their indubitably good judgment. After all, with all our intelligence, culture and alertness, we should hardly be expected to bear all the problems of state on our shoulders. Suffice it that we are experts on foreign relations, the theatre, economics and literature, financing, sports and sundry subjects. These experts were paid salaries for racking their brains over Arab affairs. As for us, our personal contact with Arab problems was restricted to the quality of the *hummous* in the Lower Haifa eateries, to shouting *badish!* (scram!) at the persistent souvenir vendors in Nazareth, or to visiting a sheikh's tent on the way to Beersheba. True, at times the problem was closer to home: is the painter's apprentice, though he calls himself Abraham, really Jewish? On the other hand, we had pleasant moments, too, as when we would see a group of Arab dignitaries, in traditional dress, strolling along Dizengoff Street; we always like to see democracy in action.

We were always aware, naturally, of the enemy on the other side of the border, but he had no face—only feet, which at times left prints at the site where the hands had planted a mine. To those who came to Israel or were born there after the War of Independence, the enemy was an intangible, without an image— much like the Pyramids or Beirut, totally out of bounds except, perhaps, for our children in some distant future, an incited and insidious enemy, reared on false propaganda, molded for murder and a ready tool in the hands of his masters. We would visualize him, at the most, as sitting in a coffee house and listening to Radio Cairo or hailing Shukeiry, but never as going to the dentist or eating chock-full-of-nuts *mahlabia* with his wife Badra and their four children. Now the Arabs have many faces, all inscrutable.

During the past two decades it never entered our minds to visit Faridis, Bakka, Garbia or any other Arab village within the state in order to ask their inhabitants what they thought about Jews in general and the State of Israel in particular. We simply drove by, along the highway, and saw the men sitting in their little cafes, or stopped long enough to buy grapes or a watermelon, cheap, and decided that no Jew need be ashamed to live in dwellings such as we saw there. Nor did we feel any compulsion to visit the towns, Taibe or Shfar'am; we found the Arabs on the scene when we came to the country and they were part of the scenery. Right after the June war in 1967, things became different. We must hurry and see the Golan Heights and the West Bank and the Gaza Strip right away, while we have the chance, for we are inbued with the lack of assurance peculiar to a people accustomed to political retreat on the heels of military triumph.

In the wake of the June triumph we have suddenly discovered all kinds of Arabs: the unspoiled, poetic Arab, the dream of every romantic soul which prefers nature to technology (for others), who tends to his black goats on the white snowy slopes of Mount Hermon, who follows the ox-drawn wooden plow in the tortuous furrows of the hilly fields, draws water from a well and reclines under his fig tree in the pastel glow of the setting sun. True, the exotic sensitivity of this child of nature is probably offset by the TV antenna atop his modest dwelling, by the transistor dangling from the handle of the primitive plow, by the red plastic jerrican which his supple daughter carries on her head, and by the Mercedes-Benz which takes him to the picturesque market place for the consummation of his business deals, but these are so much more esthetic than those horrible housing projects, the parking lots, boutiques and other abominable expressions of the degenerate western culture we had brought in.

We have also gotten to know the Arab vendor, the peddler, kin to the leech-like Arab who sprouts wherever Jewish tourists are to be found, by the Tomb of the Patriarchs, in Old Jerusalem, near Solomon's Pools and Rachel's Tomb. Invariably he is young, says "every item's a *lira*" or "cheap today" in flawless Hebrew, wants to haggle, is familiar with prices in the Jewish market. He is obviously unproductive, if he can sit all day with a stock of ten bottles of lemonade. And if you can manage to observe him from the right angle, you will be able to detect the gleam of hatred in his eyes. In general he belongs to that category characterized by the deep Jewish sigh meaning "I wouldn't trust him."

Then we have the elderly Arab dignitary who knew the late -Dr. Chaim Weizmann. Persian rugs cover the tile floors in his elegant home, and he is accessible only through the good offices of a friend in the employ of the Military Administration or through the Administrator himself or one of the old-timers who speaks the Arabic of the early pioneering days and whose life the host had saved (or vice versa) in a moment of great danger. This dignitary is visited by Israeli journalists and graduate Arabists who wish to discuss with him, over coffee served in exquisite china, the prospects for peace and cooperation. Today his words may not be dipped in honeyed brotherhood as they were when the memories of booming artillery were fresher, but he still manages to impart to his guests the hint that things could be settled—if we only knew "how the matter should be handled."

In the wake of the Six Day War, the old-timers are slipping back into their days of yore. Out of the mothballs comes the "basic Arabic" acquired during the years of labor in the Petach Tikvah orange groves, the bargaining in Haifa's Hamma Market, the memories of those good old Mandate days, of King Abdullah of blessed memory, the Zemach railway, the forgotten tastes and smells. On the other hand, the immigrants from Eastern and Central Europe who arrived after the founding of the state, are versed in the prices on the Arab market, particularly when they involve such commodities as Pyrex dishes, Chinese unbrellas,

Dacron cloth and Persian rugs—items which can be cleaned, washed, sterilized or otherwise hygienically treated, but they shy away from the Oriental dishes—*knaffa, baclava, tamarindi, labaneh*—which, in their prejudiced minds, abound with bacteria, virus and plain dirt, all under the general heading of "this Arab muck." The newcomer, the product of the diaspora and ignorant of the ways of the Land of Israel, is aware of the dirt more than of the relics from the glorious past. He is alienated by the sight of flies buzzing about a side of lamb but is oblivious to the flapping of the wings of history. He closes his nostrils to the smell of open drainage and misses the myrrh, spice and incense, all because, during his days in Israel, his eyes were turned toward the lands overseas; the "neighboring Mediterranean countries" were France and Italy. And now he suddenly discovered that he was in the heart of the Middle East. This realization came somewhat as a shock. He had been caught with his purse down when it came to Oriental trading traditions, and even now, as he attempts to haggle, his "What? Five *lira?* It's worth no more than two" lacks conviction and cannot deceive even a six-year-old street Arab of Hebron.

So long as we were in the Jewish Homeland and the only Arab name absorbed by our minds was Omar Sharif, we knew that the Arabs had to be handled, well, with a strong hand. But now we are personally involved. In East Jerusalem we met a fine boy who spoke good English and directed us to the Dome of the Rock; we saw refugees dragging a kettle, two blankets and a wash basin across the twisted Allenby Bridge; we saw the expression on the faces of the women in black when two students in mini skirts went by and the apathetic stare of the coffee house inmates in Jericho. Now we see, behind "the Arab problem," the Arabs themselves, and we are in the abyss of emotional strain; hatred and compassion, superciliousness and pangs of conscience, suspicion and curiosity.

Until now we were Jews, plain and simple. Now all of us have to be Arabists, from the Minister for Religious Affairs to the Minister of Posts, poets and entertainers, professors of plant physiology and women of the Working Mothers Association. All of us are carrying on our backs this burden of a million and a quarter Arabs, give or take a hundred thousand. The Arabs have penetrated into our everyday talk, our dreams, our Friday night get-togethers; they have replaced those carefree topics of yester-year: economic recession and party coalition, post-mortems and the ideal length of the skirt. The feature sections of the Sabbath eve editions of the press have dropped those entertaining detective stories ("I Was a Spy in Singapore") and the confessions of bare-chested actresses about truth in all its nakedness; instead, we are being fed Hebronite sheikhs and angry young men of Gaza, refugees outgoing and incoming, trials in Nablus and strikes in Rafiah. Press and radio writers and commentators on education, philately, numismatics, cooking, farming and cross-word puzzles have taken to journeying to the West Bank and ask whoever comes to hand: "Why do you hate us? Is there a way to peace?" Where, O where are those good old days of purely Jewish problems: discrimination and development towns, bureaucracy and inefficiency?

We are now the victims of the Split Israeli Personality: as security experts we are glad that our borders lie in the Sinai Desert and on the Golan Heights and along the Jordan River, but as simple Jews we aspire to no more than a state of our own with just a few, practically inconspicuous Arabs. Indeed, that was once the nice thing about living in Israel; one could speak freely, without fear that the *shikseh* might overhear and become unruly. It is no longer possible even to write a newspaper article with only our own selves in mind; they are already reading the *Jerusalem Post* and will soon get to the Hebrew dailies. Our last stand will have to be the Yiddish *Letzte Nyess* and the Hungarian *Uj-Kelet*.

The ideal situation, of course, would be to keep all the territories we are holding today—but without so many Arabs. A few Arabs would even be desirable, for reasons of local color, raising pigs for non-Moslems and serving bread on the Passover, but not in their masses and particularly not with their perennial population explosion. The pace of this procreation is such that we, with all the best intentions in the world and dedication to the task, cannot hope to keep up with it—not with all the extra work we have to do, the social obligations, the Philharmonic series, our responsible jobs and the mortgage payments. Apparently natural increase is not all nature; there must also be some incentive. Government prodding can do wonders—we see it in action every day—but in this case personal example is all-important. A highly-placed political leader with considerable progeny may inspire the masses to go and do likewise, except that our leaders, being young in spirit only, may not be up to this kind of challenge. At any rate, it is very good to know that, with the rest of the world struggling to find a way against population growth without offending the Almighty, we here must take action on its behalf. We are temporarily lagging in this respect, for reasons not entirely of our own making but rather because of one Adolf Hitler.

Our attitude toward the Arabs is most liberal, and we hold no prejudices there. When all is said and done, we never included them in the separatist category of Gentiles. It is only our speech that is at fault; we still tend to use such base expressions as "Arabic shenanigans" and "don't be an Arab." But that's how it is in all language. The English say "to Jew" when they mean "to cheat," yet they love to shop at Marks & Spencer and see "Fiddler on the Roof."

Experience says that if we are to form an affection for a people we should find something admirable about its customs and folklore, its food or girls, its poetry and music. True, we have taken the first steps in this direction: we like *kebab, hummous, tehina* and *falafel.* The trouble is that these have already become Jewish dishes and are prepared more tastily by every Rumanian restaurateur than by the natives of Nablus. Arab melodies (may Um-Hultum, the soulful singer, forgive me) are disastrous for ears which sprouted in Europe. Arabic is generally unknown, except for a few epithets which need not be mentioned here. The only Arab poet we know is Khalil Gibran—and he is an American; there was one Omar Khayyam, but he was either some Persian or is now the name of a night club. Yes, we like coffee tables of brass and mats of woven straw. The question is whether this is enough on which to base our familiarity with Arab culture. We would go out right now and buy a *kaffiyah* to use as a tablecloth, if this would bring us together around the table.

Jethro's Children

THE SIX DAY WAR widened the screen of our perspectives, and we suddenly beheld things which had previously been off the beaten track of our consciousness. We now saw the Druse community as an integral part of the Israeli family, not as mere exotic clusters in certain regions of the land. The war brought home to us the responsibility we had assumed when we established the state, toward the Jewish people as a whole and toward the Druse, who had staked their lives and all on the Israeli card, in 1948. For the Jewish people we had to win because there was no alternative; for the Druse, because of an obligation which we incurred.

The affinity between Jew and Druse (besides the kinship through Jethro, father-in-law of Moses whom they consider their spiritual progenitor) comes principally from their common fate as a minority which had learned how to co-exist with a majority that was at times tolerant, at times ruthless, and succeeded due mainly to the fact that it rendered unto Caesar what was Caesar's yet maintained its own continuity with the help of internal and separatist laws and traditions. While Jews do not welcome proselytes with much enthusiasm, the Druse do not accept them at all, saying that space in heaven is limited and cannot entertain too many claimants. Jews try to prevent mixed marriages in their midst; the Druse have forbidden them most inexorably, so that marriage outside the fold means expulsion from the community. As in the case of the Jews, the need to appear as a solid entity, at least to the outside world, has brought about considerable inner friction, in the style of the Old World synagogue wardens. The Druse refrain from airing their differences via the newspapers, certainly not in the Arabic press, for the well-known Jewish reason: no need to let outsiders in on it.

80

As in the case of the Jews, persecution by the rulers of Lebanon, Syria and Palestine impelled the Druse to pack up and immigrate overseas—to the United States, South America and North Africa —and to dream, along with the wave of rising nationalism early in the century, about a sovereign state of their own. Unlike the Jews, however, they were not blessed with a Dr. Herzl and a Dr. Goldmann. No Druse state emerged in the wake of some United Druse Appeal, and no Druse emissaries are calling out cards of Druse contributors all over the world. Both the sons of Moses and the sons of Jethro share the national hobby of discovering their brethren among the world's elite.

The basic difference between the Jews and the Druse is that, for the People of the Book, individually and collectively, the Bible is an open book, while among the Druse only a few are familiar with the principles of this secret faith; the others feel themselves to be Druse only by virtue of a common fate, the realities of life, the family, the clan, the village. Whoever detaches himself, from any of these, breaks off relations not only with a way of life but with the entire community. This explains why the Druse are more conservative in their behavior patterns than the Arabs, Moslem or Christian, even though they do identify themselves with Israel and serve in the Israeli Army (a Druse without the right to bear arms is as unworthy as one who builds his home in the lowlands). The Druse have fewer graduates of high schools and colleges; they object more strenuously to having women work beyond the confines of their own homes, and the elders insist on prescribing the laws for the young people. And when you listen to the latter complaining about septuagenarians not yielding to their juniors and about the old generation not understanding the new and about the lack of a common language between the official leaders and the native crop, all you have to do is to substitute Ziama, Golda or Shraga for Salman, Labib or Ahmad—and the tune becomes quite familiar. The young Druse may keep on fuming and trying to get something going, but the power of the elders goes on unabated, bolstered by the mutual influence of the elders and those in power in Israel.

Druse sentiments toward the Jews in Israel have undergone several crises, over the inclusion of the Druse minority with the other minorities and the fact (justified) that the Jews made light of the Druse, taking them for granted while courting the Arabs. The Israeli Army's disinclination to accept Druse soldiers into any but the minority units, and because no distinction was made between a minority and an ally, and recognition was not accorded to the Druse for joining Israel's defense forces voluntarily, all led to resentment. But all this is now a thing of the past.

With the Druse, religion, race and nationality are all one, as was the case with Jews prior to the advent of the State of Israel. As a result of Arab nationalist influence, there are some young Druse, elsewhere in the world, who maintain that one can be an Arab of the Druse faith, but in Israel itself most members of the Druse community regard the appellation of "Arab" as an insult. A small ethnic group can maintain its identity only through an abiding pride, in itself a form of defense, as we well know, but we have not practiced this attitude toward the Druse, now that we are in the position of the gentiles and the Druse are like the Jews. The father of modern psychology was a Jew, but we haven't learned much from him.

On that Sabbath of tense calm, at the end of May 1967, when the entire country was on the alert, in Daliat a-Carmel as in Tel Aviv; in those days of preparedness when discharged soldiers who had not been called up were tracking down their units, demanding mobilization, in Julis as well as in Jerusalem; in those two weeks of trepidation and the expectancy of war, the reckoning of twenty years was taken and the balance transferred to a joint account.

During those twenty years there was no sufficiently strong tie between the Jews and the Druse (omitting the mass Jewish processions to Druse weddings and hospitality, to impress the aunt from America and the guest from Switzerland), primarily because we Jews were self-centered. We were immersed in our own avalanche of problems: the dissolution of the Palmach and the elimination of partisan doctrines from the educational system, the integration of the ingathered and the abolition of the shanty towns, devaluations in our currency, fragmentation and cleavage, Who's A Jew?, "Zionism" in quotation marks. The 30,000-odd Druse seemed to be no more than a minor detail. We became aware of the importance of this detail when we discovered that the nine thousand Druse living on the slopes of the Hermon were the only ones in the Golan Heights who, in June 1967, awaited, as one, the arrival of the Israeli forces.

The Druse did not come through to our consciousness because they had no access to communications media. Any person or group that is not mentioned in the press or over the radio is out of public focus. Except where work, studies or military service provided for direct personal contact, the Druse continued to be, for a good part of Israel's populace, an exotic outlet for Sabbath excursions, for tourists eager to rub noses with the magic of the East, for eyeing supple maidens in white veils balancing baskets of *peetah* on their heads, for being served demi-tasse of bitter coffee in the company of elders with beards worthy of the Prophets, for being welcomed by little girls in long flower-print dresses and a tinkling *shalom, shalom,* and tots with traces of eye-shadow clinging to the skirts of their mothers, in the doorways, or for buying straw baskets, decorative straw trays or raw olive oil.

Personal ties between Jews and Druse are one-way, directionally: the Jews visit the Druse, but rarely do the Druse come to visit their Jewish friends, either because the Jews are forever busy or because they would rather sample the Eastern concepts of hospitality: no matter when you show up at a Druse home you will always find it open, with no need for prior notification or an appointed day and hour, ready with a cup of coffee, sweets or a full meal, and not the slightest intimation that the visit came at an inopportune time. Life may have gone modern, but Jewish time and Druse time do not go by the same clock. Jewish time is apportioned, measured, doled out, jabbing and sparring; Druse time is pliable, subdued, boundless, yielding. An hour doesn't necessarily have to consist of sixty minutes; it adapts itself to the situation, allowing for a chicken to be killed, cleaned and cooked, the dough to rise, and visits to a mother-in-law, a brother, a cousin. The day I perceive a Druse host glancing at his watch I will know that the ways of the Jews have indeed made inroads on the Druse.

On the wall in every Druse home, next to the photographs of Druse dignitaries with impressive mustaches and young men in Israeli Army uniforms, leaning on jeeps, are the photographs of the President of the State of Israel or the Prime Minister or the current Chief-of-Staff or Moshe Dayan or Dr. Herzl or all of them—a designation of honor, an expression of belonging, a decoration, a talisman. We, too, used to hang up pictures of Herzl and Weizmann and Ben Gurion, when we were beginner Zionists. Time takes care of such things.

In the Druse homes, heavy, deep couches upholstered with floral designs have given way to rubber foam sofas; tables topped with chased brass have been replaced with formica, an electric plate does the work of coals, a refrigerator has shunted aside the huge earthenware crocks, and there's an enameled pot on the range instead of a vat over living flame. Trylene trousers have replaced the cloak, and Sussita compacts have driven the donkeys off the road. Beds are used in place of mats and nylon yarn has ousted straw; a toilet with a Niagara flush has replaced the outhouse by the goat pen, the girls wear slacks, the boys wear tight jeans and colored sweaters and listen to *If You Come to San Francisco* on their transistors, and white telephones gleam on sectional credenzas. The villages near the large cities are the first to succumb, while among those in the Galilee the process is slower, but all the Druse, like all the Jews, face in the same direction—toward the unity of the brave new world.

Only in one respect has there been no change, much to the envy of the Jews: the Druse woman still knows her place. She doesn't interrupt her husband when he is talking, nor does she boss him around in front of others: "Go! Do! Bring!" She doesn't turn to a career for gratification; she doesn't go to the movies nor does she spend days in Cafe Roval; she doesn't eat with the guests, and the influence that she does exert on her husband comes by way of the diplomatic route, behind the scenes, well-known to Jewish women in those good old pre-emancipation days. The first girls who left the Druse village despite convention (this didn't hold true in Lebanon even in the days under the French Mandate), and went out among the Jews to learn a profession—teaching, nursing, child care—faced greater obstacles than all the English suffragettes. Tradition rose against them, for the Druse were familiar with precepts which the Jews learned through experience: let the woman today work outside the home, break into male conversation and take time off between pregnancies, and tomorrow you will have a terror of all males. As long as the woman is confined to the home, as long as the maidens retain their maiden-heads and as long as they are not given away as a gift but are acquired in exchange for gold and hard toil, tradition will have a crutch and a backbone and a foundation, defying the assault of modern times.

As long as the sons live, each with his wife and increasing progeny, in the large parental home, with its alcoves and entrances and courtyards and attics all attached to the next house in line, life goes on as usual. There are no such problems as who will take care of the baby or who will cook the meal or care for the sick; in case of emergency there is always a grandmother, a cousin, a sister, an older daughter. If the children are not at home for a meal, they are no doubt eating at an aunt's, this one or that one. This is the security, the warmth, the mutual aid structure of the clan, matched only by the *kibbutz*. But when the discharged Druse soldiers go off to live in separate housing projects, with green solar tanks on the roof and modern furniture in the guest room, beyond the mother-in-law's searching eyes, they tend to limit the number of children (after the third, fourth or fifth); they dress the kids on the Sabbath in Perlon shirts and bow ties, photograph the wife in color and go in for cigarettes. Eventually they come to a bad end, just like the Jews.

Life among the Jews has brought the Druse roads and water, electricity and the telephone, health insurance and immunization for the infants, free schooling for boys and girls, buses and jitneys, old-age insurance and the Labor Federation. Jewish political parties superimpose their differences on inter-clan friction; we have our first Druse artist and Druse physician, and they have our nepotism and election promises of a better life, but few instrumentalities with which to implement them. They know that the magic word is "education," but this is not easy to achieve; one must have a wealthy father with the understanding of education as the basis for a livelihood, and one must be fluent in Hebrew and live among Jews. And how is the young Druse to manage to save for the price of a wife, if he has to spend so many years in school and then enter the army? Small wonder then, as against 150 intellectuals with certified professions—school principals, teachers, Government officials, physicians and Orientalists— there are thousands of Druse boys who go through primary school in their village and go on to work in the fields, in construction, road paving, in the *kibbutzim,* into military service, into the Border Patrol, in the penal system, as watchmen in Jewish factories and workshops. It's a hard climb.

Since so few of the Jews born here or coming from Europe have bothered to learn Arabic, the Druse went ahead and learned Israeli Hebrew. They talk about *foileh shtik,* read Hebrew newspapers and write letters to the newspaper editors, and on the thirtieth day after a soldier from their community fell in action, they publish a notice, with his photograph, like the others do: "You fell in defense of the land and gave your life so that we may go on living. Your memory will abide with us forever and shall be for us an example and an inspiration."

Remembered As From a Distance

THEY ARE six million and we are two. They are the majority and we the minority, yet in the calendar of the state we have set aside for them but one day, because between them and us there is one basic and decisive distinction: they are dead and we are alive, and all contacts between us have been severed, since the final and total "solution."

Anyone with not enough sanity to go mad or anyone who shrank from sharing their fate clearly loved life more than he could love six million dead, and he tries not to show how relieved he is that fate had spared him. See, he is alive: he leaves footprints in the wet sand; he sees partridges among the orange trees; he sits back in his chair and reads a book.

Every announcement of the annual memorial observance for the six million, by their respective townspeople, echoes this attitude: the ceremonies are scheduled for eight, but the door will open at six, for the reunion. The people gather, happy to meet friends from yesteryear, talk about the family, health, the reparations payments, and with each year the dead seem to recede more and more into the unreal. The warm sunshine dulls the pain, and it becomes a tug at the heart, at the sight of a yellowed photograph or the sound of a familiar expression—and even the tug weakens with the years.

Once a year we in Israel convene in their honor, with loud-speakers and full press coverage and carefully phrased "we-shall-never-forget" speeches, with a cultural program, befittingly restrained. Once a year we dedicate several pages of newsprint to their memory, despite the loss of precious inches of space. This is done without too much enthusiasm, seeing that it's quite difficult to publish a fresh supplement devoted to the same Holocaust,

87

year after year. After twenty years very little that is new can be said on the subject—always the same stories, the same plot, the same ending. The readers of the newspapers are not looking forward to the Holocaust section anyway, either because the matter disturbs their rest and causes nightmares and insomnia (which is bad for anyone with a hard day ahead), or because it's enough, plenty, too much. How many times can we go through the same thing?

Once a year we keep the movie houses closed in their honor and the theatres are empty, despite the financial loss and the boredom engendered thereby. Kol Yisrael radio skips the Hit Parade and Paul Temple and offers the Book of Lamentations and a variety of sombre cantatas, leaving us no choice but to tune in on Cyprus, regrettably. Well, O perished ones, you've had your day, and now let us alone for the rest of the year.

Any article written about the Holocaust is a dialogue, between the living writer and the living reader; the dead stand off to one side. Such articles are left for the last, between the afternoon cup of coffee and the evening snack of sour cream, salad, white cheese and fried eggs. The article can be described as "moving" or "extremely well-written"; it was commissioned with an expert (these are Holocaust specialists who make a living from such expertise, just as there are Sinologists and experts in poultry breeding). He has measured words, effects, sentence structure and punctuation, and has given much thought as to whether he should write "seven stages of hell" or "hell on earth," then finally decided to go easy on the horror; the readers shy away from it. Whoever wants to speak for the dead cannot make words serve the purpose. Perhaps a wail, like the jackal, or a soul-rending shriek. But never words.

A magnificent Belsen memorial album, bound in leather and stamped with gold, printed on high-gloss chrome stock; an award for the most moving novel on the Holocaust which became a best-seller; an exhibit of paintings with Holocaust themes, with red dots affixed to those already sold—these are for the living, and the dead shall have no dominion.

This is not the fault of the living; there is simply no way of describing six million cases of murder, not in writing, not in painting, not in song. One can describe the horrors of things to come, the connotation of events, the particles of soot, but not the flame itself. There is no way to give expression to something bereft of all meaning, of all logic, of any sense or conclusion. The Second Temple was destroyed because of our sins, but why did the six million die? Because they had faith in men? Because they depended on God? Because they clung to life? Certainly it wasn't for the sake of a better world or for their children—the children perished in the same crematoria with the parents—nor for the rise of the State of Israel, even if it did rise from the pang of conscience which touched a world indifferent to their death itself. No reason for their death, no retribution, no sacrifice, merely an innovation: they were the murder victims not of any lust to kill or by the aggression ingrained in man, but of cold and orderly calculation. Indeed an encouraging sign for man: Behold, he is no longer an animal!

If only there were not that number: *six million!* One can empathize with the 960 rebels atop Masada: you can visualize them, in their hiding places, and they left the area marked with straw baskets, shards and coins. But six million is beyond our capacity to grasp; the figure is simply meaningless. That is why we clung to Anne Frank, not because she was more courageous than the others or because she was less fortunate, but because she had an image, a diary, a face, a name, a hiding place, parents. We can relate to Anne Frank as to one among ourselves; she was flesh and blood, while six million is from another world, an inhuman monster, a shapeless mass.

There is no love for the dead, just as there is no love for lepers or the plague-stricken. At times there is pity—the most two-faced of all traits—and at times there is fear, or disgust, or the feeling of well, they too, were to blame (for having remained in Europe or for not having put up a battle). Holocaust Day is, therefore, dedicated primarily to the rebels, the fighters of the ghettos and the partisans, though they numbered but one platoon among the legions; we admire and understand them, but beyond our comprehension is that swollen and silent river without a name which emptied into the sea of massacre, because it had hope and faith, because it clung to its family, because it failed to grasp the nature of the Master Race, because it would not believe it to be possible.

Yes, the dead must even fight for their right to die without an

89

accusing finger being pointed at them: Why didn't you fight back? Why did you go along with it? Why did you dig your graves with your own hands? Why did you go docilely? This is what we, the living, keep harping on, to satisfy ourselves that this would not have been the case with us, as it was with them. That is why we point to the ghetto elders and the collaborators and the Kapos and the uniformed Jewish policemen. They give us something to grasp, an explanation, a reason. If they would have acted otherwise . . . Now, as in ancient days, it is because of our sins that we were punished.

At first we said: We shall avenge their blood. And there were those who went forth, on the first nights after the liberation, to seeks vengeance; they killed one German, a second, a third, yet the dead were no better off. Then we said: No, not vengeance, only right and justice. Those responsible, the guilty ones, they must stand trial. And some were placed in the dockets, in Nuremberg and Magdenburg, in Warsaw and Prague. Some were executed, others were given prison sentences of five, ten, fifteen years, yet although there were verdicts, there could be no justice.

When we faced Eichmann, the pallid bureaucrat in his glass cage, begging for his life, we were almost inclined to spare him, so meaningless did it seem to be. His death was not justice, only a symbol: one pair of spectacles against myriads, one pair of shoes in exchange for millions. And we didn't touch his gold teeth.

Directors of agencies for tracking down Nazis publish bestsellers and have themselves photographed in the now-dry shower stalls of Auschwitz, and they are honorable men. Directors of agencies for documenting the atrocities fight for the status of their respective enterprises and arrange tours for representatives of all the nations, and they too are honorable men; eager Holocaust researchers are immersed in their Masters theses, and they are honorable men. But only the anonymous hunters for Mengele and Bormann in South America will be able to stand upright before the dead, even if there is no justice and no righteousness and the Judge is long gone.

Fortunate is the man who can keep on hating. We, on the other hand, have had great difficulty here, and what we learned we soon forgot. He who hates becomes dominated by his hatred, and we want to lead lives like other people, as in the days when there was no Holocaust: we want to raise children, get promotions, earn enough for our needs, see the world. Hatred is a rigorous employer, consuming all of life. We do not have the stomach for hatred, and we therefore have nothing to forgive. But the Germans have reason to hate us because they were the ones who committed the crime, to which we were witness, and yet we are alive. And if no more than one in twenty supports neo-Nazism, it would be a true sign that a new generation had indeed arisen in Germany, and that the old generation has learned caution and the wisdoms of life. There has to be another Germany, because it is inconceivable that the same feet should now be treading on grass and the same hands should be patting children's heads and the same eyes should be looking at the breaking surf. Were there not another Germany in the offing, we would have to create one; we need it more than the Germans themselves do.

Every Jew has made a pact with his feelings of hatred—so far, but no farther. Reparations to the state, yes—but no personal compensation to individuals. Accept the compensation (it's unthinkable that the Germans should have murdered and also inherited), but don't tread on German soil. Visit Germany (to arrange for the compensation), yes—but not for a pleasure trip. Relations: diplomatic, yes, cultural, no; German films, no; German cannons, yes. A Volkswagen, no, a printing press, yes. East Germans, no; West Germans, yes—if they are under 30.

The difference between those who still protest, here and there, and arrange demonstrations, now and then, and those who say "yes" right away is merely a matter of timing. We were upset when Martin Buber made a trip to Germany a few years after the war, but he merely measured time differently. We were irritated over Ben-Gurion's "other Germany," but he was only somewhat premature. Each has his forgiveness clock, and, as often as not, it's a Kienzle timepiece.

We said: we are powerless to avenge and there is no hope for justice, but we must retell the story to our last breath. But none wanted to give ear. We did find ready listeners to stories about the house of the dolls, but who can give heed to all the other atrocities? The listeners would lower their eyes, as though we were telling them something too personal, too private, not suitable for public airing. We quickly learned the formula: be an Israeli outside and a camp survivor in your own home, and perhaps not even there; why cast a pall upon your dear ones? Keep it in your closed heart. And perhaps not even there, for it is already overflowing, and other things are still trying to squeeze in.

And even when you did succeed in telling it, without the lump choking your throat, the words were no more than words, correct in their diction and grammar, yet barren of meaning. They didn't have the fortitude to bear the burden, and they disintegrated even as they were being uttered. Only photographs can tell the story. They alone are the reliable witness, without the mediation of words and artistic illustration. Had the camera been invented only for the purpose of depicting the Holocaust, it would have earned universal acclaim for that alone, as being the most important invention of the century—right after Cyclone B gas, anyway.

We should tell this story to the children, but how? Children's stories must contain a moral. Perhaps something like this: Children, whatever once took place is now gone, but you are living in the State of Israel. They walked quietly, but now we have tanks and planes, and everyone, in Israel, is ready to fight.

Do You Still Hate the Germans?

OUR RELATIONS with Germany are very much like the conquest of the wilderness: the pioneers are the only ones to suffer. Israelis always cry out against those who break down acknowledged barriers, but those who come through the breach in their wake arouse hardly any comment. One merely has to survive what is called "the outraged public," which is usually expressed through a half-dozen moralizing newspaper articles, one or two demonstrations, a threat to resign on the part of one holder of public office or another, a few slogans indelibly smeared on house walls, a batch of emotional letters to the Editor, and a temporary cold shoulder from a handful of friends. Time will then take over.

The storm has long subsided over the Reparations Agreement (1952), Martin Buber's trip to Germany (1953), the first showing of German films in Israel (1957), the sale to Germany of Israel-made Uzzi sub–machine guns (1958), the arrival of the first German Ambassador, Dr. Pauls (1965), Dr. Adenauer's visit (1966) and Chancellor Erhardt's (1968)—each in its day a travesty on eternally-sacred principles.

Where have all the principles gone? Realities have devoured them. The first German tourists to visit Israel (1955) still made news; today a German tourist, like any ordinary mortal, would have to bite a dog in order to get a line in the newspapers, and no ex-Nazi below the rank of *Untersturmbannfuehrer* is likely to evoke a demonstration.

Except for a few brave souls, Ben Gurion and his trusted Shimon Peres, who were ready to preface action with direct resolutions, most Israelis retreat from this position of principle without the honorable loophole of "planned orientation along new lines." Things just keep lumbering along through apathy or hypocrisy, lack of character or indolence, the reluctance to stand up and fight. Or the love of comfort. Don't open your heart to the Germans—but neither should you close the door.

Relations with Germany are very much like one's attitude toward religion: every Jew has his own version as to what is permissible and what is not, according to tradition. To maintain an absolute and infinite hatred, no contact whatsoever on either governmental or individual level, neither for the sake of a better world nor a better apartment—this calls for the kind of hatred that only fanaticism can generate, and ours is not a generation given to hate. Here and there some poet with a temperamental shock of hair may deliver himself of an immortal line about the "eternal chasm," and his words are enshrined on the ear of posterity on a Grundig tape recorder. Now and then the writers may make a gesture, to prove that hatred still sears their souls, and cancel a gathering in honor of Gunther Grass, chiefly in order (as it is put in Holocaust slang) not-to-rend-the-emotions-of-those-who-were-visited-by-the-tortures-of-hell, just as one does not eat ham out of deference to Grandma's feelings, as though the survivors of the camps are the only ones who should genuinely shun the Germans. In fact, it should be quite the opposite. It is enough that a man was a camp inmate or had lost there his entire family; he should be exempt from this constant emotional friction. He has earned the right to be tired and to enjoy whatever life can still offer him. Let the principles be protected by the young ones; they have the strength for it.

Half of the public utterances against . . . . . . with the Germans (fill the blank in with the relevant issue, according to the year) emanate from sheer formality, a sort of tribute to propriety, because such are the utterances to be made in decent Israeli society. Slowly, however, a distinction is setting in between the Holocaust and the Germans, the ache is being pared away from the hatred, and the murderer is set apart from the victim. Use of the term "murderer" is in itself a negative connotation, exaggerated and fanatic. In this respect, "Holocaust" suits the mood of the people much better; it does not infer cruelty, it does not identify atrocity, it does not sob and whimper. "Perished in the Holocaust" does not grate on the ear as does "murdered in the gas chambers"—and it does not demand commitment.

The issue of our relations with the Germans has in general lost much of its importance, especially since the Six Day War, not simply because of the passing years but also because there is a wide open field regarding whom we should shun, despise, abhor and hate. Once we go into an analysis of the behavior of the people of the earth toward us, in the small matter of the annihilation of the Jews, the whole world becomes eligible to be hated (the Danes and the Bulgarians are the exception): the British for having shut the gates of Palestine; the Americans for having kept back the dollars that would have bought Jewish lives from the Nazis; the Australians for refusing "to import racial problems to a place where it still does not exist"; the Ukrainians for having welcomed the Nazis; the Czechs for not having lifted a finger; the Poles for their active aid to the annihilation, to this day. As more and more details are revealed about the world's acceptance of the "final solution," the list lengthens and includes entire peoples as well as great and revered personalities, with Churchill and Roosevelt at the very top. The doomed Jews on the other side of the Cyclone Gas Curtain once said: "If the world only knew . . ." —and they didn't know that the world did. The awareness we had, during the days immediately preceding the Six Day War, that the world was ready to witness, for the second time, an attempted annihilation of the Jewish people and to do nothing about it, somehow mitigated the position of the Germans. True, there is a substantive difference between those who perpetrate a crime and those who stand aside, but the differences tends to fade, with the years.

As against the gradual reconciliation with the Germans, people cite the boycott of Spain, which was kept in force by the Jews for five centuries. However, we do not have today a central moral authority, and the proscription by religion finds only a comparative few who would obey it; (most of the rabbis have shown more tolerance toward the Germans than toward Reform Rabbis), and the few attempts by secular authorities to influence relations with Germany (such as the clause in Israeli passports, in the '50's, "good for visiting all countries except Germany") could not withstand realities. Some look to the intellectuals for a moral authority, and these offer a selection of a wide spectrum: Max Brod's love from a distance, Natan Alterman's "relation-yes; culture-no,"

95

Uri Zvi Greenberg's emphatic ostracism, with each offering a level and a category to suit the disciples' character, personal stake in reparations, professional career or general ambition. And if the desired dispensation is not available in the intellectual inventory, at the moment, there will always be some Government Ministry that will issue it, in the name of the national interest. The Foreign Ministry is all for stable relations; the Ministry of Commerce and Industry is all for stable trade; the Finance Ministry is all for a stable Reichsmark, and the Ministry of Tourism is all for stable tourists—each Governmental trading post is eager to do business. But if they are all interested in maintaining good relations with West Germany, out of a thousand and one considerations, who the devil fosters the annual rehash of hypocritical attacks on Germany, come Memorial Day, on the part of Ministers and legislators?

Our emotional attitude toward Germany is riding a see-saw, but we are not the ones who supply it with motion. As in the exilic days of the Jewish people, our attitude is generated by others. It all depends on what is taking place within Germany itself: a flurry of Neo-Nazism—and our attitude hardens; a procurement of arms—and it softens; the Germans yield to Arab demands—thumbs down, but if they hold fast against Arab demands, thumbs up; the arms deal is off—way down, but they *do* rejoice in our victory, and the barometer's fine.

In his "The Vow," poet Abraham Shlonski talks about "unto the tenth generation"; the Lord is satisfied with the third or fourth, but we are not capable of shunning even the second generation. You gaze at German young people, and they are like all other European young people—beatniks or peaceniks, looking for a good time or unable to decide what to do with themselves, and you simply cannot blame *them* for the deeds of their parents. At times, when you see their faces flushed with drink and their eyes fixed in a watery stare, and when their raspy voice brings back a haunting note from the past, you are overcome with a sense of abhorrence, but soon civilized and cultured logic takes over: tsk, tsk; one must not hate collectively—that's racism, even when those involved are Germans.

A first meeting between young Germans and young Israelis is usually more of a shock to the Israelis than to the Germans, precisely because the latter appear to be so normal, so far removed from those monster images in the long green jackets and black leather boots and flaying the Jews with their whips, about whom the Israelis had learned in school. The entire attitude toward the Holocaust is put to test in these inter-youth confrontations.

There is distortion in the very idea of shifting the emphasis from the Holocaust to the heroism of the Jews in the camps, a shift intended to create a closer bond on the part of the young generation with diaspora Jewry; it is as though we, too, have no interest in recalling the millions who perished because they clung to life, and prefer to dwell on the thousands who managed to fight back. This may be at the root of our rapprochement with the Germans: neither they nor we like to hear too much about the atrocities of the Holocaust.

Only absolute separation can assure absolute and adamant dissociation. The moment that people are brought together into one framework, be it political, commercial, professional or intellectual, the relationship ceases being static and evolution sets in. The memory of the Six Million, it seems, should not enter into the issue of our relations with the Germans. We can relegate the feeling of loss to the depths of the soul, where the years will dull its edge, and still manage to bear a rational attitude toward the Germany of today. But in reality this is not the case. The wrath is muted along with the pain.

Whoever has ever argued that one can approve of reparations to the Government and can receive personal compensation, without it influencing his attitude toward the Germans, either deludes himself or echoes rampant hypocrisy. Money covers a multitude of aches. In this case, the Germans visualized the evolution of the matter much more clearly; they called restitution *Wiedergutmachungen:* it hits the nail on the head more squarely, in the practical sense, than "reparations"—when something becomes *wieder gut,* there is no longer any need for *Wiedergutmachungen.* Reparations carried the illusion of timelessness.

German newspapers, German books, a German theatre (Austrian, to be exact, for the sake of sugar coating the pill), German tourists, German merchandise, German films, a German Ambassador, the German flag, the German coat-of-arms, the German national anthem, German cultural undertakings—Israel's doors are open to all of these. Only poor Wagner and Strauss have not as yet been taken in out of the cold; they are the last stone upon stone left in the crumbled wall of principle.

And now what, little Israeli? It is quite unlikely that the present Government will have the courage to chart this course in accord with principle, to close the gap between Holocaust speeches and daily behavior. As individuals, then, we shall have to depend on either ourselves or the Germans. Should Neo-Nazism rear its head in Germany, and should anti-Semitism there rise above the international average, and/or should the Germans adopt a clear-cut anti-Israel line, we would be absolved from all decisions and calculations. We shall simply say: "We knew it all along; once a German, always a Nazi," just as it is said: "Once a Pole, always an anti-Semite," after twenty years of mouthings about socialism and progress. But, should the Germans insist on being democratic and being more or less friendly toward Israel, then we shall be faced with the problem of how to continue hating the Nazis without offending the Germans. On the other hand, the road to solution is already partly paved: you separate the Nazi Era from the epochs preceding and following it, as though it were some lonely island completely detached from the mainland; then we shall have no difficulty admiring and respecting the Germany of the other epochs, the Germany of Bach and Brahms, of Goethe and Schiller, radiating culture and knowledge; we shall find a common tongue with modern Germany—blooming, expanding, the Germany of Grass and Hochhut and Böll, and treat the twelve years of Nazi rule as a temporary vacation from human civilization.

Trade Marks

The Kibbutz Has Many Faces

Kibbutzim, like people, have their own peculiar features and characteristics. There are the affluent ones and the subsistence level ones, those that know how to enjoy life and those in a state of perpetual crisis, the orderly and the distraught, the progressive and the treadmills, the ones that frown and the ones that smile. The collective physiognomy of the *kibbutz* is not merely the aggregate features of those who inhabit it. Affiliation with one *kibbutz* sector or another may have a bearing on the ideological context of a particular *kibbutz* but not on its day-to-day characteristics. The layout of the terrain, age in the settlement's register, and the number of its members all carry a certain specific weight, but these are not the decisive factors. There is something in the personal character of a *kibbutz* which eludes objective analysis. Apparently *kibbutzim,* like people, are not created equal; they must have a little bit of luck in life, a portion of heavenly grace, a smile from fate, an ace in the hole.

The character of the *kibbutz* membership may have a determining effect on its makeup in the early years, but in the course of time it tends to evolve its own independent life and to mold the image of the membership rather than the other way around. The same young people from Hungary, Czechoslovakia, the United States or South America who have come here as more or less homogeneous groups and become dispersed among various *kibbutzim,* become—five, seven or ten years later—totally different one from another: apathetic or diligent, ambitious or inert, maximalists or minimalists, reflecting the *kibbutz* they had joined.

Relations between the *kibbutzniks* and the urbanites have undergone many changes in the past twenty years, especially

101

between the *kibbutzniks* and past members of pioneer youth movements who balked, at the critical moment, and instead of entering a farm training center or joining a settlement nucleus, turned to the sidewalks of the city. In those days they did it with a vengeance, like the renegade *yeshiva* student who broke with his past by eating ham, on buttered bread on Passover.

Withal, we were comforted by the ideologists with the right psychology, who glibly assured us that one can be a pioneer in the city as well, by mastering the golden sands of Herzliyah beach, by fructifying the subdivisions of Savyon (the Westchester of Tel Aviv), by encouraging the intrepid entrepreneurs of steak joints and fighting the gallant pro-Bikini swimsuit battles. Briefly, we were assured that each of us could contribute his or her share to the development of the land, each in his own way and as his status of prosperity allowed, giving a little to the left or to the right. From the day that the abdicators to the city were thus rehabilitated, it has been possible for them to re-visit the *kibbutz*, heads held high, arriving in a Peugeot 403 (high-octane) without any visible signs of embarrassment or inferiority, especially since everything was going well, financially, vocationally and otherwise. It doesn't pay to betray the *kibbutz* past if one is to live in the city in austerity, work hard in some uninteresting occupation, a small cog in an insignificant office, having to watch every penny. Betrayal must be worthwhile.

Graduates of youth movements, training farms, settlement nuclei and others reared for *kibbutz* life, who dipped their toes in collective waters but held back from the plunge, have various ways of assuaging their stricken consciences. Some of them (like the smokers who know that they should be sucking mints instead of doing away with two packs of Kent daily, but who lack the strength of character to fend off the lung malady) will readily confess that the *kibbutz* is a wonderful institution, even if it's not for them. Others, on the contrary, will try to talk themselves and others into believing that collective life is no good in the first place; it grows people like flowers in a hot-house and produces pampered creatures who couldn't make a go of it elsewhere; all are cut along the same pattern; their personality wings are clipped even as they are waiting for the first chance to get out.

Kibbutzniks with individualistic tendencies, if and when they

102

feel the limitations of the *kibbutz* closing in on them, can leave it (at least on weekdays) as spokesmen for the movement to which it belongs, to represent it in the Knesset or on a mission abroad, thereby gaining for them both worlds: a career with a chauffeured limousine thrown in and meals at the Tour D'Argent and, on weekends, the lovely natural setting of the *kibbutz,* a reserved seat at the Passover Seder. Thus they will enjoy that something for which their pioneering spirit yearns while they valiantly cope with the madding crowd outside the *kibbutz*.

There was a time when a man from the *kibbutz* could be spotted in the city, at first glance: the thick, hand-knitted grey sweater (the proud handiwork of his spouse, accomplished during the lengthy general meetings). The woman from the *kibbutz* could be identified with equal ease by her black Sabbath skirt and white blouse with the round filigree pin at the throat. *Kibbutz* attire nowadays is unmarked (except for the khaki pants of the Last of the Mohicans, flapping about their legs as though they were the banners of socialism); in the *kibbutz* and in the city it's the same blue jeans and knit blouses, the same tight cotton dresses and the same stretch pants.

The *kibbutzim* are now more open to outside influences. This may whet the appetite of the young for the temptations of the city, but it also furnishes them with a certain immunity. The *kibbutzim* have apparently adopted the tactics of the modern parent, who, instead of shutting his adolescent daughter up behind bolted doors after nightfall—which only enhanced the chances of the first enterprising male to embrace the maiden with the first unguarded flick of the bolt—teaches her the facts of life, with special emphasis on the vagaries of the male character, bachelors and married men alike, then flings the doors wide open, hoping against all odds that virtue will prevail.

The city dweller is generally pleased to see encouraging signs of bourgeoisie and affluence present in the *kibbutzim* with which he is personally acquainted; it relieves him of any feeling of responsibility for the austerity which once marked their existence. Only millionaires and *kibbutzim* can afford a swimming pool next to their residence, tennis courts and horseback riding. Of course, this affluence should not be overdone, especially in the younger *kibbutzim*; there's a limit to dispensing with frugality. Somebody

103

in the country should be the prototype of Modest Living, and the *kibbutz*, where status does not hang as heavily as it does for the toiler in the city, is just the locale for it.

Things which the *kibbutz* old-timers tend to regard as being contaminated with bourgeoisie or a threat to the path of socialism are more things of habit than of ideology. At one time these foes were the electric kettle and a private shower, now it's a private refrigerator or air-conditioning. Unbelievers cannot understand why God should want women to wear long sleeves and kerchiefs in the summer heat; similarly, the city dweller cannot understand the contradiction between socialism and apricot-colored lipstick or a miniskirt or a bottle of Lord of Carmel brandy (all of these being bourgeois items which have, nevertheless, become quite popular among the young people in the *kibbutz*).

Tourists, volunteers from abroad, Gentiles, new immigrants, guests from the city and relatives from overseas have nothing but boundless praise for the *kibbutz* collective mode of living. They go into rapture over the attention given to the children, the care bestowed on the sick, the freedom from fear of later years, the leisure hours for hobbies, the well-tended gardens and the intensive cultural experience. The reasons that hold them back from packing their suitcases, liquidating their affairs in the city, and joining a *kibbutz* are really minor ones—a whiskey-and-soda, a private car, a wide bathtub or a home-cooked meal—but items without which life would lose much of its pleasure. Another barrier to the enjoyment of *kibbutz* bliss is Ideology, the core of the *kibbutz*. Actually, one can live quite comfortably there, were it not for the tiresome nuisances of socialism, partisanship, movements, politics, missions. The time may yet dawn, in the Utopian end of days, when people will choose to live in a *kibbutz* as in the city (after all, one doesn't have to be ideologically motivated to buy a two-and-a-half-room apartment in a Tel Aviv suburb). They would dwell under the collective vine and fig tree because it would be the natural thing to do; right now, living in a *kibbutz* is like living in Israel—you cannot do it without the involvement of Zionism, socialism, and the rest of the isms.

Just as we, the secularists, would be willing to come closer to religion were it not so demanding, that is, without the rules of Sabbath observance and synagogue attendance, without "proper" attire and *kashrut* restrictions (God is O.K., but He should be a liberal, broad of outlook and unconcerned with minutiae), so would we, the city dwellers, be willing to assume *kibbutz* life—but without its limitations, the endless discussions at membership meetings, the work allocation headaches and the other problems. Life in the city grows on you like any other bad habit; the passing of time only makes it more difficult to become weaned away from it and live within ideological confines. Young people join youth movements without any overly ideological motivation; they choose a movement which has a den near their home, or one to which their closest friends belong, or because Dad's friend, a real nice guy, is one of the leaders. Ideology comes in later, in a sneaky sort of way. None of us in the Pioneer Scouts Youth knew exactly why it was the best among the movements, but we did know that it was incumbent upon us to best the Young Revisionists in fist fights.

An isolated city dweller, cloistered in the confines of the small modern family, far away from helpful uncles and grandmas and groaning under the burden of his multiple responsibilities, may tend to regard the *kibbutz* as the substitute for family warmth, the many-branched family of yesteryear which was both the Social Welfare Agency, the Help for the Oppressed, the Security Fund and the Free Loan Society, in many ways similar to the socialist collective (but a form of membership from which one could never resign): the same crutch in times of stress and the same duty to bear the burdens of others, the same compulsion to live with the foibles of the other fellow, the same dislikes and resentments which vanish when the chips are down.

The Ministry of Tourism hasn't yet awakened to the realization of what a treasure trove the *kibbutzim* can be. Instead of dragging the poor tourists to all sorts of ancient sites which look alike (time-worn stones sunk in the ground and weeds growing in the crevices), they should be taken to the *kibbutzim,* universally peerless, and not merely for a blitz half-hour tour, sandwiched in between a real live Bedouin sheikh and the ruins of a Roman amphitheatre; at least for a day or two, the tourist should experience the slogan, "Be a *Kibbutznik* for a Day, Live the Utopian Way!"

Obviously, if we could foster free love in a few of the *kibbutzim,* just as a matter of familial cohesiveness, tourism would shoot up like blood pressure. After all, the staid married life prevalent in the *kibbutz* is something that visitors from abroad enjoy at home as well; when they travel they want to learn all sorts of strange customs, as described in "Hawaii" or "El Mondo Cane." Sad to say, the conventional morality of the *kibbutz* dwellers has simply made them useless to sociologists: weddings as prescribed by the Rabbinate, sleeping with one's legitimate spouse, gossiping when any extraneous flirting is involved—phooey, it's the same rubbish that one finds among those rotten bourgeois!

Over the years, *kibbutzim* have been the targets of carping criticism, to the effect that, one, they employ hired labor and are therefore in the vile category of exploiters, or, two, they refuse to employ hired hands and have therefore been shirking their obligation vis-a-vis the new immigrants; they are either inefficient and therefore exist only by virtue of loans made from public funds, or they have waxed rich as the result of their marketing acumen; they either hold themselves aloof from the realities of life in the country, or they stick their collective noses into too many places. The lines of morality and good behavior to which the newspaper people want the *kibbutzim* to stick are very tightly drawn.

But when all is said and done, the country's trials and tribulations—shelling, conscription, constantly on guard, war itself—have pointed up the full import of the *kibbutz* for all Israel, as military post and bastion, a reservoir of combatants and a living bulwark against the foe, a peg on the map on which hang our boundary lines.

Against a hundred complaints about what's wrong with the *kibbutz* movement, we must consider the figures of the Six Day War casualties. Eight hundred Israelis were killed in the June 1967 war; two hundred of these, or 25 per cent, were *kibbutz* members, although the *kibbutz* population of Israel is a mere four per cent.

The War We Thought Was The Last

WE BELIEVED, in that first exuberant flush of the Six Day War triumph, that a new era was about to dawn for Israel in general and for each one of us individually. We made optimistic statements about peace-in-the-offing, about the mass-immigration-to-come, about essential alterations in the national character-to-take-place. Then a year passed, and almost another; we matured a bit more and gained further knowledge and experience, yet everything remained as it was, or nearly so: hostilities are still going on, mass immigration has not materialized, the same Establishment is still with us.

Peace seems to be distant and obscure. And as much as we look forward to it, so are we apprehensive about it, for the proponents of "stability in the Middle East" are cooing peace with their voice, but their hands are dabbling in war. Back in that fast-receding month of June we thought that the outcome of the war would act as an electric current, galvanizing the Arab states to see the Great Light; belligerent regimes would crumple like paper tigers, and the Arab masses would join hands with us in building a better future for the entire region. But behold! All the Arab rulers are still astride their steeds; their subjects are still rattling the same belligerent sabre, while their armies are being equipped with the most modern weapons, and gradually we find ourselves talking about a "fourth round," without our heart skipping a beat every time the term is mentioned. Expectations are no longer attuned to war or peace, but swing between war conducted from our strategic vantage points and theirs. The concept of genuine-and-permanent peace has given way to one of an armistice for-the-time-being. And again we are told that the next war will be more destructive than the last, and this we know to be true, yet refuse to consider

107

the fact in our life's reckoning. Twenty, fifteen, ten, five years—as many as we shall be granted, until the next war, we shall regard as a gift. We are beholden to Syria, the most detached of our foes, for its unequivocal stand; this frees us from the fear lest we yield secure borders in return for a receipt signed by two guarantors and a Security Council stamp affixed thereto. Hostility doesn't frighten us; friendship Levant-style does.

Ever since the Six Day War there hasn't been a moment of peace: the sinking of the destroyer *Eilat,* the disappearance of the submarine *Dakar,* attacks by the El Fatah, here and abroad, mines hidden in dirt roads, shelling of the Bet She'an and Jordan valleys, ambush, assault, attempts to wreak havoc and spread destruction. The dead are there all year long, and today we are no longer surprised—only amazed that we should have believed otherwise, in that summer long gone by.

On the anniversary days of the fallen, black-bordered notices appear in the newspapers, and the young faces look at us, without complaining. Their friends put up personal exhibits and publish memorial writings; families establish prizes and plant groves in their names, but they keep slipping away from our awareness. The mothers are still wearing black, the widows still imagine that they hear a familiar step, but the all-consuming ache is buried under the daily problems: the unpaid mortgage, tax exemption, municipal easements, the death certificate, a final notice from the bank, looking for a job, tuition grants, and the crushing emptiness when evening falls. Surprisingly, life has not stopped. The current of time keeps flowing over the sunken pebbles, and starlings chatter in the weeping willows near the water's edge.

Yes, we were sure, many long months ago, that never again would we be upset by such minor things as a car breakdown, a rise in prices, a messy bathroom or a refrigerator going haywire. We were sure that, henceforth, we would dwell in a fortress impervious to mundane minutiae and look at life below us in the true fashion of war's veterans. But again we are put out by the same petty things and argue over nothing and figure at length about purchases and payments. These tangibles are again besetting us, and we find ourselves taking comfort in the very fact that we are as we were prior to those days of June of 1967, bores or petti-foggers, misers or gluttons, quarrelsome or honorable people—

because in this may be the strength of the state, that life can go on, though wars come and go, the *fedayeen* go and the El Fatah arrive, the United Nations condemns and the world expresses regret.

Following the war we quickly realized that Gentiles would never bear the same love toward us, as victors, which they did when we were on the brink of annihilation. But when we go abroad and sense, at first hand, the lack of sympathy and understanding, and listen to the outbursts of criticism, accusation and condemnation coming from people otherwise of liberal mind and cordial sentiment, we feel our isolation much more sharply than when we are in Israel, behind the protective wall of our sense of belonging there, and all we hear are the distant echoes of demonstrations, mud-slinging or condemning resolutions. We can analyze the reasons for this shift of sympathy with cold logic, taking into account that victory in war is not becoming to a people which has known nothing but defeat for two thousand years. To this we can add the fact that we arrived on the scene just after the International Grab-Bag-Department window had slammed shut —yet we find it difficult to reconcile ourselves to this situation. When all is said and done, we are more enlightened conquerors than the British, more trustworthy custodians of the Holy Places than the Arabs; our administration is more democratic than that of the French, and our socialism is more genuine than that of the Russians, yet we are condemned right and left, especially left.

The world is wagging a threatening finger at us, and we feel the complete loneliness of the small boy who was punished unjustly and now, from his seclusion behind the wardrobe, holds the entire world to blame. On the other hand, we walk about with the notion that it could have been otherwise, had we only known how to explain our reasons and motivations. If the approach to public opinion really constitutes a second front, it should be treated as a military operation, along with the mobilization of the reserves. Scientists and researchers, philosophers and literary figures, *kibbutzniks* and students, athletes and artists—all should be mobilized for the public relations campaign, with each man fighting in his own area. After all, in our sophisticated world of communications, the offerings of the professional public relations men and the varieties of spokesmen carry no weight; that's their job and they are paid to write official letters of reply to the editor. In this world, where public opinion is subjected to salvos of pronouncements from big people in high places, pea-shooters are of little avail. It may well be that no explanation on our part will be able to alter the fact that we won and conquered and are not prepared to give things up, just like that, like good children—but we must make the effort.

Love can never rest on its laurels. One has to contend for it anew, time and again, as every individual learns in private life. It is the same with international relations. At one time it seemed that Holland and the Scandinavian countries would be on our side forever, but even there we have had demonstrations against us, when the subject was the unification of Jerusalem. The attitude of the younger generation toward Israel is invariably linked to its attitude toward the Establishment in its own country: the fathers sympathize with Israel, and the sons challenge the wisdom thereof; the elders proclaim animosity toward Israel, and the young ones clamor for the reestablishment of relations.

But along with the solitude we still feel the repercussions; nothing happens, in this world, without its specific implications for us—the Robert Kennedy assassination and the student revolt in France, the change of governments in Canada and Dubcek's struggle in Czechoslovakia, the warfare waged by the Kurds and the imposition of sanctions against Rhodesia. No matter how deep your yearning may be to live peacefully in your own back yard and just be a backward provincial citizen, they just won't let you alone, because the whole world is in one boat and everyone is retching from the same storm.

We have been inclined to believe that truth will out, in the course of history, but now we have our doubts. What will happen if the Arab-Russian-Pakistani-French-etc. version, i.e., Israeli ruthlessness, aggression, pogroms, Nazism and assorted oppression, should take hold? What if the truth were to be quashed into oblivion, so that if an enterprising researcher should ever uncover it, no one would believe it? Even we, who have often promised ourselves never to forget the unnerving hesitancy during that month in May, the partisan jockeying, with death staring us in the face, and the mumbling of the panicked legislators, we, too, swallow a daily dose of this amended history as though it were a pesticide, to show its effects only with the years. But even though many beliefs have fallen by the wayside, to this one we shall stubbornly cling: *this* truth must be preserved.

So many of the things we now do are obvious of themselves: we can phone Jerusalem (the Old City) and reserve a room at Hotel Inter-Continental atop the Mount of Olives; we drive to Jerusalem via the Latrun highway; Gadot, at the foot of the Golan Heights, is no longer a border settlement, and Kfar Saba, within earshot of the West Bank, is no longer on the boundary line: we eat *hummous* in Nablus and decide that, in the entire West Bank, there isn't a single good cook; the Sea of Galilee has two shorelines, east and west; the Egged Bus Line serves Bethlehem and Osem noodles are sold in Gaza; Ramallah has an Israeli broadcasting station; we buy Dubek cigarettes in El Arish and pay for it in Israeli currency; the Dead Sea does not end at Ein Geddi. We no longer tour the West Bank, the Golan Heights or Sinai like sleep-walkers, merely to feel and breathe it, but go there with a specific purpose: to visit the ruins at Sebastia or bathe off Coral Island, buy lace in Bethlehem or drop in on the homesteaders in the Golan. We no longer ask the residents of the West Bank, as we did when the honeymoon was on: What do you think of us? Isn't it true that we are not the monsters you were told we are? The astonishment caused by the discovery that the Israeli is a human being is gone and forgotten; the dread has vanished. Now they are allowed to hate, as they become accustomed to the situation, if they could only be sure what we ourselves consider this situation to be: annexation is no good because of world opinion; to return the territory is no good for security reasons; a Palestinian state is no good because of Israel's own Arabs, and a bi-national state is no good because it conflicts with our Jewish consciousness; we must not take the refugees back for demographic reasons, yet they cannot be left to languish in the camps, for humanitarian reasons.

Semantics can also be troublesome. We didn't like the connotation of "conquered territories"—though this is the fact—and we weren't sufficiently hypocritical to designate them as "liberated"; we were wary of "occupied" because the inference is excessive temporariness. We therefore chose to designate them by their geographic names—Judah, Samaria, Golan, the Strip, Sinai—

which carry no inherent danger of finality, until we arrived at the innocuous expression, "the territories beyond the green line," and saved the situation.

We learned one thing from those days preceding the Six Day War: public opinion carries weight, and people in power are afraid of it. This is the time for loud and clear shouting, applying pressure, circulating petitions, putting up giant posters, calling for gatherings and issuing proclamations. Whoever does not exert pressure is made the victim of pressure. At one time the wise man was exhorted to keep his own counsel; now the wise men—and the less wise—hold forth, issue statements, address symposia, call for meetings, all because the Establishment's meteorological station is always checking to see which way the wind is blowing. This may well be the principal drawing card of the Land of Israel Movement, even though we may not go for the term "annexation"; it's good to have someone raising his voice, and it's good to have someone who is hard of hearing.

In the interim we have made our contribution to Arab-Jewish rapprochement: we bought up all the Chinese parasols and English fabrics and Japanese dishes and Persian rugs that they had in stock, for which we left with them seventy million Israeli *liras,* so that they should appreciate us. Now that the bargain shelves are empty we have shifted our co-existence activities to another front and are learning Arabic from Kamel and Zuzu over *Kol Yisrael* and are already able to order *zalata* and *hubez* and *zivda* in their restaurants.

With us, no revolution took place; the population of Tel Aviv has not taken up residence in the Negev; the doctors have not hung up their shingles in the border settlements; the political hacks have not given up their posts and testimonials. A few went up to the Golan Heights, a handful settled in East Jerusalem, some scores went back to the Etzion Bloc, but for the rest everything is as it was. Perhaps the Finance Ministry shouldn't know this, but deep inside we are happy over its request that we participate in the new Security Loan; by doing so we assuage our vague pangs of conscience for having remained what we were and where we were, after the storm had subsided. Officials go on guzzling tea, and the pious go on fighting against post-mortems. The Sick Fund still hands out numbers; emissaries are still circling the globe, and immigrants continue not to come in droves.

We still find it difficult to comprehend Yitzhak Rabin in the post of Israel Ambassador to Washington; Shuli Natan's voice still carries over the echoes of *Jerusalem of Gold,* from the day that the city was liberated and the entire nation wept; we still pounce on every story about the war and every combat diary, the moment they are published, grateful for the renewed confirmation that all these things really happened and that we were witness to them, at least as emotional partners. In the bookstores, the special shelf devoted to war albums kept lengthening, until the official Israel Defense Forces album brought the process to a halt. We bought all of them, at first out of some feeling of intoxication and later because we wanted to digest it all once more and pass it on to the children, as a souvenir, and always with the feeling that time is slipping away from us and can be grabbed only by its coattails, here, between the book covers.

To Zahal, with Civilian Love

THIS WAS not a case of love at first sight; far from it. The people in the Israeli community who took exception to "Zahal," the Israel Defense Forces, during its early years, outnumbered those who were for it. Arrayed against it, in principle, were the members of the disbanded Palmach, who found the idea of a standing army repugnant; the former fighters in the rightist underground groups, to whom Zahal was an ominous arm of the party in power; the old-time pioneers, recalling as they did the Czarist army, rebelled against the show of militarism; pious Jews who feared the inroads of secularism among observant young people. But while the attitudes of the old-timers toward Zahal were polarized—pro or con all the way—the hundreds of thousands of immigrants who came after the birth of the state, and were too old for the draft and too engrossed in the tough struggle of earning a livelihood, did not relate to Zahal at all, except for the momentary exultation at Independence Day parades, by way of remarks such as, "who would have thought that we, too . . ." etc.

The passing years saw an increasing number of Israelis directly affected by Zahal: sons, sons-in-law, husbands, grandchildren, who garnered military lore along with the customs of the land, such as how to enjoy the balcony and *falafel*. The apathy turned into kinship, into affection and, following the Six Day War (or the three weeks before it, to be exact), into a deep and abiding love, at times irrational and bordering on religious faith—the sole religious sentiment which an enlightened Israeli, Class of 1967, can allow himself to have—the last bastion of faith for the Israeli who had slammed down the receiver on the celestial exchange. Zionism and Socialism, once the substitutes for faith, are now encrusted with quotation marks; global brotherhood is a staff on

114

which only the very young tend to lean, impressed as they are by the international nuances of the protest demonstration against American intervention in Vietnam, capped with the singing of "We Shall Overcome."

Israel's Jewish community was once subject to spasms of innocent faith in the nations of the world—civilized, progressive, enlightened or democratic—a childhood disease of which we were finally cured with the help of Dr. De Gaulle. The Six Day War starkly illuminated for us something that had previously been an obscure feeling: there is no one in whom we can place our trust, no one in the big wide world and no one in our little one; we have to rely on our strength—and its name is Zahal.

Our conviction that the conduct of the state is infallible, like the Pope, at least on less crucial occasions, which gave so many of us peace of mind in the bygone days when Ben Gurion was at the helm, was buried under the avalanche of stones which drove him into retreat at Sdeh Boker: in May of 1967, when confusion gripped the Government, this conviction breathed its last. Now only Zahal was regarded as the embodiment of good sense and capability, the fine and noble savior from ills and evils, a talisman in khaki.

In recent years the tendency has been growing to lose interest in politics and in all its inferentials, except for the diatribe and gossip which it foments. "Political dealing" has become a repugnant term, connoting unclean hands, a stab in the back, personal vendetta, vacillation, lust for power, heavy-handedness, an unwillingness to step aside—traits diametrically opposed to those that make up the Zahal image: practical, efficient, bright, swift, fair, unselfish. Faith in Zahal leads one to view Israeli realities in black or white, without any intermediate shades, just as people once viewed capitalism vs. socialism, assimilation vs. Zionism—as though there was never any bureaucracy in Zahal nor any efficiency in a civilian agency (which is not impossible).

The first Independence Day parade in East Jerusalem after the Six Day War was a red-letter occasion for the Israelis no less than it was for the Arabs. The discipline and precision demonstrated in the parade was the most extreme antithesis imaginable of the chaos and confusion at the Central Bus Station—the well-planned and diligent military vs. the confounded and helpless civilian

115

sector. Behold! To conduct a military parade, with half a million spectators on hand, in partly hostile territory, despite the Security Council ban and the Al-Fatah threats—that's a simple matter, but to plan a transportation schedule for a few hundred buses—that's beyond our organizational capacity.

Once upon a time, five long years ago, to be exact, when General Ezer Weizmann, then commander of the Air Corps, prognosticated that the next war, should it break out, would be swift and crushing, he was assailed for his braggadocio. Today no one will question any conjecture made by any Zahal commander, including one about a war with the Martians. The faith is boundless.

This love becomes more demanding as it grows, and it saddles Zahal with heavy responsibility, other than the good feeling and the encouragement that it engenders. What is there in Zahal, you ask, that the people so adore? Certainly it is not the trim and impressive uniform or the measured military step, not the insignia nor the smart salute, nothing of the features which distinguish the spit-and-polish standing army. At times it seems that the love is not for the individual soldier, judging by the time he is left to stand on the highway, waiting for a lift, as hundreds of cars, half-empty, whiz by. This love is not for the ordinary mortals—the bald or paunchy, who like to fish or take a drink, drive the kids for a picnic or go with the wife to the movies (which is what Zahal officers are like in civvies); but to some mystic entity made up of supreme beings, over whom no enemy can triumph. This faith, particularly touching when expressed in flowers and cakes, harbors the danger, not of militarization, but of an idolatry whose offering altar is bound to explode from interior pressure. There must be some shortcomings to overlook, if one is to love completely.

The bothersome question: if so many Israelis pass through Zahal ranks and remain associated with it for years, why is it that so few of the military traits (and, in Israel's case, all of these are positive) have carried over to the civilian sector? Is it because civilian life is a direct continuation of the past, the diaspora, petty leadership, party strife, while Zahal is an outgrowth of the Israeli soil? Perhaps it's because the threat of death is a cleansing element, absent in civilian life, or perhaps because the army, from a certain standpoint, is unreal and beyond the bounds of reality. It may be that the army extracts the best that is in the Israeli individual, so that when he does go back to civilian life he reverts to his usual sloppy self, until he is called to reserve duty. It may also be that, in the tilt between the military and civilian traits the latter comes out victorious because the game is played on its home grounds. But it is a fact that when Zahal officers, having attained the benign age of forty or fifty (in contrast with their friends in civilian life who remain young, if necessary, until seventy and beyond), go into the labor market, blessed with all the good habits that the army implants, they are swallowed up without a trace, other than an occasional tiff with the politicians. Those who find themselves, after years of service in the army, in the new world of civilian realities, discover that things there are more stringent: responsibility for salaries or apparatus is far less significant, to them, than their former responsibilities for people's lives. In the case of most Zahal officers—other than those engaged in professions which they practiced while in the army and to which they subsequently returned—the spark simply died out.

Anyone who served in Zahal sees the map of Israel in a different light than does the civilian. To the latter, the map is divided according to the quality of the highways, the fairly good roadside stops, the residences of friends and relatives, moderately priced hotels, convenient beaches, attractive picnic grounds. Zahal maps carry memories of forced night marches and sequestered glens which, at the end of a hard day, were safe harbor; it is a map on which the circles stand for danger and the black lines mark the path of death.

Youngsters have always played soldiers, but Israeli children can copy reality and come up with exploits and adventures which put cowboy-and-Indian clashes in the class of a sleepy adobe: they lead charges against familiar targets, parachute down from warehouse roofs, stand bare-chested in wooden turrets, use names of live heroes and dream of becoming just like them: pilots, paratroopers, tank commanders.

It was only a few years ago that parents, asked "Would you like to see your son an officer in the regular army?", would have stared back their disapproval, especially if the parents in question were at the top extremes of Israel's society: the *kibbutz* fathers and the well-entrenched bourgeoisie. There was a time when

117

young men of the *kibbutz* who signed up for regular duty were regarded as heretics and traitors to the *kibbutz* ideal, and many of them left their *kibbutz* and slammed the door behind themselves. Today, particularly since the Six Day War proved the relative superiority, viewed numerically, of the *kibbutz* product over the urban material, Zahal is regarded as an extension of the *kibbutz,* and (if the young man insists) is preferable to any other occupation outside the collective. Even a manufacturer or the owner of an import-export business is now more inclined to accept the refusal of his son to go into the business, provided that he joins a prestige corps: the Air Corps, the paratroops, armor or intelligence (which has made the top rung of the popularity ladder only recently), but not—God forfend—that he should become quartermaster, paymaster or PX manager.

It is less difficult to determine what in civilian life has *not* been influenced by Zahal: food habits (other than the immunity that Oriental boys develop to Occidental foods); attire, since khaki antedated Zahal by many years; physical fitness, since, from the moment of their discharge, they become gluttons and ride instead of walking. Zahal's influence on driving has been negative: the kind of driving that militates in the army is even wilder, more inconsiderate and road-hoggish than is generally to be found. Withal, it is impossible to imagine how the nation would have looked without Zahal—if there were still a nation in existence. But you do know that even the *yored,* the selfish brat, the criminal, the worst shark in the business world—all bear a spark of purity and faith towards Zahal, the commander, the fellows in the unit.

I don't know whether Zahal should feel complimented or should sue for slander the people who maintain that most of the entertainers in this country come from the military troupes. It all depends on the eardrum: you may not see what's going on, but you can hear it, from a considerable distance. Obviously this reflects the influence of the top sergeant, whose mellifluous voice turns raucous by evening. The images in the skits portraying army life become, in the course of the years, irrevocable prototypes, as in the Comedia del Arte: the pert secretary, the dumb private, the screaming top sergeant, the mixed-up recruit, the innocent girl soldier, the strict commander, the golden-hearted cook, the battalion oaf. Perhaps this feeling of "we've seen it already, we've heard it before" is an indication of our cumulative years. After all, Zippi the Secretary is reincarnated by every fresh batch in the Women's Corps.

If language is a mirror of life's processes, then the army has penetrated into our civilian bones much more deeply than it would appear on the surface. Besides the professional terms—confrontation and reserves, operation and division, citation and radar, which civilians have learned to use with comparative ease—our vocabulary has become enriched with scores of down-to-earth terms, born in camp, aside from the long list of expressions which my innate sense of propriety keeps me from putting down on paper.

Popular tunes, like slang, need the realities of life and an appeal to a distinct group, if they are to spread, something which the fragmentized civilian experience cannot produce (except in the *kibbutzim,* for internal use only). Going over the list of the tunes which gained longevity since the establishment of the state one finds that they deal mostly with war and the military: "Dudu," "Bab el-Wad," "Uri," "Hey, the Jeep," "The Day Will Come, Believe Me," "Patrols, Patrols," "Dina Barzilai," "Three Soldiers," "At Mount Sinai," and the songs of the Six Day War, "Ammunition Hill," "The Straits of Tiran," "Whoever Went Forth Won't Ever Come Back," plus "Jerusalem of Gold," which burst into glory with the war. Perhaps this is because tunes are for young people, and the young are bound up with army service, or perhaps because the army is the most powerful reality, other than love, that young people here experience. Perhaps it is because our automated world does not afford too many opportunities for honest sentimentality, and tunes feed on sentimentality like garden flowers on fowl fertilizer.

There are but few things in life that can cause a sedate, intelligent and rational person, as each of us considers himself to be, to get a lump in his throat and moisture in his eyes at the sudden sight of a flight of Mirages flashing by overhead or squads of dusty and tired soldiers singing as they march along the shoulder of the highway, especially now, when the memory of the Six Day War is still sharp and vivid. This is one of the dependable criteria of age: the younger and more vulnerable that the soldiers appear to us, the older we ourselves are becoming and the more difficult it is for us to contemplate another war. There is no logic in the wish that Zahal should ever remain what it is today, bold and sure of itself but at the same time unnecessary: obviously Zahal has achieved its position today only because it *was* necessary, through battle, danger and sacrifice. And this is the source of the split in the soul of the Israelis: all of us yearn for peace, if not for ourselves then at least for our children, and at the same time we take fierce pride in Zahal, in the image of the fearless Israeli fighter, for, in some small way, all of us have a share in him. We all want free borders and friendly relations with the neighboring states, and yet we dare not ask ourselves: what will we look like, in a world of peace and tranquillity?

Sing to Us the Songs of Zion

WHEN THINGS are quiet, at least on the surface, even the Rolling Stones and Petula Clark are capable of giving expression to the emotions coursing through Israel's habitations. But when a state of emergency comes upon us, the melodies turn inward and become introspective, like the nation itself. During the Six Day War the songs of the world were stilled, as was the world, and we discovered that the Hebrew tunes which, in time of peace, serve merely as fillers in the broadcasting schedule, those tunes which hover about our ears but do not penetrate inside, these melodies are an additional signature to the deed in our possession.

In days of suspense we tend to see the future in danger, and we seek to probe into the past for answers, to look to it for a crutch, to find some sustenance in the good old days—good primarily because they are known and have nothing of the mysterious about them. Songs from the War of Independence and the Sinai campaign, of the pioneers and the Palmach, even "On to Zion With Flag and Banner" which came from those serene days of long ago, in the spring of 1967, seem to be much closer to us than the offerings of the tunesmiths, such as, "Who Can Count the Curls?"

At times, events may pick up a song which is struggling to keep alive and sweep it up, into a symbol, a battle cry, an anthem; at times, a songwriter may rise to the occasion and set it to music. But when a new song, fresh and unused, is on the spot for its shining hour, like a banner which is readied before the charge into battle and which then enters the pages of history along with its bearers, it is blessed by a singular stroke of good fortune, reserved for the chosen few only. As long as the liberation of the Old City of Jerusalem by Israel's forces is recalled, so will Naomi Shemer's "Jerusalem of Gold" be its expression; this is almost like having a personal chapter in the Bible.

Most songs are like fireworks: they illumine the skies for a brief moment, give voice to fleeting emotions, to a touch of genius and two months' royalties, then fade away. Only a few are filtered through the sieve of time, and this is quite as it should be; each generation should compose its own songs, as though it were the first to do it. It might be more gratifying if we could be certain that the selection is based on quality, that is, the mediocre fall away and only the choice remain. But here the element of chance comes in, as it does in determining which heroes are remembered by history. Circumstances also take a hand. *Bab el-Wad* remained the symbol of the fighters of the War of Independence on its own merits, perhaps, but also because of the fact that Bab el-Wad, entrance to the ravine along which runs the highway to Jerusalem, is something tangible, as are the wrecked armored cars still lying by the wayside; every time we go up to Jerusalem or back down to the plain, our thoughts are in communion, for a few brief moments, with those who died there.

At times a gifted singer can save a song from oblivion. A song may be rescued by a single word or a few bars. A song exported without fanfare may return in a blare of triumph; few will claim that *Hava Nagilah, Hevenu Shalom Aleichem* or *Tzena, Tzena* are the pride of Hebrew melodics, but since the Gentiles took a liking to them, why spoil their enjoyment?

There is no rod by which one may measure the longevity of a song. If a dozen certified experts in music and lyrics were to be asked as to what would be the chances of a song becoming a national anthem, if the lyrics went, "As long as, deep within the heart, the soul of a Jew is murmuring," (imagine a soul within a heart which is afflicted with a murmur; clearly a case for a cardiologist), set to a borrowed Slavic melody, their answer would certainly be a unanimous "nil." Naftali Imber, adventuresome, a rebel, a character worthy of immortality who circled the globe from Galicia to Vienna to New York, Daliat a-Carmel and Africa, wrote much better songs, but his *Hatikva* alone has endured, together with his interred remains on Jerusalem's Mount Herzl.

The effectiveness of a song, like a sacred site, lies not so much in what can be read or heard, but in the thoughts and emotions that it evokes. The years pass on, and the words of *Hatikva* no longer apply to the times, but pure sentiment keeps the song going strong. The voices which sang *Hatikva* during the seventy years since its composition, in Rumania, Basel and Tel Aviv, in Auschwitz and Sharm a-Sheikh, have molded it into something quite different from the original. The more that the song means to you personally, the less are you concerned with its textual contents.

Songs, like custom and tradition, depend for their longevity on the conservative bent of the individual: despite the steady surge of new tunes, there remains at the core a solid island of songs impervious to time. Certified kindergarten teachers by the hundreds, wholesale producers of verses and composers for the very young, have brought a flood of children's songs upon the world, yet the very first ones that a modern tot learns are *Ooga, Ooga, Ooga, The Little Bunny* who forgot to close the door and consequently caught cold, and *I Have a Lovely Garden*, which their parents once learned as well and now sing along with their progeny, possibly because the doting parents had done nothing, in the span between childhood and parenthood, to expand their trove of basic songs; some may sing along because it gives them the gratifying feeling of continuity. The parents once sang, *We Have a Billy-Goat*, to which the offspring add continuity by way of *Our Billy-Goat Has a Beard*.

Parents and governesses fall back on Little Red Riding Hood and her Grandma, who is very careless about safety in the home, and on Cinderella and her stepmother, who exploits her under extremely poor working conditions; the ideological implications may be suspect, but they are part of the realm of childhood. Similarly, children tend to go back to songs of former generations, even if the words are just so much abracadabra: Shireleh dances a ballet, followed by Moshe Sharett; "Shireleh Tempil" dances in this fashion and that; Hitler's dead, his wife is ailing—all echoes from a dim past. One finds it hard to believe that only eight decades have elapsed since Eliezer Ben-Yehuda went about rearing the first Hebrew-only-speaking child, in the face of a jeering Jerusalem.

The meticulous like to differentiate between songs and tunes, as one differentiates between literature and journalism, fixed assets and merchandise for sale. A tune is allegedly derived from melodies of other peoples, i.e., American, French, Italian, Spanish;

123

a song emanates from pure Hebrew culture, and any similarity to a Slavic, German or Armenian song is purely coincidental. Songs are written primarily for sopranos who, for some incomprehensible reason, didn't get to the Met and were therefore foisted on us; a tune can be rendered by any scamp. We also apparently have something called the Israeli folk song, since a festival is held annually to stimulate it. A folk song is like any other song, except that it exudes the fragrance of farm and wildflowers and portrays the beloved as a deer loping along the hillsides.

Elsewhere, people framed folk songs, over the generations, on manual labor, the rough life and robust, when nature was still untrammeled. But we, having dedicated two thousand years to prayers and biblical cantillations and, at most, to songs in Yiddish (a purely exilic tongue which dealt with subjects no less exilic: matchmaking, mothers with a Jewish heart, and prancing rabbis), now feel it incumbent upon us to catch up with more proper themes: galloping horses, fishermen's nets, shepherds' pipes, wildflowers, fallen leaves and other natural impediments, using the technique of assembly line production.

When the Spaniard sings about *Mio Caballo* and *Curacon,* and when the Hungarian emotes about *Yoi Tzigan,* they bear direct reference to their historical past. In our case, if we are to go by the multiplicity of Israeli songs dealing with flocks, flutes, ewes, and wool being clipped meh-meh-meh, we must be the most pastoral people in the world, except, perhaps, for the people of Tibet. Obviously these pleasant musical settings have little idea of animal husbandry: it's fine for sheep to meander along evergreen meadows, but there is also the hoof-and-mouth disease and the high price of salted cheese.

Our songs are generally behind the times, technologically speaking. The only motorized Israeli song which really caught on was *Hey, the Jeep*—and that was twenty years ago. Otherwise it's the hooves of a mare, camel caravans, foot patrols, we are hiking, hoppa-hey! No living creature apparently rides in a car, and songs about a Lark, Fiat or even a Vespa are still to be written. Nor is there any ado about mechanized farm equipment: combines, tractors, portable sprayers; our composers are still behind the wooden plowshares, harvesting with the scythe, squashing grapes in the winepress with their feet (ugh!), tying sheaves by hand and generally behaving like *felaheen,* primitive tillers of the soil.

The volume of seltzer, juices, Tempo, Oranjada and cider that we consume in this country exceeds the amount of wine a hundred-fold, but our folk songs ply us with red, red wine, with a chaser of sparkling water from a jug. Plastics, of course, are out. We are in the twentieth century, in the age of the atom and space, but the songs, like our longings, bask in the secure past of the man who lived according to the season of the year.

The only sector in Israel which generates true-to-life songs is the army, perhaps because its ballads grow out of Israel's realities, without the tradition of lofty verbiage and pious hypocrisy, which has replaced truth in public affairs, in speeches, writing and song. Army service is still the most impact-laden phenomenon in the life of every Israeli.

The physiology of the young female has evidently undergone no startling change over the centuries. No need to bring these facts up to date, therefore: the same curls, the doe or chocolate eyes, the same freckles, the same like-two-apples breasts, the same lilting feet, ever since the days of King Solomon. The image that songs ascribe to the Israeli female did not change during the war, but the approach did. No more impassioned pleas, flattery, compliments, courting, but outright demand for a more sympathetic understanding of the man in service (well does he know that the way to a maiden's heart is through a uniform and a packed knapsack): wait for me, hold your fingers entwined for me, be faithful, O my faithful one!—exactly how warriors wailed when the slingshot was first invented. Only the tactics and the armaments change; the man is the same, and so are his songs.

Community singing, other than in religious worship, was popular prior to the Industrial Revolution and chiefly among those who toiled like mules. Singing came naturally to the Volga boatmen, the Sicilian fishermen, the Mississippi Valley cotton pickers, the Manchester weavers. When a man is hungry, wrung out, humiliated and hopeless, the song wells up of itself, but one is hardly moved to sing in the lobby of the Tel Aviv Hilton or in the Shalom Tower elevator, next to an IBM machine, or in Café Nitza. It is hardly becoming for a man in a Dacron suit and fragrant with Ice Blue, with the keys to a Mustang in his pocket, to sing like a savage. There must be the atmosphere of mobilization and war; anyone of public or other prominence must go back to uniform and messkit and sand in his teeth before his mouth will open in a community sing.

A man is capable, if necessary, of eating in the company of a thousand strangers or even people whom he dislikes, without developing ulcers, or to work alongside a hundred faces which repel him, but to sing with them is more difficult, for group singing calls for a sense of belonging, of identification. Forced community singing is therefore more of an infringement on personal freedom than is forced labor. The Germans claim that *boese Menschen kennen kiene Lieder,* "evil people do not know how to sing," but they themselves proved the opposite to be true. Singing with others is no guarantee of a lofty character: it can be an outlet for hatred as easily as for love, for fears as well as for hope, for pangs of conscience as much as for faith. It all depends on who the singers are, on what and where they are singing.

During the Six Day War, when we tried to tune in on foreign newscasts, between our own, we felt Israel's isolation in the world even more strongly. Wavelength upon wavelength, cycle upon cycle, station after station with blaring Arab marches—inflamed, threatening, hysterical—and all we had, by way of rebuttal, was *Believe In Me, A Day Will Yet Dawn.*

Today (wartime excluded) a mature person will not sing aloud, even if he is alone, unless he is in love with his own voice or is in love generally or is taking a shower. Humming along with the radio is fine—but not a decibel more. Only the conservatives, the household helpers among the Orientals and Russian expatriates with deep bass voices, are ready to shout down the trend of the times. Serenading 'neath a window will get you a ride in a police wagon for disturbing the peace. Singing aloud calls for innocence, an ingredient long lost in one of life's byways. Yet we were once among those who copied songs into blackbound books; we were the ones who swallowed tears to the melody of *Perhaps These Things Never Did Happen* under the evening sky. Either Rahel's poems are not what they used to be, or we are not. The war alone revived those days of song, if only for a few days. That's how it is: in wartime, the older folks become younger and the young ones become old, overnight.

126

Heroes Remembered and Forgotten

JUDAISM CALLS for a good memory. For two millennia we have been exhorted, at all times: "Remember that which Amalek did do unto you"—remember the exodus from Egypt, the stance at Sinai, the destruction of the Temple, the thousands of details which, in their aggregate, comprise the history of the Chosen People. This memorizing is chiefly a matter of repetition, the same things said or done time and again, year after year, one generation after another. The Holy Scriptures are immune to forgetfulness and will so remain as long as they are an integral part of a religion which embraces all of life.

In our day it is obvious that we must remember the War of Independence and the Six Day War, the siege of Jerusalem and the Battle of Tel-Fahr—we and our children, as though each of us had gone forth to do battle; our continued existence is built on this remembrance, but no new Bible is being written and no divine command tells us: Remember! Human memory, when not subordinated to celestial decree, does not like to put itself out. Perhaps this foreshadows the perfect world, in which there will be no obligation to remember anything and no bar to forgetting everything.

In the eyes of the world, it does not befit the People of the Book that the principal memory of its restoration to sovereignty should involve the bravery of fighters and that the first twenty years of the State of Israel should form a long list of wars and battles and clashes and death, in its defense, all along the line. We don't like it, either. But the outlook of universal liberalism, unencumbered by nationalism, is a luxury to be experienced by citizens of old, well-established countries, with boundaries clearly defined and generally acknowledged; this luxury is beyond the capacity of a

127

20-year-old state, saddled all those years with a situation that is neither war nor peace. We, too, would like nothing better than to be noble of spirit, enamored of global humanity, with no need for a single thought for our narrow interests—were we not forced to be nationalists of a sort in a small state, fighting for its life like a crazy cat.

The age in which we live has neither time nor inclination for war heroes and brave deeds in battle, and if we were perched on the Left Bank (of the Seine) or ensconced in Cambridge University we, too, would dismiss such notions with a delicate wave of the hand, as something which belongs to a narrow-minded and chauvinistic past. But here, in the Middle East, we still tend to be primitive; we must have heroism as a matter of life and death. This fact no doubt impairs our standing among the liberals and the advanced intellectuals of the Bertrand Russell type, wherever they may be—as though we were still wearing loincloths while the rest of the world is already attired in Dacron suits. But we cannot help it; we achieved modern nationalism rather late, with all due regrets.

Much as the fighting individual is appreciated, no one name from among those who fought in the War of Independence has been singled out by the entire nation as its outstanding hero—no one image, or two or three, to symbolize the aggregate of the six thousand who fell in 1948-49. Perhaps twenty years is too short a span, or this may be the price of democracy, which pares away top layers and lumps them with the rest. Perhaps only a totalitarian ideology and regime can turn out a national hero in a matter of years, as did the Germans with Horst Wessel or as did Franco with Primo de Rivera, and that is why we steer clear of national heroes. Or it may be, as Emerson said, that in the course of the years every hero becomes a bore. The trouble is that we tend to remember history through individuals, and that without this personal identification the past has no face. Accounts of the War of Independence, at times without the complete names, without personal evaluation, without preference of one over the others, have rounded up the fighters in this war into one contingent, for better or for worse. No symbolic images.

This may explain why, in Israel today, people still remember the names of the *Irgun* or *Lehi* underground heroes, Dov Gruner

or Yair Stern, more than the valorous men of the War of Independence; the latter fell on the battlefield, while the others were
alone. Also, rightist organizations lend greater weight to individual
exploits, and the memory of the individuals has been fostered
consistently and with aforethought. Forty-seven fell in defense of
Kibbutz Yehiam, and they were no less courageous, if courage
can at all be measured, than Yair Stern, hero of *Lehi,* but they
were many and they died in similar fashion, while he was all alone
against the British police.

It may be that, in this twentieth century and in line with modern
combat tactics, the flashy heroes are a burden and a risk; a commander would prefer courage in the ranks, according to plan, to
daring exploits which at times run counter to orders. However,
folklore (where heroes play a major role) prefers the extraordinary.
For this reason Orde Wingate stirs the imagination of the young
people in Israel more than do all the Haganah members who
fought along with him in his Special Night Squads, for he was
different from the others, in name and origin, blessed with the
stuff of which heroes are made: personality, uniqueness, zeal,
courage and a tragic death at an early age, and he is, furthermore,
the subject of several biographies in the English language which
describe him as a man of flesh and blood, with all his problems
and idiosyncracies.

The writings about the Six Day War show a definite shift in
attitude. We now have published accounts of the recipients of
the citation for valor, the life stories of these heroes illustrated
with their photographs; scores of war books based on individual
exploits; descriptions of commanders with a definite image,
photographed and interviewed. The Israel Defense Forces is now
torn between two contradictory objectives: to have its renown
set down in writing, and at the same time maintain the sense of
equality of the fighters.

It may make little difference, in the long run, who is remembered
and who is forgotten, but with us Israelis immortalizing a memory
is an obsession, as though one may grasp eternity by its coattails
through a biographical work or a collection of memoirs, by
naming a street or an institution or establishing an award in the
name of the dear departed—as a sort of modern interpretation
of faith in immortality. Regrettably, a nation can memorialize

129

just so many images, as proof of its continuity and of faith in the future; all the others (and no plaque on any building will help) will become, at best, listings in the general encyclopedia volumes, known only to people whose professions call for it. The name of a street, a prize, a museum, which does not conjure up the image of the man behind it, is no more than a combination of letters: Beilinson is a hospital, Nordau is just a street, Kaplan is a prize, Gordon is a movie theater—for all who know neither of the man nor of his deeds. Anyone seized with the desire to have a street named for one dear departed—a pleasure reserved, in Israel, for those who have gone on and beyond, and obtainable through due pressure on the municipal council—can be eased out of this urge by having him listen to the radio program called "Who Knows This?" People reside on Kisch Street or Abba Hillel Avenue ten years and do not have the faintest notion as to who and what was the bearer of the name.

A street must have luck, like anything else in life. A main street in Haifa named, many years ago, for a revered Zionist leader, is today a mere connecting alley; on the other hand, a low-ranking Zionist functionary was honored, at that same time, with a dirt road in an outlying section of the city—today a busy main artery. Heinrich Graetz was a greater historian than Simon Dubnow, but his street is small and forgotten, while Dubnow Street was, for a period of time, the symbol of residential status in Tel Aviv. Judging from the streets, Ibn-Gabirol was greater than Bialik and Soutine more important than Rembrandt.

When a person of renown departs—a hero, a leader, an artist, an author—we gather up his belongings, his table and chair, books and photographs for safekeeping in his memory, unto future generations, yet if there is no image of the man behind all this, the objects remain no more than objects. What distinguishes Hayim Nachman Bialik's watch (the one that plays *Hatikva*) and old bric-a-brac is the sound of his poetry. Dr. Weizmann's hat, diploma and Bible are endowed with a soul only for those who regard him as more than a photograph on the wall of the Board Room.

At times it seems that we forget more quickly than preceding generations, perhaps because our tempo of life is swifter or because we have inherited an interminable name list of the great

130

and noble and dedicated and meritorious men, the fathers and architects of Zionism, all of whom deserve commemoration. Or it may be that our memory is like the modern museum: no longer are there thousands of paintings, jammed in rows from floor to ceiling, but only a few works on otherwise blank walls—and these stick in our memory. Of all the fathers of Zionism, the only one who rises out of the sea of forgetfulness is Theodor (Binyamin Ze'ev) Herzl, he of the long beard and the eyes of a seer, driving himself, interceding with king and sultan, neglecting his family, his health—an ancient prophet in modern dress. All the others who stood by the cradle of Zionism, J. L. Pinsker and David Wolfson, Max Nordau and Nahum Sokolow, Shmaryahu Levin and Nahman Syrkin, are merely names attached to villages, avenues, quarters, or in the books one comes across in the National Library or in the school texts, learned today and forgotten tomorrow. A few are remembered because of their descendants living here, only a few, because most of the Zionist stalwarts, then as today, were ready to do anything for Zion's sake except for that one small item of settling and raising their children there.

Herzl's family is gone. "He is my son," noted Dr. Herzl, on his son's birthday, "my eternal continuity, my guarantee that I shall inherit this earth for all time, ever-rejuvenated in my son, my grandson, forever young, forever handsome, forever strong." This eternity lasted exactly fifty-five years, from the birth of his son Hans, who committed suicide at the grave of his older sister, in Bordeaux, to the death of his only grandson, Stephen Theodor, son of Trude (nee Herzl, who perished in the Theresienstadt ghetto), who took his own life by drowning in the Potomac. And even though children are no longer named Binyamin Ze'ev or Herzlia, Herzl's picture, sad, lonely, brooding on a parapet above a river, is ingrained in those who grew up here, like the Lag Ba'omer bonfires or the cries of the watermelon peddler.

Herzl is the sole Zionist leader to have been accepted by Jewry here and abroad in equal measure. In the case of most of the others, the Israelis tend to be cool toward those whom the diaspora Jews hold in high esteem. This holds true for Dr. Chaim Weizmann, who was indelibly stamped "Zionist" rather than "Israeli," a man who belonged to the world more than to Israel. It also holds true for Abba Eban, the darling of American Jewry, whose

English is superior to the Queen's and whose Hebrew is purer than the Hebrew spoken by the Israelis (this does not require much effort), yet who is not looked upon as being "one of us"— perhaps because we are still imbued with the impression that leadership and true conviviality must be within the formats of Labor *aliya* and the principles of Labor settlements or within the ranks of the military, and that whoever didn't get his upbringing there will always remain an outsider.

The most controversial figure of them all, and for the longest time, is David Ben-Gurion. No man, in the two decades of Israel, has been so revered yet so attacked. Even today, past eighty, and known to all as "The Old Man," he continues to arouse the same polarized emotions of admiration and antagonism. Only four years separated the slogans "Vote Yes for the Old Man" and "The Old Man's for the Old Folks Home," but between the two runs the entire gamut of feelings that Israelis have towards Ben-Gurion. Freudians may shake their heads and call it a typical case of the tribe rising up against patriarchal rule. True, many Israelis did allow themselves, in the early years of the state, the expensive luxury of exalting Ben-Gurion, in a measure of adoration undeserved by mere mortals. In the destructive Atomic Age, each of us feels the need of leaning on someone who appears strong enough to bear up under the weight and stand up to the demands of the hour, of having perfect faith in the capabilities of at least one man, whether his name is Ben-Gurion or Buber or Che Guevara. This faith finds expression in many ways, each man according to his educational level and maturity. As long as Ben-Gurion stood at the helm, many Israelis felt that no evil could possibly befall the state; a most comforting thought.

The Ben-Gurion Era—the first fifteen years of the state—was, for a considerable segment of the citizenry, a period of political adolescence. On the day that the Great Father-Messiah-Prophet was reduced to appearing to them battling for his influence, demanding but not getting what he wanted, as vulnerable as his antagonists, they felt disillusioned and steeped in a black void. Since then we have matured a bit and now regard Ben-Gurion as a great man rather than a demigod, and we can appreciate him as he is and not as we conjured him up to be.

Those of us who came here with the establishment of the state found Ben-Gurion already at the pinnacle of leadership, very much a fait accompli. We therefore can't play the old-timer's game of "were *he* alive today"—if Berl Katzenelson, Haim Arlosoroff or Z'ev Jabotinsky were alive today—Ben-Gurion would be merely one of the bunch, a peer among his peers. Dr. Weizmann expressed this evaluation through an intentional oversight in his *Trial and Error;* in all of his detailed memoirs, Ben-Gurion's name appears but thrice, as coincidence and aforethought. As to the eternal question of whether man creates his times or vice versa, relevant to Ben-Gurion as to any other leader, Ben-Gurion himself has given an answer, albeit with reference to Churchill, yet with a personal connotation: "I am sure that he felt that, at the particular moment, he was the only man who could save Britain. History would be quite different, had Churchill not then been in existence."

Ben-Gurion has always regarded himself as the bearer of a mission. Here is the source of both his greatness and his weakness; his conviction is at the base of his willfulness and strength and the capacity to bear responsibility, and it is probably the source of the antagonism on the part of his contemporaries: he lacks the flexibility to adapt himself to convention, to reduce himself to *I'm-just-a-small-cog-like-all-the-others,* and to let others decide, in due course and by themselves, that he was their superior.

At times it would seem that the admiration or animosity that people have toward Ben-Gurion is not so much a matter of political acquiescence or opposition as it is his character. Ben-Gurion is not congenial, neither as a leader nor as the Opposition, neither as an enemy nor as an ally, not in his prime of life nor in his elderly days. He threatens, he demands, he keeps harping on the same fifty-year-old themes: the role of Zionism, the Chosen People, the significance of sovereignty, a change in the electoral system. He is stubborn, he says things which rub people the wrong way, he remembers who said what forty years ago. He is not to be looked to for tranquility by the man relaxing in his chair or going over his accounts. It is so much easier to read about heroes than to live with them.

Our Man in Havana

SMALL COUNTRIES ordinarily get on the international espionage map only as the locale of the plot, the rendez-vous of secret agents and ravishing women, hardened government sleuths and shrewd gold smugglers. Cities that wish to qualify as centers of espionage activities must be adequately vice-ridden and supplied with dingy bazaars, hashish dens, night clubs and brothels, like Hong Kong, Casablanca, Tokyo, Tangiers, or they have to be located strategically, more or less neutral politically, and within the spheres of interest of two hostile powers, e.g., Istanbul, Havana, Vienna, Berlin. The agents themselves, however, are in the pay of the major powers, rich and powerful, who can afford to train them as gentlemen and supply them with unlimited expense accounts for putting up at de luxe hotels, driving fast cars and keeping glamor girls in line (all this if the spy is Anglo-Saxon), or to provide them with ultra-modern equipment, a highly scientific kidnapping system and ruthless superiors (if he is Russian). The machinations of a Greek spy on Turkish soil or the adventures of an Indian secret service agent in Pakistan may be material for local spy literature in Turkish, Greek, Tamil or spoken Urdu, but any spy aspiring to international stature must work for a Great Power, or against it, otherwise it makes little difference who emerges triumphant, the Secret Service of Nicaragua or Ecuador.

The fact that Israelis have been breaking into international espionage literature—not as contact men for some British agent of the Master Race but as equal partners or even as the heroes of the action—is a compliment to the Israeli security men, of which every Israeli may well be proud. Would that a James Bondy of our own arose in our midst!

Spy story lovers are not concerned with purity of soul and are

134

not interested in prototypes of morality and friends of the human race, so important to progressive and liberal authors. They want s.o.b.'s, master schemers, and it makes little difference if they are shrewd or tough, so long as the basic motivation is more or less noble: love of country, or faith in justice, or at least professional pride and love of adventure. A spy does not live by money alone. And this is the trump card that the Israelis hold and which has given them entry into the big time: the motive is always lofty (to defend the homeland or to avenge the Six Million who perished in the Holocaust); the actions are daring (kidnapping a top Nazi halfway around the world or planting a spy among the big brass of an Arab state). Add to this the exotic backdrop of the Mediterranean, an atmosphere right out of the Bible or secrets from the past hidden in the ground (scrolls, the Temple candelabrum or other unusual souvenirs), and scientific standards approximating international espionage demands, and you're made.

The trouble is that, in true life, the world seldom gets the information about Israeli security and intelligence from successful missions which eventually come to light, such as the Eichmann episode or the lightning strike against the complex of Egyptian airfields in the first hour of the Six Day War. All too often the sources of this information are the missions that failed or came to light before they were fully done, as was the case of Eli Cohen, our man in Damascus, or the hunters of the German scientists in Switzerland. There seems to be something rather illogical about the espionage story addicts: their admiration goes not to the local security forces, who succeeded in uncovering the plot, but to those who managed to elude or outmaneuver them, for a while.

The path to glory in a security services system is very much like the beginning of a movie starlet's career: she must fight for it every inch of the way. Take, for instance, the vaunted British Secret Service, world-wide pride of the profession, the subject of hundreds of books and films. Its public image today, in the wake of the spy who came out of the cold, of George Blake and the Philby affair, reminds one of a mixed up old aunt or a dormant gentlemen's club. The English allowed Philby to slip away because, up to the very last moment, they couldn't believe that a real gentleman, scion of an honorable family, a product of Cambridge with the right amount of heartiness and the proper accent, could be capable of betraying not only his country but also his colleagues in the warm, cheerful and exclusive club of the British Secret Service.

A possible Israeli counterpart of the Philby affair, albeit in part only, is the episode of Dr. Israel Beer, a member of the Labor Party, a lieutenant-colonel in the Israel Defense Forces, trusted by Ben-Gurion himself, but who never belonged to the tight circle of the people in power. At times I am inclined to believe that here, too, had the suspect been a pioneer of the Second or Third Aliya, a native of Minsk, Pinsk or Chelabiansk, a veteran and pillar of the Labor Movement or a founder of a labor settlement, a lover of pot cheese drowned in sour cream and of anecdotes in Yiddish, no one would believe the accusation—reminding one of the remark made by a matron of the Second Aliya when she first saw a prostitute on Hayarkon Street:"She can't be one of ours." The first reports about Israeli Jews in Arab intelligence employ also came as a jolt; murder, rape, robbery, embezzlement, forgery—in this we were ready to be like other nations, but betrayal of country? Perish the thought!

Those who count security men among their friends—and this happens in the best Israeli families—know that they look like any other people, and you wouldn't give a single tarnished Egyptian coin for them. Most of them are like their counterparts all over the world: office workers behind desks and seniority ratings, clerks, researchers, experts, whose private lives contain no more romance and adventure than a poultryman's. According to our notions, gleaned from detective tales, an agent's life begins only when he is already on his mission, beyond his own borders, when he is no longer his own self but altogether someone else, when he puts on his disguise, nurtures trust in order to betray the trusting, eavesdrops, opens letters addressed to others, keeps tabs on what they are doing, and generally engages in ventures which are forbidden to us mortals, much to our sorrow, by the rigors of morality. The secret agents are today's knights of old, in shining armor of technology, heroes bearing the badge of courage bestowed by epic literature, who contend with fate, elude danger, ward off their pursuers, leap from ramparts, overcome every obstacle, and finally stand revealed in their true identity, this being no more and no less than a version of Little Orphan Annie's real father.

The status of most professions undergoes some change, in the course of generations, moving up and down the ladder of prestige. There were times when stage actors were not given burial in proximity to respectable folk; clerks were once regarded as the *intelligentzia*, and a secret agent was no more than a plain spy or the minion of the Czar or some other tyrant, just one degree above the ordinary police stoolie. True, the Bible considered spying to be necessary military strategy, particularly when contrived by the Lord and innocent of moral elements. The thrill of spy spectaculars was evidently known in those days. The account of Madam Rahab has all the ingredients of a film box office hit, especially with Gina Lollobrigida in the title role. In Europe, however, the level of the profession has degenerated greatly during the last few centuries.

The hour of glory struck again for the intelligence operator with the advent of technology; the urgency of obtaining immediate information about enemy activities, the tempo of warfare, sophisticated weapons, the heavy stakes and the meaning of failure, the tremendous technical knowledge demanded by warfare—these caused espionage activities to be transferred from amateurs of the type of Mata Hari to the real professionals.

In the Land of Israel, the attitude toward the secret agent also underwent change. The first contemporary spies were the members of *Nili*, a group of young intellectuals (Sarah Aaronson was the heroine) who, in World War I, spied on the Turks for the British, and were shunned for it by most of their own people. Back in 1932, when David Tidhar published his series of twenty-eight detective novelettes (based on his experiences as a member of the British constabulary in Palestine), the populace turned up its literary nose (and bought 10,000 copies each week), and the pioneer of detective tales was obliged to publish a long apology. In his autobiography Tidhar later contended that from the ranks of the readers of "Bombs on Mount Carmel" and "In the Claws of the Human Monster" there came the tacticians who directed the struggle against the enemy, during Mandate days and particularly after the birth of Israel.

Popular acknowledgment of the importance of security intelligence came with the struggle against the British, the organization of the Haganah, possession and concealment of arms, and running the British blockade. The acquiescence held strong as long as the operations were against the British, the Arabs, the Germans; but when it became known, after the establishment of the state, that the security forces were empowered to act against Jews residing in Zion as well, to listen in on their conversations, keep track of their activities and take them to court, the sensitive Zionist heart was quite shocked. The "dark forces" were rehabilitated in the community and gained worldwide acclaim only when Eichmann was brought to justice.

The world visualizes the Israeli secret operator in two roles: he is the avenger, a survivor of the concentration camps or at least someone whose entire family was wiped out in the Holocaust, pale and with burning eyes, zealous and ascetic. In Morris West's *Tower of Babel* he even carries, sewn into his pocket, a metal Shield of David engraved with the names of the concentration camps and the number of inmates who were put to death in each respectively, and, thus fortified, he goes to Syria to face death while murmuring—as was to be expected—"the Lord is our God." The second image is that of the *sabra:* sturdy, tough, daring, resourceful, the end-justifies-the-means type, no great intellect but persevering.

Issar Harel, former head of *Shin Bet* (Security Intelligence), built the organization on teamwork and discipline, and he would find it distasteful to go along with the popular notion of the Israeli secret agent as the organizer of orgies (such as "the pink ballet" in *Our Man in Damascus*) or the exploiter of the body of an innocent Jewish maiden in order to obtain the secrets of a counterspy (*Funeral in Berlin*). One of *Shin Bet*'s ironclad rules is to avoid using the bed as an instrument for eliciting secrets, unless the agent is a gay bachelor to begin with or the situation calls for the employment of a professional hostess. If we bear in mind that Samantha, the *Shin Bet* girl in *Funeral in Berlin,* sacrifices herself to the embrace of Michael Caine, we might agree that the *Shin Bet* should reconsider its regulations regarding female operators.

The problem which all epics with an Israeli locale are likely to face (or where Israeli actors play leading roles) is the same as L.B.J.'s: the credibility gap. If a top-notch author like Muriel Spark tells her readers in *Mandelbaum Gate* about Pakistani students attending the Hebrew University in Jerusalem while living in Acre, can we blame a small-time writer? The fragrance of orange blossoms fills the air (in October!), and the *Shin Bet* man with the impeccable Hebrew name of Edom Ronen calls his infant daughter "Golda"—not to mention the gross tendency of all Israeli intelligence people to think aloud about the issues of Zionism, the manifest destiny of the Jewish people, the Holocaust in the light of the Holy Writ, in compliment to the erudition of the reader. Imagine a conversation between General Aharon Yariv, head of Israeli Military Intelligence, and one of his aides, on a morning after a *kibbutz* has been shelled, as follows: "We lost six million dead in the Holocaust, Captain! Israel is built on their ashes! Remember that!"

The *Shin Bet* and military intelligence men scattered all over the globe are generally called Yitzhak, Moshe or Yaacov. The family name is unimportant, unless the operators are top echelon people, in which case they are assigned tough–sounding patronymics: Baratz, Barzilai. *Shin Bet* men would presumably like to set things straight and to draw an image of the Israeli agent as they see him: efficient, direct, disciplined, dedicated to the goal, patient, and so on, down the list of noble traits, but this is beyond their reach; they are subject to the same rules of behavior imposed on children being reared in the British tradition: one is aware neither of their voice nor of their presence. This is the sad antithesis in the life of a *Shin Bet* man: he is valuable only as long as nobody but his superiors is aware that he is alive. Once a secret agent wins world renown, his career, as far as assignments are concerned, is over, as witness the case of Wolfgang Lutz, who operated a horse-riding school, was arrested in Cairo, tried, released, and never went back into the cold.

The best course is to allow folklore to grow; realism is poor stuff for thrillers. If you are too close to an entelligence employee, you will never enjoy a spy tale. We know this from the Eli Cohen episode and the men condemned in the Cairo trials. The moment we say to ourselves that the secret agent is no different from any of us, more talented perhaps, but no immortal and, furthermore, one who is likely to die in depressing circumstances, we begin feeling responsible for him. Espionage must keep its distance, if it expects to remain a thriller.

139

The Tempting Earth

IT IS no mere coincidence that one of Israel's former chiefs of staff, Professor Yigael Yadin, is an archeologist by profession, and another, Moshe Dayan, is one by avocation (and almost lost his life on one of his digs), or that the Israeli Army at times participates in archeological surveys, providing equipment, security measures and personnel. Archeology today is the top national hobby, being much suited to the Israelis generally, and particularly to the men in the military—no bloody bullfights or boring cricket for them, but probing into the past, a sort of Zionism in reverse, a *post factum* assurance that this land is indeed ours.

There is, of course, an essential difference between the scores of professional archeologists in Israel and the two thousand certified amateurs registered in the Palestine Exploration Society, on the one hand, and the many thousands platonically attached to archeology, on the other. These are not interested in the Pliocene or the Pleistocene Age or the Inca civilization in Quechua or the Mohenjo Daro excavations in the Valley of the Indus, but only in the history of the Middle East region as it relates to the Bible, the Jewish War of Josephus, and other written evidence. The imagination is challenged not by stones but by words, wherever literature is substantiated by reality.

If a visit to an archeological site is to be more meaningful than the usual passing glance of the tourist, the visitor must relate personally to the culture imbedded in the site. To anyone who has not drunk from the fonts of Hellenic civilization and has not read its mythology, in breathless suspense, the Acropolis is merely a beautiful spot of charming scenery and ancient pillars and, nearby, Greek vendors offering linen handbags, Royal Guard dolls and other souvenirs.

If Masada were no more than the ruins of Herod's magnificent palace in the heart of the desert, then the spot would draw tourists by virtue of its incomparable panorama, but inasmuch as Masada is tangible proof of the Jewish revolt which Josephus describes, and is the evidence of drama, of the final moments of men known by name, it is not as an archeological site but as a saga that it has retained its power to this day. What draws us to archeology is that dramatic moment, and you must have someone who can combine the two elements, expertise in the subject and the ability to write for the non-professionals, in order to convert archeology from the business of the few into an attraction for the masses.

Archeology is, in a way, akin to a film: thousands of extras digging under the blazing sun, sifting soil, classifying fragments of pottery, lugging baskets, brushing dirt away from stones and doing all sorts of things which, to the non-archeological eye, look like hard, dull labor, and among all of these there is only one, the star, who announces the great discovery to the world. The relatively brief history of archeology is the story of the top stars: Schliemann, Evans, Champoleon, Wooley, Yadin.

The drawing power of archeological digs or underwater exploration for the amateur (nor are the scientists indifferent to it) is as old as humanity itself: the quest for treasures. Every find legally belongs to the country where the site is located, and this holds for archeological discoveries as much as it does for all other tests of honesty. Now, as long as the find consists of bones of prehistoric man or an Aramaic inscription on a tablet of stone, one can more or less rely on the high civic-mindedness of the average Israeli. However, and we say this hypothetically, if a man strolling along Achziv beach were to come upon a Phoenician female statuette and not a living soul is in sight, he would have to be possessed of character of steel to hasten with it to the Department of Antiquities. He is more likely to rationalize that our museums are crammed full as it is, that they already don't know what to do with the stuff they have and simply keep storing it away in cellars; on the other hand, the same ancient little statuette, in a private home, would be infinitely more appreciated, not being among a hundred and fifty similar items, in the museum, where visitors flit by unappreciatively, anyway; as for the researchers, they do nothing with the items but classify and catalogue them, then write dull books about the whole thing. These arguments naturally hold true only when there are no hostile witnesses in the area. Otherwise, honesty is a round-one winner.

Archeologists thrive on tragic occurrences; the more sudden and overwhelming the disaster, the better. A city that has been inhabited for many hundreds of years, like Jerusalem, provides no opportunities for extensive explorations and major sensational finds. Even a few meters dug up adjacent to the Western Wall aroused a debate on the Cabinet level, and were it not for the giddiness of those first days following the June 1967 war, when the bulldozers were able to work unimpeded, even this would not have come to pass. The ideal conditions, from the viewpoint of the archeologist, combine the eruption of a volcano and the complete and immediate destruction of an entire city, which is thereupon buried under a thick protective layer of ash, covering washerwomen at work, dogs, dishes, for-men-only paintings on the walls. However, the mass annihilation of an entire community, like Qumran, if located in a dry desert climate, also has possibilities. The archeologist dreams of dead cities, put to the sword, burned down to the very foundations and emptied of their inhabitants, for as long as a city remains alive it continues to consume its past, building layer upon layer, using ruins of one period as building stones for another, destroying the old to make room for the new.

Gone are the good old days, when archeology was the preoccupation of wealthy gentlemen interested in history and hungry for adventure, when the world was still replete with forgotten civilizations. The natives, having no idea of the worth of the ancient treasures in their midst, allowed the wealthy gentlemen from the west to cart them off at will, in return for a tip or token payment (Venus de Milo was acquired for some $180 plus $5 to cover handling charges, and at that time she still possessed an arm). Today archeology is the business of professionals, of organized research expeditions, scientific and systematic excavating, charitable foundations, universities, permits, legislation, restrictions. Archeology, like hunting, has fallen prey to the Bureaucrats. The lone wolves can't afford it.

The entire Land of Israel is one single archeological site, and we are only adding a layer to the cake of history (imagine how

142

the future probers into antiquity will torture their poor brains over the significance of the wooden African statuettes — one of our more recent fads—unearthed in such immense quantities at the excavations of Tel Aviv of the Plastics Age!). The Israeli archeologists are, therefore, infinitely better off than their colleagues in most other countries: there's enough here to go around. Each archeologist has a personal ancient site, perhaps even two or three: Tel-Dan and Arad are in the province of Dr. Abraham Biran; Tel-Gat is Professor Yevin's domain; sole archeology shareholder in King Solomon's mines is Dr. Nelson Glueck; Jaffa is Dr. Y. Kaplan's bailiwick; Jerusalem gleams golden for Professor Mazar; Megiddo, Hazor and Masada are General Yadin's plums. Then there's Bet-She'arim and Bet-She'an, Avdat and Subeita, Ashkelon and Gezer—the entire country undulates with these mounds, and each archeologist is king of his hill, until his sovereignty is challenged by the mass of the population converging on the site in quest of yet another bit of national pride.

The connection between archeology and the military is not accidental, nor is it true of Israel alone. Military men at times dabbled in archeology (Lawrence of Arabia worked at the Carchemish digs) and archeologists have often served the armies of their countries as advance patrols and intelligence scouts. The denominator common to both professions, when operating outside their own land, is the hunger for adventure, the drive to conquer worlds extant and forgotten. Many important archeological finds were made by a conquering army, especially by the British and the French in their advance eastward, only in those days a general was able to enrich his private collection with an Egyptian mummy or a complete temple, if he had the room for it, without a voice raised in protest. The English, French and Germans sallied forth eastward with the conviction that the natives —Greeks, Persians, Arabs, Turks—were too backward to be entrusted with the cultural treasures bequeathed by their predecessors, and that the natural place for these treasures was western Europe. This was a most sanguine approach to the matter, and it moreover enriched the British Museum and the Louvre with priceless collections. Only the luckless Americans had to pay, with good dollars, for every item in the Metropolitan Museum of Art, yet they are being accused of exploiting the world's masses.

Archeological deciphering of aerial photography, today a branch of science in itself, also came to archeology from the military. The first to engage in this activity, in World War I, were German and British officers. The Germans, fighting alongside the Turks in Sinai and southern Palestine, found time to do some photographing within the framework of the Preservation of Ancient Sites Command, of El-Arish, Agua el-Hafir and many other sites in the vicinity. The aerial photographs were subsequently published in a book authored jointly by General Kress von Kressenstein, commander of the German and Turkish troops in the region, and a professional archeologist.

In Israel, the connection between the military and archeology (and the Israel Geographic Society) has a further basis—call it the quest for rootedness or nationalism or identification with this land, to each his own lexicon. New states in quest of self-aggrandizement begin with fostering research on their early civilization within their sovereign borders (the Czechs, in the sovereignty of their new First Republic, tried to stress their Slavic origins and play down the German influence). It was the lack of national cohesion of the Eastern populations that made it possible for the invaders from western Europe to make off with their archeological spoils. Today, no self-respecting state, and this includes each and every one, would allow any foreigner to dig without a special permit and a full guarantee of its own rights. Here and there, one item or another is spirited away, to reappear in the private market, but that's already part of the profession, thank God. Otherwise, where would the private collector be?

One of the first Israeli projects in the territories taken in the Six Day War is a complete archeological survey of the regions, with special emphasis on Jewish sites. The expeditiousness is explained by the fact that experience bids us to do our research while the sites, which further substantiate our historical claim to the area, are still in our possession.

Less than a hundred years ago, most of the ancient sites in Palestine—Megiddo, Hazor, Bet-She'arim, Masada, Avdat, Subeita—were virtually unknown. Only the sites sacred to the various faiths were on record; religion needs a long memory to stay alive. The first excavations, chiefly by British explorers sponsored by the Palestine Exploration Fund, were like journeys into the unknown—excruciating, dangerous, marked with toil and hardships; compared with them, today's work is more like a hobby.

On the global map, the archeological excavations in Palestine, with all their historical importance, constituted but a small mound, and their finds, from the viewpoint of scientific study of the history of civilization, belonged in League "C" of the International All-Stars, until that summer day in 1947, when a Bedouin shepherd threw a stone into a cave, above the western shore of the Dead Sea, and heard the sound of breaking pottery. The story of the acquisition of the Dead Sea Scrolls and their wanderings all over the globe is proof that despite all the laws, permits and governmental supervision, the era of private motivation in archeology is still with us, and that the incentives thereto have merely grown with the passage of time. Now it is obvious that bits of decrepit leather are more valuable than jewelry, because the power of the word is greater than the power of gold. Score at least one point in favor of *homo sapiens*.

Equity Shall Not Prevail

It's A FACT and we don't deny it: we have given to the world the Bible, the *kibbutz* and the *tembel* (dunce) cap, but let us not be carried away by chauvinism, justified though it may be: we did not invent *protectziya*, "pull." Influence as a means to one's advantage is older than both the People and the State of Israel, but we should be credited with giving this antiquated and circumscribed concept a broader meaning and a more liberal interpretation.

Protectziya, in its ancient format, meant "patronage," extended by a ruler to a subject and contributing more to the latter's success in life than a college degree does nowadays, even more than a winning lottery ticket and a Federation of Labor passbook, all rolled together. A protege of Tiberius Caesar or the Sun King had naught to worry about save a falling out of grace or the loss of his head or both, in one fell swoop. This patronage was conferred in the form of a lofty and well-cushioned post—an ambassadorship to the Court of Spain or collecting taxes in the Dukedom of Milan or the governorship of Omsk, Tomsk or Krasnoyarsk, which automatically supplied the favored one with anything to which a man may aspire: status, money, women.

Protectziya in Israel is totally democratic; myriads of Israelis are in a position to confer it, each in his own sphere and according to his ability, at any particular moment. Every Israeli is also entitled to seek it, according to his character, ways and means. It has ceased being the asset of the few in power. The average citizen can engage in it, as well: the ticket collector extends *protectziya* when he lets you into the bus by the center door instead of by the one at the rear, where the push is on: *protectziya* practiced by the registry clerk will arrange your passport extension in one day; *protectziya* on the part of the stadium attendant will put you into an otherwise inaccessible seat at the soccer game. *Protectziya* is no longer a medium for getting a job; it abides with us everywhere in life, from the nurse to the hearse, as we strive to get a telephone or housing, a hospital bed or a bank loan.

The affinity of the Jewish people to *protectziya* did not arise all at once: it is the result of a long national history. In fact, the Almighty was the first to sanction it; his Book attests to the profusion of divine favor to be conferred on his people when and if it walked in his path. And didn't Joseph use *protectziya* to get his family into Egypt? And didn't Esther wield *protectziya* when she had husband Ahasuerus appoint Uncle Mordecai as satrap?

The dispersion gave *protectziya* a new dimension. The laws and ordinances were enacted by the Gentiles—not for the good of Jews, naturally. Helping a fellow Jew circumvent those decrees was not so much *protectziya* as it was a good deed. This has implanted in the consciousness of the Jew, to this very day, the firm conviction that any decision and any law or decree can be altered or evaded if one has the right approach to the right person.

Any member of organized society inevitably comes to a juncture where his will is bound to clash with law and order, customs, administrative procedure, fixed arrangements and limitations which define his existence. *Protectziya* is one of the numerous ways of evading these impedimenta. For generations and across the globe, from the Siberian taiga to the Arabian desert, from the Wall of China to the minarets of Istanbul, there has been a simple method by which one can achieve his ends, despite all difficulties and prohibitions: greasing the right palm.

The form and fashion of bribing has always been correlative with a country's state of development. If the gold coin goes directly from the applicant to the agent of the authority, the country in question is bound to be quite backward. Currency slipped in between the pages of the petition, as it is being handed to the official in charge, denotes improved methods of administrative communication. In a truly progressive country, a bribe is never given directly. There are go-betweens and intercessionists whose job it is to pick up the money at the home of the applicant and deliver it to the home of the favors dispenser, in return for a

147

commission which included a premium for the risk of becoming the scapegoat, should anything go awry.

There may be some countries where everything proceeds without partiality or bribery, where each and every citizen receives exactly that to which he is entitled, and where the sole criteria employed by the custodians of society are the laws of the land and its ordinances. People do say that such a social order does exist in the Scandinavian countries, but this I can neither confirm nor deny, since to date no travel agency or airline has attempted to bribe me with a free round trip flight ticket to those regions.

In Israel one can depend on the prevalence of absolute equity. Any man can apply for a position and rest fully confident that his thorough training and knowledge-in-depth constitute a sufficient guarantee for his getting the post in question. Anyone can also apply for a telephone and sit by, without any further effort expended, until his turn comes around according to the official priorities list. Nor will anyone be prevented from asking the Sick Fund for a number to see the orthopedic physician or from waiting several months until that number is called. It is entirely possible that the respective individuals will get the job, the telephone, and a session with the doctor—if they live long enough. Be that as it may, Israel definitely has no law which prevents a man from going after what he needs through the channels of justice and equity, free from discrimination, just as there is no law which forbids a man to subsist on grass or sleep on a bed of nails. This *is* a democratic country. On the other hand, there is no law which says that a man may not try his luck with just a little bit of *protectziya*.

Any study attempting to measure the influence of *protectziya* on life in Israel will be unable, unfortunately, to base its conclusions on proven facts and figures. The researcher would have to depend on his instinct only, for two reasons: first, revelations of partiality come to public note via letters to the editor, written not by *protectziya*'s "haves" but by its "have-nots" or those who tried to get it but failed, all of which understandably obviates all fair attitudes toward it: secondly, no one has thus far found it necessary to devote to *protectziya,* the central pillar of our existence, a statistical study in depth. The Bureau of Statistics does research on the labor force, but it gives no data regarding the percentage of employees who got their jobs because a good word had been put in for them. We have statistics about hospital bed occupancy, but not the faintest hint as to how many got there on a stretcher and how many gained entrance by picking up a telephone.

Nor do we have any authoritative definition which would set the demarcation line between *protectziya* and other forms of human relations. If a youth comes to a God-fearing Jew with a letter of introduction from the Grand Rabbi of the locality, then the fulfillment of its contents is obviously a divine commandment. If Abrasha from Kibbutz Kinneret appeals to a Labor Federation stalwart, how can the latter refuse an old friend with whom he once shared both folk dancing and malaria? Certainly this is not *protectziya* but the fulfillment of a basic tenet of comradeliness. If the request involves taking care of a brother, a son, son-in-law, uncle or maternal cousin, *protectziya* obviously doesn't come into the picture at all; this is merely natural selectivity. If the seeker of the favor comes from the same town (in case of the Polish) or the same country (Hungary) or speaks the same mother tongue (of Mother Russia) or wears the same school tie (British Commonwealth), no one would even as much as insinuate *protectziya;* this is true brotherly aid. *Protectziya* prevails where partiality is not an expression of natural emotion but of cold calculation—whether it's worthwhile to grant it or not; what the advantage would be in acceding to the request or what troubles would be invited by turning it down.

Functionally, *protectziya* is divided into two principal categories: the direct and the third party. Direct *protectziya* operates along the healthy line of "you do something for me and I'll do something for you." It involves just two people: one who is in the position to confer the favor and one who, in time, will be in the position to return it: a reduction in the Burial Society fees/housing for a young couple/admission to a mental institution/expediting an import license/a travel ticket/a low interest loan. This kind of *protectziya* calls for contacts, and contacts are a matter of whom you know—which still guarantees nothing. It is not enough to know the right man in the right spot in order to get from him what you want. The right man must have cause and reason to respond to it. This cause and reason has many faces; at times the influence of the one who is asking for the favor must be measured not by what he can do in return but by the harm that he is capable of doing if his bid is not granted.

Protectziya by way of a third party is more complicated, and one must be familiar with what gives in Israel in order to be able to distinguish between the different shadings. *A* may not always genuinely intend to get from *B* what he is asking on behalf of *C*. *A*'s action may be just a formality, made with the knowledge aforehand that his request will be turned down, the idea being that *C* would be convinced that the will to help was there, but, alas, it came to naught because of *B*'s refusal. Such requests are usually made in writing, so that *C* (a new immigrant, a welfare client or one in similar straits) could see with his own eyes that everything possible was being done on his behalf. Such a written request was once popularly known as a *petek* (a slip of paper) and was generally addressed to the Labor Bureau, the Welfare Bureau and the Jewish Agency. However, as these petitioners became acclimated, their exaggerated respect for the written word, as well as their naivete, underwent radical change. Today they demand that favors be requested vocally, or at least by phone, in their presence and hearing, although a request by phone also has various shadings. An approach in a hesitant, almost apologetic, tone, to the effect that "I have an old friend here in my office, a Mr. Yacobowitz, who has some problems with your department" is an intimation to the man on the other end of the line that he need not put himself out. Finally, it appears that the most effective channel of communications for *protectziya* is the Eustachian tube, or four of them, to be exact. Eyes mean nothing here; the communication can take place at a cocktail party or an official reception. Actually, social events serve the ends of *protectziya* the way a stock exchange serves securities.

Happy is the man who, in quest of *protectziya,* does not have to resort to the services of others but can demand it on his own, who doesn't have to introduce himself as "the friend of" or "the cousin of" but simply states: "This is Eliezer Suchinsky," in a tone which denotes both the status of Mr. Suchinsky and the urgency of his request. There are in Israel several thousand of these fortunate individuals who are personally acquainted with all the right people, know all the important positions, who never have to wait in line at the clinic nor scurry about for six hours at customs to clear a shipment, who never had to genuflect in front of a municipal clerk in order to get a license, who know nothing about the grim wheels which grind the little man. These fortunate ones are usually the little man's spokesmen and guardians.

In the crooked mirror of society it may appear that *protectziya* is particularly prevalent among the Ashkenazi, chiefly those of Russian or Polish extraction. I am happy to be able to state, on the basis of thorough personal research, that in this sphere, at least, there is absolutely no difference between the communities: the people of Israel as a whole are much taken with *protectziya*, the sole distinction being that this attachment, among the Orientals, is still in its platonic stage, but as the newcomers learn to find their way to the fonts of *protectziya*, the frame of reference grows wider, in the same manner of penetration as was achieved by the electric refrigerator, the gas range and the television set. The day may come, at the End of Days, as the cow will graze with the bear and the lion will eat hay like the cattle and equality will roam the countryside, that *protectziya*, too, will not be around, since there is an ironclad rule which says that a plus added to a plus is a minus—when two enjoy *protectziya* in equal fashion, they tend to cancel each other out, with a third somebody, enjoying a more preferential *protectziya*, picking up the prize.

But life is undergoing changes here, and so is *protectziya*. There was a time when you had to have it in order to be admitted into an *ulpan;* today these crash-Hebrew institutions are running after students. At one time you needed *protectziya* to wangle an exit permit and a foreign currency allocation, in order to be able to travel abroad; today even the Labor Federation can arrange your jaunt to any part of the globe. Formerly people needed *protectziya* to get any kind of employment—building, road construction, house work. Later, as prosperity set in, you had to have it with the Labor Bureau to get a housemaid or to attract the attention of a house painter. Came the recession, and the wheel of *protectziya* spun around, made a complete turn, and now, God willing, it's time for another fling.

An individual who has no merchant prince ambitions (that is, with no need for connections in either the Ministry of Commerce and Industry or the Ministry of Finance) and is not a new immigrant (whose status calls for all kinds of *protectziya*), today requires good contacts in two instances: telephone and health, the latter including mental disturbances, birth and death. Any man who can count among his friends a few hospital directors and the secretary of the Burial Society has nothing to worry about in life; moreover, he can pass away in serenity and be accorded a good plot, perhaps even in a preferred cemetery.

Protectziya is a means of getting something that cannot be purchased. You don't need it to get a table through the night club waiter; the instrumentality in this case is a five-*lira* note slipped into his palm. You don't need it to induce the tailor to do your suit before the others; a promise of extra payment for his effort will obtain the same results with equal dispatch. But if over-and-above attention is not obtainable through payment, you must perforce seek other ways of persuasion.

A person faced with adamant refusal when he believes his request to be justified—accepting a retarded child into an institution or getting a building permit—can go home and reconcile himself to the situation or he can smash a chair over the head of the nearest official, but *protectziya* still remains the more civilized approach.

Let us assume, for a brief and morbid moment, that there were no *protectziya* in Israel. The results would be disastrous. What would be the standards for handing out jobs, granting permits, awarding bids? The need for *protectziya* grows even more crucial when the demand exceeds the supply; how is one to select the man best suited to manage the soda fountain? Certainly not in the order that the applications were received; this is not at all objective. There are people to whom a day equals a year and others in whose eyes seven years are but as one day. Should we go by psychotechnical tests? Can we maintain with certainty that the man who is best at placing square pegs in a round hole is also the most proficient when it comes to carbonating water or shooing the flies away from the sesame bagels? No, no, here equity shall not prevail!! *Protectziya* is the way of natural selection, the way Darwin had it: the weak go off abroad, and only the strong pull ahead.

In So Many Words

Yiddish: Its Fall and Rise

ONE WOULD be hard put to tell what Israel's visage would be today if, consequent to the heated debate at the Tchernovitz Conference, 60 years ago, about the national language of the Jewish people, or later, in the wake of the Hebrew vs. Yiddish conflict on the soil of the Land of Israel, Yiddish would have won out as the official tongue of the dwellers in Zion. The Knesset would have discussed the issue of discrimination (against the Oriental communities) in Yiddish; Top Sergeant Salah Ben-Hamu would bark to his soldiers, *"Forvertz, marsh!"*, and the Kameri Theatre would produce the Yiddish tear-jerker, *"Der Kenig Lear."* Anyone not brought up on the lap of Yiddish culture would regard such eventuality as ridiculous nonsense; to the generation reared in Israel and to the immigrant devoid of "the Jewish spark," Yiddish is a marvelous medium for transmitting songs, anecdotes, Hassidics, vituperation and food, but it hardly suits politics or the military; yes, a likable, refreshing, expressive and entertaining tongue, but definitely not to be taken seriously.

The champions of Yiddish were sure, in those days of debate, that Hebrew couldn't become the everyday language of the people. Even today there is the feeling among the extreme Yiddishists who braved assimilation and survived the Holocaust that the sacred tongue is too meager for national use. However, relations between Hebrew and Yiddish have undergone major changes during the past twenty years. As Hebrew took more permanent root and its sovereignty no longer hung in the balance, it became more tolerant and permitted Yiddish to grow and develop in this land. Yiddish, on its part, realizing that the battle was over for good, no longer strived to regain lost positions, and concentrated on salvaging that which could still be salvaged.

Every few years, Yiddish writers and journalists renew the hue and cry about some fresh insult or deprecation or indifference shown by the Israelis, and every once in a while a storm in a teacup is brewed over the historic rights of Yiddish and the outlook for its existence. The protagonists and protectors of Yiddish are so jealous for its honor because, deep down, they know that time has pronounced the death sentence on their culture, even though a stay of execution has been granted for another twenty or thirty years. Because they are a minority fighting against time, 99 per cent of the standard-bearers of Yiddish are engaged in matters of honor and status (the remaining one per cent is engaged in nursing ulcers).

Thirty-five years ago, Tel Aviv newsstands handling Yiddish newspapers were threatened with the torch. In the eyes of the generation then in the process of maturing, Yiddish was the tongue of the decadent diaspora, of the residents of the miserable Jewish townlets, of peddlers, fishmongers, beggars, the Rabbi's hangers-on. Today it is even fashionable, among the native born, to have a warm spot for Yiddish, and a *sabra*'s personality is not one whit diminished if he enjoys anecdotes in the language or attends readings of Itzik Manger's poems or displays an affinity for *cholent* or *gefilte fish*. It may be that the affection for Yiddish and what it represents—the 700-year-old Jewish culture of the East European diaspora—reflects (as do so many other things) the American influence. Isaac Bashevis Singer, who wrote some of his works in Yiddish thirty and forty years ago, became known in Israel only after the ascent of his star in the English-speaking firmament. The same happened to "Tevya the Dairyman," which, translated into Hebrew thirty years ago by Sholom Aleichem's son-in-law, Y.D. Berkowitz, and made a basic subject in the school curriculum, nevertheless came into universal prominence only thanks to *Fiddler on the Roof*, produced originally in America. If non-Jews are moved by the *tzores* besetting Tevya and his spouse Golda and their daughters, may they all live and be well, then it's a sure sign that the diaspora can't be such a terrible affliction.

The changing attitude toward Yiddish on the part of Israel's younger generation is tied in with its uncertain gropings toward what is called "diaspora culture." When Zionism was a struggling movement, it stressed the culture of the ancestral home, chiefly the Bible, the repository of incontrovertible authority and proof and basis for the return to Zion. It laid emphasis on the new Hebrew literature of the past century, as the foundations of modern Hebrew. Today, with no further need to be concerned over the vitality of the language (merely over its quality), it is permissible to bear a positive attitude toward Yiddish in the diaspora as well, even toward life in the *shtetl,* now that it has been obliterated in the Holocaust.

The quasi-affection for Yiddish now suffusing the state is also due to the advanced age of Israel's architects. Take the foremost advocate of Hebrew among the old-time ex-Europeans and scratch his linguistics; below the surface there is a Yiddish soul. Even the Hebrew literary greats were afflicted with a chronic longing for the warmth and the human quality of Yiddish. Hayim Nachman Bialik, the poet laureate of the Jewish people, admitted: "Hebrew is spoken, Yiddish speaks of itself." Give most of Israel's Cabinet ministers an opening, and they will gush forth with Yiddish anecdotes; find some free time for the actors of the Habimah National Theatre, and they will do a Yiddish bit; bring a Yiddish-speaking guest from abroad to an editorial session of *Davar,* the Hebrew daily of the laboring class, and the roomful will break out in smiles.

One factor favoring Yiddish in Israel is the relaxation from the stringent principles of the past that it affords. Once upon a time one had to talk Socialism; now one can live like the bourgeois. At one time one had to strive on behalf of Hebrew; today it's pleasant to fall back on the beloved jargon. The rejuvenated love for Yiddish emanates, when age sets in, from the longing for those childhood years, the old house, the demolished yesterday.

Outward indications prove that Yiddish, like the Jewish people, is blessed with indestructible vitality: a daily Yiddish newspaper and a literary periodical, half a dozen theatre troupes (which disband and merge every once in a while), a Yiddish Department at the Hebrew University in Jerusalem. Scores of Yiddish writers now settled in Israel are continuing to create in the language; the radio has a Yiddish program, and at least one high school includes Yiddish in its curriculum. One out of every five Israelis knows Yiddish, and some of the country's most prominent personalities are devotees of the language—but there is no generation of continuity. Yiddish, like scalding tea on a hot summer day, belongs to the elderly.

Lovers of Yiddish, in arguing for its vitality, offer in evidence Aramaic and Latin, which remained alive even after they had ceased being spoken. However, these tongues were preserved because they were adopted by ongoing religions—Latin by the Catholics and Aramaic by Judaism. But what can be the fate of a language which is not used in prayer? Its works are preserved in libraries and universities; it will serve candidates working on their Ph.D.'s and using it in research, but it will remain lifeless.

The last fortress of Yiddish in Israel in the Neturay Karta, the ultra-pious disciples of the Satmar and Belz rabbis, who have never made peace with the profanation of the sacred tongue into the language of commerce, the home and of everyday life; their children use Yiddish in both speech and studies. At times, walking through a religious quarter, in Jerusalem or B'nai Brak, you see boys in long black cloaks, white stockings and large, stiff, over-size hats set on their heads, and you hear their Yiddish—and you feel that time has taken you back to the heart of the old *shtetl*.

The Yiddish theatre is enjoying prosperity in Israel, not simply because half a million people speak the language here (most of them speak Hebrew as well) but because the Yiddish theatre fills a role which the Hebrew theatre wouldn't touch with a ten-foot stage prop—unless its financial situation is catastrophic. The Yiddish theatre gives the public what it wants—no avant garde stuff and no Theatre of the Absurd, no black comedies and no plays without beginning or end, no communications-gap between man and his neighbor, and no endless probing into the soul of the playwright, only plays that touch the heart, and standard and familiar characters, like in the Japanese theatre: the luckless orphan maiden, whom everyone treats most cruelly; the rebellious son, who insists on marrying the *shikseh;* the wealthy wretch whose soul became blighted because he didn't want to share the wealth; the garrulous uncle, the nagging mother-in-law, the lovable rascal, the sage rabbi, and, above all, the true love that triumphs in the face of all obstacles, distances, prohibitions, class distinction. A Yiddish play which does not bring on the tears simply has no Jewish flavor.

The Israelis, imbued as they are with the sense of eternity that comes with four thousand years of recorded history, assume that Yiddish culture can be preserved for generations only as part of the Hebrew, in translation. It may be true that some of the fine points are not done justice by translation, and that whoever reads Sholom Aleichem or Leivick in Hebrew "kisses his bride through the veil"; on the other hand, all of humanity is today kissing through veils, thick or thin, Dostoyevsky and Shakespeare and Kafka and Proust, and the flavor is not so terrible.

Hebrew has taken on quite a few Yiddish expressions, especially in its treasury of expletives, verbal obbligatos to blows, deprecations, which it has been lacking all along—much the same as a finishing school maiden who was not allowed into the wicked world: *lekker, shvitzer, nudnik, shnorer.* How can you give gratifying vent to your antipathy toward someone without resorting to Yiddish? Even an immigrant from North Africa or Iraq, who has at his command the rainbow verbiage of Arabic, is compelled, upon going into the used clothes business, to proclaim the fact with the standard call of *alte zachen.*

Prophets of doom are met by Yiddish loyalists with vigorous denunciations, from New York to Buenos Aires. They will point to the Yiddish schools in South America and "three hundred thousand readers of Yiddish in the United States." They cite the prestige currently enjoyed by some living Yiddish authors (who are dismissed by all the other Jewish authors with one wave of the hand); 18 universities have chairs in Yiddish; the language has been undergoing resurgence; miracles have visited the Jewish people in the past. But we here in Israel, though prepared (despite our religious shortcomings) to accept a divine miracle here and there (especially in military matters) are pretty sure of our ground: God's language is Hebrew, but—the righteous who surround His throne, as they pause between one Hebrew prayer and the next, tell one another magnificent anecdotes—in Yiddish.

159

It's All Hebrew to Me

THINK OF how much history you create, just like that, and your ego will inflate like a balloon. You berate the youngsters, chew out the bus driver, quarrel with your spouse, boo the referee on the soccer field—all in hearty Hebrew, the sacred tongue, which but eighty years ago was the exclusive property of literature and the liturgy. The Irish, Welsh and Basques strive to follow our example and revive their own dormant tongues. The English, French and Germans envy our ability to read what was written two and a half millennia ago as though it was penned today, with no barrier separating the archaic from the modern. We take it for granted. We say *Hassneh* and have in mind the insurance company by that name rather than the flammable (but unconsumed) bush in the wilderness; we talk about "a coat of many colors" as a modern item of fashion.

Years after a non-native has begun speaking Hebrew, he realizes that it was crass nerve and sheer daring that got him into it. Had he known, then, how rich the Hebrew language is and how numerous are its sources, what is inherent in it and how lofty is its philological pedestal, he would have never dared to use it for conversation, for writing, for contemplating. *Ulpan* students are fortunate; the little promises so much. When they set out to learn Hebrew they are sure that, with the aid of a limited Hebrew vocabulary ("yes, no, thank you, stupid ass"), plus the international vernacular used by the intellectuals *(reactziya, oppositziya, rehabilitatziya),* a few cuss words in Yiddish and technical terms in English, they will be able to converse in Israel, on any and all subjects. In the course of time they do come aware of the truth of "I know that I do not know," but by then it's too late; Hebrew has become a habit.

In their first days of jousting with Hebrew, people feel that the language can be reasonable and quite pleasant to the ear, if it would only align itself a bit with such human tongues as Hungarian or Slovenian, and particularly if it were to be written with Latin characters. This proposal doesn't seem impractical at all; if one can write in Latin characters, with no difficulty at all, *amen* and *halleluja* and *Gabriel* and *meshugga* and *kibbutz,* why not *beresheet bara elohim* and go on with Genesis, all through the Holy Writ? But with the years we have become more Jewish, and we sense the indivisible affinity between sound and letters, between the letter and the religion; we learn how to write Hebrew —illegibly, like the natives; we become accustomed to reading a Hebrew newspaper, sometimes even a book. At times, though, as eventide closes in and the eyes grow tired and the brain is weary, the Israeli-by-choice reverts to the Latin characters, like the cavalryman who takes off his riding boots and thrusts his feet into a pair of worn house slippers.

The greats of world literature who come to visit us, or writers abroad with whom an Israeli comes in contact, always trot out the same nag: Hebrew! That's the language of a small handful, read by a million—good, two million!—people, or the population of a medium-size metropolis, as though an author would write strictly for the people of Liverpool or Marseilles. And indeed, Israeli authors and poets and playwrights and journalists do tend to walk about most of the time with the feeling that, if they were to create in English or French, they would have long ago gained international renown, outstanding prizes and a sterling reputation among the intellectuals on the face of the globe—like Saul Bellow or Françoise Sagan. When Yael Dayan, daughter of the Minister of Defense and a native of Israel, decided to write her novels in English, the entire country was up in arms, but from the vantage of practicality she was proven correct: she is today the only world-known Israeli writer of her sex. On the other hand, writing in Hebrew gives the writer the assurance of continuity, of one letter interwoven with the next, each individual and each generation adding a letter of its own to the one inscription: "The People of Israel lives on." Civilizations came and went—Assyria, Babylonia, Egypt and Rome; languages flourished and withered, and no one today argues in Latin and no one writes any more amorous letters in Assyrian, but in Hebrew a young man is, at this very moment, saying to his fair lady, "You are beautiful," exactly as did King Solomon, almost thirty centuries ago. Yet it was as recently as in 1906 that a Jerusalem newspaper, *Hashkafa,* in announcing the marriage of a Miss Goldberg to a Mr. Walichen, congratulated the couple for being the first in the country "to make love in Hebrew."

We forget, at times, that it was only eighty years ago that Eliezer Ben-Yehuda took the Hebrew language out of the Holy Ark, where it had been reposing for generations, dusted it off and fashioned it into a spoken tongue. Children still come across the story of his son, Ittamar Ben-Avi, the first child to speak Hebrew exclusively; how people were worried lest he remain a mute and mentally retarded because they had to address him in Hebrew which, at that time, had no word for "dolly" or "bunny" or "seesaw" or "pacifier." Of course, even now one hears moans from psychologists or meteorologists or cardiologists because Hebrew has not as yet come up with certain terms which they need in their professions, but these are en route: etymological innovation is as much a national hobby as discussing politics or hunting bargains. No one can argue, today, that Hebrew cannot be the everyday language of a vibrant people. When all is said and done, we can now play volley ball in Hebrew and run a brothel in Hebrew and repair tanks in Hebrew. It is those of us who grew up with a foreign tongue who at times mourn for a missing word, flinch at an inaccurate expression or dig around for nuance, but anyone steeped in Hebrew will never be at a loss for an expression in Hebrew even if he has to *fabrek* (yes, fabricate) it.

And so, for the past eighty years, our philologists have been having a field day, ferreting out from days of yore the words for everyday use: handkerchief, towel, pressing iron and brush, newspaper and editorial room, as well as words peculiar to the twentieth century, e.g., escalation, frustration. Some of the new words are absorbed immediately, and one finds it hard to imagine how we could have gotten along without them (challenge, confrontation). Others remain academic (a painfully ironic word, since the foremost Hebrew language "institute" is called *academia*), and the language rejects them like indigestible food. A language is apparently like a child, capable of absorbing only a certain number of new words per day, week, month or year, channeled through books, newspapers, radio programs and public utterances, while others are the castoffs by the wayside. As yet, no one has discovered the secret of why one word becomes the darling of the public in a single day (like *hashlacha,* projection, from "to throw"), while another is stillborn before it can make a proper debut. Perhaps words, like people, need that touch of heavenly grace.

It is to be expected that the language of the Hebraists who came here out of their own free will, out of love and a feeling for destiny, should be much richer than the native vernacular, which consists in the main of four verbs: show up, arrange, be engaged in, proceed. With the natives, Hebrew is in no competition with any other language; it is self-understood and does not have to be courted. The man who knows Hebrew grammar and can actually distinguish between the usages of a quiescent *shva* and a mobile *sheva* is either an Israeli professional in the field or is not a native. After all, since when does one have to know grammar in order to be able to speak a language?

Today there are in Israel a few score vowelization specialists who apply their expertise to poems, juvenile books or advertising copy directed at recent immigrants, and they serve the entire nationwide demand for vowelization; the others simply ignore the matter. None but a beginning Israeli is put out by the thought that he is reading a language without vowels, a sort of secret speedwriting system, as though it involved the deciphering of STRCTL FRBDDN or WNSTN CHRCHLL. Chills run up and down his spine when he realizes that only the structure of the sentence can tell him whether ספר (*sfr*) refers to a book, someone counting something or border country, or whether עבר (*ovr*) means "foetus" or "he passed" or somebody's "past," or *Eber* (Gen. 11,14). When he catches himself making the wrong choice, after ten, twenty or thirty years with the language, he is likely to be ashamed of it, but by that time he no longer insists that the spelling must be changed, and he accepts Hebrew, with all its idiosyncracies, as his very own language. However, in a cry of pain or a seizure of anger, in the embrace of his beloved or bending over a cradle the old abandoned tongue breaks through, that

163

language of childhood days; emotions inundate reason, and the barrier separating those who grew up with Hebrew and those who accepted it looms as thorny as ever. *Maminka moya* or *ach Du lieber Gott!* is still audible in Israel.

Currently some million and a half of Israel's populace speak Hebrew. While this is not an overwhelming number, it still outstrips the Welsh, the Latvians or the Albanians who speak their native tongues. About a million can read a Hebrew newspaper, but the number of those who read Hebrew books only the God of Authors knows. This does point to a distinction between the immigrants and the natives; it is precisely among the *sabras* who studied abroad that we find English to be the literary language, while Hebrew is the daily speech used in communicating with the grocer and the mailman, the bus driver, in the coffee shop and on the beach—but not for reading belles lettres. This is certainly a mark of success, for only fifty years ago people were concerned lest Hebrew remain too literary and never become the tongue of the vendors in the market place, which it is today: "Cheap today; everything's a *lira.* Prunes like honey sugar."

Spoken Hebrew is today far more natural and precise and much less flowery than the way the old-timers spoke it. Our parents studied in the old-fashioned *heder;* they were familiar with the sources—the Bible, the Talmud and its commentaries and homiletics. Hebrew was caressed and showered with attention as only a suitor could do it (it is not by chance that Vladimir Nabokov performs more linguistic acrobatics with the English language than any Englishman would dare to do), but the offspring did not inherit the deep love for the beauty of the language; perhaps love for a language can be transmitted only with the love for its literature, down the generations; in our case, this love was not transmitted because the literature was mostly religious in nature and content. Furthermore, the young spurned the flowery language of the elders, perhaps as part of the total sense of rebellion or because they who must take to arms have no time for linguistic ornamentation. Today the simple, direct vernacular is regarded as a trade mark of the *sabras,* and he who is carried away with words is regarded with suspicion. Facts are the thing, not words.

People concerned with the purity of the language move about all their lives in fear and trepidation, lest Hebrew absorb too many foreign words or be overly influenced by English or Arabic or Yiddish, or lest the spoken and the literary Hebrew come to a parting of the ways, as is the case in Arabic (although there is no sign as yet of this coming to pass), or lest the people here end up with speaking a sort of Basic Hebrew—a poor, inferior and lame excuse for the language. But Hebrew pays them no attention. It thrives, grows, expands and gets around. Take, as an example the simple word *bool,* etymologically meaning "crop," "parcel," or "segment." Today *bool* is primarily that colorful postage stamp on which the Philatelic Service makes a fortune. Eliezer Ben-Yehuda took a Turkish word, in its Arabic pronunciation, and added it to the national assets. *Bool* also means hitting the target, a direct bit of bull's-eye plagiarism from the English. Here, then, we have gained two new expressions and Hebrew has remained unscathed.

Foreign languages fill the void if there is as yet no proper, pleasant, convenient and well-rounded Hebrew counterpart of the term. Since *telegramma* is mentioned neither in the Bible nor in the Talmud, *mivrak* (from "lightning") had to be invented. The same happened with *mimsad* (the Establishment, from "base" or "foundation"), a word without which no intellectual journalist would dare open his mouth or take pen in hand. Today it's *mimsad* here and *mimsad* there; people toss *mimsad* around day and night and will do so until the time will come for the *mimsad* to topple, like a preceding regime or last year's dress, and take its place in the dictionary, properly and quietly.

Not only is Hebrew, like sex, here to stay; it is indispensable. Hebrew has unified the speakers of seventy languages; in Israel it is not too far-fetched to assume that in every store and little office you will easily find twenty languages per every forty square feet. Hebrew has given them all a unity and uniformity toward the outside world. There is no feeling more gratifying to an Israeli wandering abroad than to be speaking Hebrew with a compatriot and to be sure that none of the Gentiles around has any idea of what is being said, unless, suddenly, in the London subway an African in national dress may rise and say, in perfect *sabra* vernacular, *"Ahlen, chaver"* ("hi there, friend"), a by-product of his study of biology at the Hebrew University in Jerusalem or mechanics in a vocational school in Netanya. Or it

165

may be a gentleman of Japan who will state, very correctly, *"Anee mayvin Ivrit"* ("I understand Hebrew"), the result of his one-year sojourn in Kibbutz Dalia.

Hebrew has become a symbol of solidarity of diaspora Jewry with Israel, after the religious ties had weakened. Danny Kaye, Leonard Bernstein and Enrico Massias address their audience here in Hebrew, and the Israelis go ga-ga. Hebrew is today the language of all the Israelis (including, in large measure, the Arabs who had been living in Israel since its inception); Hebrew—and not Arabic, the tongue of the inhabitants of the locality to which the Zionists came, not French, the language of the educated circles in the Middle East, not English, the tongue of the regime of Mandate days, not Yiddish, the mother tongue of most of the early immigrants, not even German, which had been used as the language of instruction in several educational institutions in the Land of Israel (and was originally slated to be such at the Technion in Haifa). This may have contributed to the feeling of detachment from the rest of the world, but it has served Israel as a prime cohesive force. Had the same Jews chosen English or German for the national tongue, the image of the nation today would be far different.

There is an ingredient of symbolism in the fact that although the Ashkenazis were the ones to develop Hebrew as a daily language, the pronunciation comes from the Sepharadi. It was apparently a happenstance which occurred to Eliezer Ben-Yehuda when he was in Algeria for treatment of tuberculosis and chanced to hear the Sepharadic Jews there at prayer. For some reason he decided that the sound was more germane to the tongue of the Hebrew ancients (though no tapes or recordings from the days of the Hebrew monarchy are extant to verify it). Still, there must be some significance to the incidence—as there is in every event that led to the establishment of Israel, from the chance presence of Theodor Herzl at the Dreyfus trial to the either-way vote of the United Nations in November of 1947. Those who have it in them classify this incidence as Divine Providence, while others exclaim: "What luck!"

People of the (Practical) Book

PEOPLE WHO read go through life with pangs of conscience: they should have been reading Hebrew novels, poetry in the original, the new translation of Plato; they should have gone back to the classics, delved into the Book of Legends, kept up with world literature in general, attempted to decide, for themselves, what it was that Marx had *really* said, reviewed daily a chapter of the Bible, taken more interest in Freud's writings, looked into what the young people were reading—in short, they should have been more careful about the methodology of their reading habits.

It would seem that man is basically a disoriented creature; nature alone forces some orderliness upon him. He must observe the axioms of morning and evening, childhood and adolescence, marriage and children (not always in that order), lunch at noon and slumber at night. Reading, on the other hand, is an activity within man's exclusive control, and nature is out of its element here. In this age of freedom, there are no laws against or limitations on reading, no restrictions and no disqualifications, no directives nor traditions to go by. Each man is free to do what he pleases and as he chooses—and that's where the trouble lies: what should we read first—what next—what, in general?

Herein, perhaps, is the secret of the success of "popular library" publishers—*Sifriya La'am* or *Dukhiphat,* for example—book clubs which save their readers the decision as to what they want to read. This also accounts for the popularity of the small lending library around the corner; the advice it furnishes is a dike against the flood. "Three new books have come in," confides the proprietress. "Here's a historical novel about Catherine the Great; you won't be able to put it down until the end."

Three new books, not a hundred, the Lord be praised. Israel

publishes some 120 books every month (England, some 1,500; America, over two thousand). Granted that many of these are in special fields and intended for special use, and that some are undisguised trash, we still come up with ten, twenty, thirty books very much worth reading and which you'd like to read, not to overlook the long list of excellent books which you failed to read when they first appeared, plus those published before you were born. And there's nothing as aggravating as those lists of a hundred or two hundred or a thousand books which every intelligent person should read. These lists confront one with the same dilemma (as my fertile fancy suggests) as having two dozen beauties in one bed. Quite overwhelmed, you retreat to the kitchen and read the newspaper.

You do read, of course. You filch the latest *Inspector Maigret* from Giora, purchase *Darling* for the train trip, borrow *Day of Fire* from a neighbor. You pass by a bookstore and see a one-volume edition of Parkinson's works. The Broides volume of poetry you receive as a gift. It's all very casual, incidental, as it comes along. You solemnly promise yourself that you will read them—when vacation time rolls around or when you take that sabbatical, when the children are grown, or when you go on Social Security. (Hell must have a special department for readers who wanted to make good on the promises to read that they had made while still on earth).

Really, why should authors exert any authority over us? Are we to suffer because they want to be creative or to give vent to the stirrings of the soul, or to change the complexion of the world—assuming they did have something to say? Our forefathers displayed great sagacity when they concerned themselves, over the period of an entire lifetime, with no more than a dozen tomes, which supplied them with thought and content to last them for years and years; nor were they interested in innovations or in having the world in the palm of their hand. Reading, after all, is like taking a stroll. One man can walk to nearby Tel-Baruch and see an entire world: the death of a cat, a child crying by himself, the lonely figure of an old man crossing the highway, a housewife beaming over the white of her laundry. Another man may circle the globe and see nothing but himself.

It is not by accident that, in America, nearly every book with a

Jewish setting hits the bestseller lists. We Jews still retain something of the spark in the legacy of a faith inextricably bound up with the Book. We still bear some respect toward it as evidence of the Covenant and as the repository of life's values, and this respect extends to the Book as a physical entity, as well. Some among us still remember that a book that fell to the ground was to be picked up and kissed (like bread which had fallen); a book must not be brought to the dinner table, nor used to shield one's head from the sun, nor handled when one is not dressed, nor burned (even when the leaves no longer hold together) but stored away—a tradition to which we owe the survival of the famed Cairo *Genizah,* which yielded so much material for historical research. We do longer have inhibitions—only allergies. Some of us cannot bear seeing a book lying upside down, or a book in torn condition. Some cannot bring themselves to read second-hand books; others cannot tolerate lurid jackets, and still others can't toss a book into the trash can, even a softcover edition of *Unbridled Passions.* Each to his own rules.

As long as books were hand-written they were quite expensive and commanded respect by virtue of that reason alone, even when they were not on religious subjects and even after the invention and development of printing. As recently as some seventy or eighty years ago, when the demarcations between the lowly and the wealthy were more clear-cut, books were owned by the wealthy, the scholars, the people of culture. In this respect, Jews anteceded western peoples by hundreds of years; the bookcases in the *bet hamidrash* (the "house of study" attached to the synagogue) were accessible to the poorest Jew in town, and he could sit and read there, in light and warmth and good company, at no cost; all this at a time when in the Christian world the concept of public libraries was unknown, and even reading the Bible was forbidden to the lower classes unless an authorized overseer was present, lest it incite the readers to intellectual ferment.

It is only in the current century, in the Age of Technology, that the book has come within the reach of us all—and thereby lost its exclusivity. It seems so long ago, but it was no more than just prior to World War II that people were clipping chapters of serialized novels from the newspapers, stringing them in sequence, and passing them from hand to hand, one aunt to another, one neighbor to the next. They bought novels in installments, a pamphlet at a time, the way people buy the *Tarbut* Encyclopedia today in chain stores and supermarkets. In the end the people paid more, for the poor printing on inferior paper, than they would have paid for an elegant volume with cloth cover. The first such example in Jewish life relates to the printing of the Talmud (Constantinople, 1583), by Joseph Javitz who promised his readers that "we shall issue a pamphlet of this Talmud every week and distribute it to the public, thereby making it possible for everyone to acquire it, paying a little at a time".

In our subconscious, we still tend to associate books with learning and knowledge. The written word is still more highly regarded than the spoken one, and the book is more authentic than we are. The very thought that, some day, the written word will yield its importance to the movies, TV, records, microfilms and technological achievements yet to come robs us of the desire to be around when that sad day dawns.

But the signs are clear enough. It is imperative that we revise our approach to the book, now that it has become an item on the weekly shopping list, like a can of apricots or chocolate-chip cookies, available at the drugstore or the supermarket, and when any idiot can publish a book (and some such do) and when the same advertising formula is used for deodorants as for Truman Capote. There are no longer any hard and fast rules for books, and the literary profession as such guarantees nothing. In appearance and format there is no difference between (cheap) journalism and (serious) literature. The pocket-size book, which once intimated an account of stormy sex or the adventures of men of steel, can nowadays contain the introduction to Jung's philosophy or the history of means of payment. The jacket can show a couple locked in deathless embrace and can also camouflage Hemingway's *A Farewell to Arms* (even the Israeli Army has resorted to this lowly technique for its *Tarmil* publications). Politicians have become authors, and writers go in for politics. In short, when you choose a book these days, you must depend on common sense or a literary critic, and only the Lord knows which of the two is the less reliable.

It is believed that only the person who lacks something in life needs to read "a book" (this book being something other than a textbook, phone book, cookbook, dictionary or encyclopedia). The robust male whose profession calls for physical fitness (James Bond, etc.) limits his reading to confidential reports from Smersh. The current exponent of *La Belle Otero* has no need for books, except as something on which to rest her glowing eyes, as she reclines on her couch of yielding foam rubber, in her see-through morning gown, and awaits the arrival of her lover. A book for reading substitutes a reality other than the one that surrounds us. The individual who drains the cup of life to the last drop, who fights, loves, eats, drinks, rides, swims, dances and issues orders, has no need to immerse himself in the lives of others. Perhaps. But where does one see such supermen around? In our neighborhood everyone has some gaps in life, and these must be plugged up with reading.

Former contentions no longer hold true. We used to say that people seek escape, in a book, to something which they don't possess in real life. Housemaids used to read in their beds in the kitchen (made up with colored sheets, white linen being then the symbol of the middle class) about unfortunate orphan girls who became members of the nobility by "virtue" of their fathers. The staid well-to-do reclined properly in their upholstered chairs and swallowed tales about Jack the Ripper and Molly Pitchum; busy housewives plunged into the adventures of Amber, and lecturers in botany showed preference for Agatha Christie. Today, however, the sadists read Sade, *kibbutzniks* turn to *Hedva and I,* advertising men peruse Vance Packard, and the wealthy read *The House of Rothschild,* or they read nothing at all.

All this holds true in varying degrees in different places. In comparison with most countries, including those with high cultural standards, such as England and France, where a book appears initially in an edition of 3,000 copies, we still do read a great deal, but only a little more, compared with what the book once used to mean to our people. Today, with Israel's Jewish population at 2,400,000, a Hebrew book is published in 2,000 copies, poetry in 1,000—no more than was published thirty years ago, when the population was one-fifth of its present size. On the other hand, there are books in Hebrew, chiefly documentaries and particularly those dealing with the Six Day War, which have sold 20,000, 30,000 or even 50,000 copies (hard cover; minimum pocket-size editions are 20,000 copies). Today we have Hebrew poets—Natan Alterman, Avraham Shlonsky, Uri Zvi Greenberg, Leah Goldberg—whose works can attract 15,000 buyers. Comparing these figures with their counterparts abroad, our Jewish hearts glow with pride; this is tantamount to a contemporary English poet selling a quarter of a million copies of his works in his native land.

For whom are books a "must"? For children, naturally, since they are learning how to read; they study physics, geography and things of importance in life. Books come in handy in keeping them quiet on Sabbath mornings and in the early evenings. Vacationers must read something since one cannot spend the whole day at the pool nor just sit around and wait for the clock to move from afternoon nap to dinner. The bedridden must have books, if their condition is not too grave, in order to pass the tedious time away. There are people who cannot fall asleep unless their eyes travel over a few lines of print. Books are more salutary than sleeping pills and no less effective; (newspapers are liable to soil the bed linen and create quite a nuisance, with their rustling).

We should very much like to comfort the publishers, the authors and the educators who are debilitated by the ceaseless decline in popularity of the Hebrew book. In another generation or two, we should like to be able to tell, illiteracy will disappear, everyone will be reading Hebrew, and the Golden Age will come around again. However, the difficulties do not stem from the development towns or the immigrant settlements. Like the British aristocracy and its disinclination to read, the fact is that we have an ever-increasing, higher stratum of people who simply do not read, that is, not for the pleasure of it and particularly not in Hebrew. All the lawyers, architects, corporation executives, politicians, scientists, businessmen are immersed in their work and barely manage to read their professional journals (plus *Time* Magazine, to be up on things) and an occasional book which everyone is talking about, *Sinai Diary* or *In Cold Blood*. Yet there's nothing wrong with reading professional publications—except that the soul tends to shrivel up a bit. On the other hand, inasmuch as the soul is not visible to the naked eye nor is it something which hangs in an ornate frame in the living room, the damage isn't too serious.

Interior decorators have finally been able, therefore, to do away with the hallowed tradition of bookcases and bookshelves in assembled cases in the living room, that is, the salon. We can now dispense with the anecdote about the society *grande dame* who ordered six yards of beige-and-black books. If one has a study, that's where the books are; if he does not, so much less the trouble. Books, like an astringent or salve for scaly skin, are a person's private affair; there's no need to show them off. Except for a negligible cult, they have no status.

This is as it should be, really. Your library is a dead giveaway; it exposes your personality for all to analyze. An expert in such matters can "libranalyze" you in two minutes: Bialik's *Collected Works*—a Bar Mitzvah gift (today, the God of our Fathers be praised, people give checks or underwater diving gear); the few books of poetry are the ashes of young dreams; the books about the Haganah are in memory of glorious days of yore; the Album, Hebrew-English and English-Hebrew dictionaries, *Dr. Zhivago—wonder where he keeps Frank Harris and the Kinsey report? In that back row, perhaps?* A bookcase is like a personal confession.

An economic consideration holds that a book for reading isn't worth buying, because one doesn't read this type of book more than once (indeed, the number of the books that are read twice is very small, and the number of people who have the time for it is even smaller). This means that buying such a book is a one-shot yield, at best. According to this line of thought, of course, buying a ticket for a concert or the movies is a criminal waste, since you see the performance once and no more. Now take pencil in hand and—here's something, as advertised in the catalogue:

SHAMIR, MOSHE, *The Border*. A new novel by the author; time—the present; place—the Jordan-Israel border in Jerusalem. A multi-faceted adventure story. 304 pp. Cloth cover. IL 7.50.

That's two and one-half agorot (0.7c.) per page. Reading speed is an important factor; let's say, twenty pages per hour. What a bargain: half a Pound per hour! That's much less than an amusement park or "Holiday on Ice"—and no transportation costs or baby-sitter charges.

The People of the Book has become the People of the Practical Book. No more one-yield items but recurring dividends: a dictionary, an encyclopedia, a lexicon, an atlas—reference books required, now and then, for solving crossword puzzles, answering a child, phrasing an official letter. The advantage of an encyclopedia is that no one really expects you to know what's in it. The decorative book is also still in demand. An art or photo album, Modigliani or Toulouse-Lautrec, tossed careless-like on the low coffee table, also looks very good. Even though the recurrent dividend does not militate here, the art album is good for smoothing out currency, drying flowers, or engaging the attention of the young man whom the daughter brings home for the first time. Baby-sitters like them, too.

Whoever takes the trouble to build up a library, or has his heart set on books, is, like any collector bitten by the bug, incapable of appraising books rationally. He is not deterred even by the thought that, some day, he will have to leave everything behind: books, and paintings, sculptures and stamps. He may try to coat the bitter pill with thoughts of bequeathing these treasures to a museum or to some institution, or to heirs who might enjoy them, when the time comes. But the fact is that the collection is enjoyed by the collector only, and he builds it up as though it should last for generations—row upon row of books, stacked according to height and/or subject matter, in flamboyant jackets or conservative covers. It's the same temporal gratification that one gets from a neat row of mud pies or rows of ripe strawberries or drawers full of ironed and folded shirts.

It's an awful emptiness that descends on the person who has nothing to read—the helplessness, the terrible longing for a printed word, regardless of what it may be: the Mailmen's Annual or a brochure about insecticides or a two-year-old newspaper or a story about Little Dolly Yemima, *anything* on which the eye may rest, to make sure that the world did not begin that morning and won't end that night, and that there's life and a future beyond the wall. Anyone who has ever felt this emptiness will gather books as a squirrel gathers nuts. The hard winter may not even transpire, and even if it does, the squirrel may not remember where he has sequestered the nuts, but there is great comfort merely in looking at the glistening pile.

In days past, when books were very expensive, every Jew was morally obligated to let scholars use his books, and it was considered a major *mitzvah* to buy a book with the intention aforethought of lending it to people who could make use of it. One has to feel an abiding love for the Lord or faith in his fellow man to be able to suppress his own love for the book and entrust it to alien hands, with no assurance whatsoever that it will be returned to him in the same good condition. As far as the collector is concerned, humanity is divided into those who return books and those who do not, the latter being in the majority.

The Eskimo custom of lending one's wife to an honored friend need not be surprising. Any way you look at it, this custom is more logical than lending a book. The wife will return, if she is so inclined, under her own power, but the book, even if it were to yearn inconsolably for its owner, and even if the space it had vacated on the shelf glared like an open wound, cannot come back by itself. This is the horrible dilemma which haunts every owner of books: how to display them, how to show them off a bit, without being asked to lend one. In this area it takes years to learn how to say "no".

Our bookstores: We have been taking them for granted, like the soda dispensers and the gasoline vendors, and then the tourists drew our attention to them, marveling at their number, all along the streets of Israel's cities. Even considering the growth of Israel's population, the number of shops and stalls along Tel Aviv's Allenby Road and its tributaries is amazing. Here we shall make a count: between Steimatzky's and Ma'ayan, and taking in Nachlat Binyamin Street, there are twelve bookstores in less than a one-mile span. But this phenomenon is a relic from the past; the book trade is no longer a lucrative investment. It no longer enjoys the prestige of days gone by, and there's no money in it, to compensate for the lack of honor; it's almost like teaching.

Perhaps we shall follow the English example, where a single bookshop, neat and fashionable, takes care of the needs of an entire neighborhood. Perhaps, as in so many other things, we shall strive for the American level, where the ratio of material published in periodicals to books is 200 : 1. Perhaps the authors will go back to the method of selling books from door to door, as custom once dictated in the diaspora. Perhaps, in the sphere of the book we shall not be like other peoples; after all, there must be something unique about the Jewish book, if all Jew-haters began their careers by burning it.

By No Other Name

THE AUTOMATIC distinction between names in general and Jewish names is so deep-seated in our consciousness that we tend to overlook its similarity to the basis of anti-Semitism. Whenever names of actors are flashed on the screen, or a news item comes through about offenders against the economy of the Soviet Union up for trial, or whenever we run down a list of names: the new members of Britain's Parliament or Nobel Prize winners, the first impulse is to look for the Jewish names among them, camouflaged though they may be with thick layers of assimilation. In the course of the years we develop a special flair for spotting Jewish identity, whether it is a look in the eye or the sound of a name.

From the day that Jews began to dwell among the nations, which is to say the larger portion of their history, in Aram, Babylon, Greece, Rome, Arabia, Spain, Germany, Russia, America, some of them, particularly among the erudite and the highly-placed, were inclined to adapt their name, or one of their names (at least phonetically) to the nomenclature of the lands of their sojourn, deriving them from the people or the rulers: Esther (Astar), Hyrcanus (son of Joseph), Alexander (Yannai), Bahya Ibn-Pakuda, Meyerbeer, Heine.

For many years a change of name required no special rigmarole, since in the good old days bureaucracy was still in its infancy. No one was obliged to hold on to a fixed family name, and every individual adopted a patronymic or a supplementary name as he desired and saw fit, in line with his language and locality. Reuben Henriquez came to Germany from Portugal, in the fifteenth century, and settled in the town of Glückstadt. His son's name became Michael Portuguese; his grandson bore the name Reuben

Glückstadt; the great-grandson was Michael Reuben Heinrichs, and his descendants retained the name Heinriksen.

The custom of answering to definite family names came only in the eighteenth century. The family name often related to the occupation of the paterfamilias, or to its origin, parent's name and family tree, or the emblem or coat-of-arms on the door (Rothschild). In the days of the Austrian monarchy, including most of Poland, the Jews were obliged (in 1787) to have civil names—by order of Kaiser Joseph II. This move came from primarily economic and military considerations, designed to facilitate taxation and conscription procedures. The rest of Europe took its cue from the Kaiser. Jews in various German states welcomed their permanent civil names with enthusiasm, as a harbinger of emancipation, but in Galicia and elsewhere in the Austrian monarchy, the Jews greeted the measure with suspicion, irresponsiveness and even resistance. Quite a few names were selected by the royal officials, determined at times by the size of the bribe that preceded the act. If one is to judge by the hordes of descendants named Bigeleisen, Ochs, Kuh, Butterfass and Rotschwanz, there must have been quite a number of impoverished Jews at that particular juncture of history.

Along with the obligation to register one's civil name which accompanied the release of the Jews from the ghetto, there emerged the inclination toward making the change a thorough and decisive one, as a means of changing identity altogether. Rosenfeld evolved into Roda-Roda, Samy Rosenstock became Tristan Tzara, Pincus became Pascin and Saltzman turned into Slansky, Bronstein became known as Trotsky and Sobelman became Radek. A counter-reaction then set in, which forbade changing a name without the permission of the authorities (this holds true in Israel as well). Thanks to this regulation, every change of name became public property, known to all via the Israel Government publications.

Within one six-month span, the Government registry showed some ten thousand petitions for choice or change of names. In proportion to the total population of some two and one-half million souls, this, I am sure, comprises the highest percentage in the world, even if we assume that, in some of the instances, the petition referred to the first name only, usually from foreign to

Hebrew: Firosa became Ayala, Salim converted to Samuel, Gotke to Gedalia, and Benvenida to Zippora.

Diplomatic representatives of the Ministry of Foreign Affairs have to Hebraize their names before assuming their posts abroad; for others, the decision to do so is regarded as a purely and strictly personal matter. A change of name is not merely a matter of reshuffling several letters. It incorporates a person's attempt, or desire, to change his entire personality, his way of life, his image in the eyes of others, his children's future. It represents a determination to break with the past, with origins, with the diaspora.

To me it seems that the desire to retain the family name, even if it has a decidedly foreign sound—Weizmann or Toledano, Lishansky or Alterman—is generally to be found among Israelis of religious inclinations, to whom the prestige of the name back in the diaspora is still a factor of consequence. The name—Hager, Teitelbaum, Hildesheimer, Karlebach—means more to them than any Hebrew name possibly can. The same holds true for people with strong emotional ties to their family's past, or for those who made a name for themselves abroad, or for those who consider the ties with diaspora Jewry to be no less important than the revival of the Hebrew personality on his Hebrew soil.

Generally, a person's desire to shed his old family name is at its peak in the first years of his *aliya,* when, as a newcomer, he imagines himself as an emerging new personality in his homeland. But if he has no such equations and only feels himself growing more tired, more nervous, less restrained and more impudent— in brief, if he feels that he has weathered the first shock of *aliya* and has not changed his name in the process, he is likely to hold on to his old name. Any subsequent impulse toward change will probably come for or from his children, born in Israel, who will have no truck with such hybrid names as Doron Zilberzweig or Tal Kapulsky.

Integration with the Israeli nomenclature begins at the personal name level. Names recognized as expressly Jewish—Abraham, Sarah, Isaac, and the rest of the Patriarchs and Matriarchs—are not in vogue at the moment. We are currently deep in the botanical period and in the category of unusual biblical names whose origin is a mystery known to Bible scholars only. The originality of these names tends to fade as they become more and more widespread.

A name change usually expresses the desire to forget the diaspora, to sever all connection with this past and to erase its footprints, to bolster the dream, the ambition, to echo the names of the models, the heroes; in Israel, these are the native-born, or the old-timers of Ashkenazi stock. This change brings on the others: clothes styles, furniture, taste. Ami Yisraeli bears no resemblance to Abdallah Ramzi; David Ben-Zvi has little in common with Zorel Hershko, Dina Zamir is a far cry from Diamantoni Koroptva, and Nurit Shimoni is worlds away from Taria Sa'id.

The common tendency is to pick out a name which is not too compromising, not especially outstanding, not scintillating, not too long and not chauvinistic. As in the modern song, emphasis is not on content or the meaning of the lyrics but on the tune. The consideration is not what the name implies but how it would sound, abroad as well as in Israel. The choice is therefore in the direction of names with an unmistakably Israeli sound but which would not scare away a Gentile. The name as such means nothing to its owner or to anyone who has close contact with him, but no liaison officer of any foreign ministry should have any difficulty with the spelling. But this category is not limited to Israeli diplomats; it is equally popular with journalists, lawyers, economists, promising young men with ambitions of climbing ladders. The identifying mark of this category is the letter "n" at the end of the name (four consonants is the limit): Naton, Ribon, Doron, Rimon, Givon, etc.

The Ineffable Name has also gone out of style. No longer do we witness its popularity among the first immigrations, when its evidence ("El") was most widespread, as the long lists in the telephone directory indicate: Elyashiv, Elyakim, Eliraz, Elizur, Eliram, Elyashar. The few who still take Him into account when they change their names are the Orientals.

Cohen, from the Jewish viewpoint the designation of nobility (our *von* and *de la*), yielded in the early days of Emancipation to such sound affiliates as Collins, Cowan, Colmers and Conrad. To the credit of the Israelis it should be said that very few Cohens change their name, although in Israel the change may have more reason behind it; the Cohen who bequeaths the name to his progeny may also leave a legacy of trouble, should any of his children wish to wed a divorcee (a Cohen, a "priest," is prohibited from doing so by the Bible). Also, looking for Cohen in an Israeli telephone directory is like wading through the pages of Smiths and Joneses in London or New York. On the other hand, there is a definite tendency to be rid of the widespread name of *Mizrahi* ("easterner"), which points to the origin of its bearer; the motivation here is no doubt akin to the impulse which produced, in the diaspora, such Jewish names as Montague or Reinhardt.

There is also a penchant for short names, preferably monosyllabic and at times consisting of no more than two letters (albeit, in Hebrew, two letters will spell "Leigh" or "Schey"). Perhaps it's the age we live in, where time is money and money is everything. If you reckon the amount of time saved by a corporation treasurer who signs checks with "Paz" instead of "Zlatopolsky," you will readily acknowledge the wisdom of the change. Rosenkopf, Resnick and Reiser become Roz; Teuerthal, Landrat, Taranto decide to be Tal; Goodman and Weinstein choose Gat, Likover and Barabi go forth as Bar. Haim Zimenkopf and Rudolf Potz went for Paz (how Rudolf managed to exist in Israel with that four-letter word is a mystery). To this category of formerly extended names belong Dan, Gal, Mor, Rom, Kol, Tzur, Ziv, Niv, Nir.

In various parts of Europe there were certain periods when Jews were forbidden to adopt Christian names or those of the nobility (a German Jew who, in 1814, attempted to adorn himself with the name of a famous military figure, Von Tatenborn, was forced by the authorities to settle for the more modest Pollack). In Israel there is no such restriction; any citizen who is so moved may call himself Eshkol or Rabin, Garadian becomes Sharett and Shirazi is no less than Shazar, Gamliel picked out Dayan and Saposhnik chose Sapir.

Custom, non-Jewish as well as Jewish, often attaches the name of the father to that of the son. This evolution of the patronymic became, over the years, a major source of Jewish family names. The name of the father, with the prefix "ben" or "ibn" or the suffix "son," "kin," "witz," "scu" or "les" gave birth to dynasties of Abramson and Yacobowitz, Dworkin and Hankin, Abeles and Pereles and Davidescu and hordes of other variations. This used to be the accepted method for Hebraizing a name and an admirable way of immortalizing the memory of a parent. Recent indications are that the number of Israelis who hold their fathers in such esteem has been dropping. Here and there we still come upon Ben-Hanan or Ben-Yitzhak, Bar-Yaakov or Ben-Abu, but the paternal stock is falling.

Jewish names are also signposts along the trail of Jewish peregrination. It is estimated that half the names adopted in Germany and Poland were derived from geographical localities of origin: Pollack and Breslauer, Alfez and Posner, Shapiro (from the German city of Spier) and Dreyfus (from neighboring Trier, once Tribas), Krakauer and Dubnow, Kalisher and Lifschitz. Nomenclature experts can therefore identify family origin even if the descendants had, in the interim, wandered on by half a globe. Clearly, no new Hebrew name could possibly have anything to do with such origins. One cannot Hebraize a name and still have it refer to extra-territorial localities.

The mode of verbatim translation gave Israel its long lists of Kochavi ("Stern"–Star), Duvdevani ("Kirschenbaum"–cherry tree), Caspi ("Zilberman"–silver), Zahavi ("Goldman"–gold), Shchori ("Schwartz"–black); these, too, are far from being snapped up. The "I" ending, which suggests an affinity with Israel's Mediterranean neighbor, Italy, is also vanishing. In a few fortunate cases and by pure chance, the original name has a synonymity of sound with a Hebrew word, albeit the meaning is different; by stressing the second syllable, "Rosen" becomes the Hebrew for "nobleman"—not an unattractive coincidence.

A popular mode of Hebraizing a name, advocated, among others, by the late Moshe Sharett, is to arrange the letters of the original name so as to obtain a similarly sounding Hebrew name. This method has endowed us with long lists of names of esthetic sound, properly and syllabically arranged, but usually without any meaning in reference to the bearer. There is nothing wrong in this, if we assume that a name is of importance only to the generation which selects it. Orlovsky, in line with the mode, became Uryan, Sheinhorn became Shenhar, Kleinman—Kenan, Neurath —Nur, and so on, like a crossword puzzle.

Jacob's blessing unto his children brought, from the animal kingdom into the Jewish fold, such names (both in Hebrew and Yiddish) as Zvi/Hirsch ("Naftali is like a *doe* sent forth"), Arye/ Leib/Leon ("Judah is like a *lion* cub"), Ze'ev/Wolf/Lupu ("Benja-

181

min like a *wolf* shall rend his prey"). In due course these personal names developed into patronymics: Lupovici and Wolfson, Herzl and Hershkowitz, Lionel and Leibush. The animals kept on going: Karp and Fishel referred to Ephraim, Taub and Golomb related to the dove. In Israel, the animals no longer hold sway; the deer emblem of the Israel postal services appears to be hobbling, and the lion in the zoo has grown fat and weary. We are out of the Zoological Age and into the Botanical, out of the fauna and in the flora; flowers are for girls (Iris, Sigalit, Vered, Nurit) and trees, as one may expect, are for families (*Dekkel*—palm, *Shaked*—almond, *Geffen*—vine).

Initials once served as a popular source for purely Jewish names, though with non-Hebrew sounds: Katz (*Cohen Tzedek*—a righteous priest), Zack (*Zera Kdoshim*—seed of the righteous), Segal and Chagall (*Segen Levaya*—adjutant), Schein (*Shaliach Ne'eman*—trustworthy emissary). President Shazar (*Shneour Zalman Rubashov*) is one of the few who turned to this source, which typifies his role in the State of Israel and emphasizes his deep roots in the diaspora.

Fruit from the Tree of Knowledge

TODAY, THE injunction against partaking from the Tree of Knowledge is known as censorship, or news blackout, but the principle has not changed since the Garden of Eden gambit: somebody, up there, knows what should be known to us, better than we know it ourselves. As long as the Almighty himself was the Chief Censor there was little sense in picking an argument with him, especially in view of the fact that he can be hard of hearing, far out in firmament space. But now that mortals have deigned to take over his domain, we are within our rights to question their actions.

All our days we live under the supervision of trustees who concern themselves with our spiritual chastity. One supervisor of purity departs, and another succeeds him; they come and go. Doting parents and municipal librarians decide what the child should read, what books are proper for him and which should be deferred to the category of you'll-understand-when-you-grow-up; they decide at which age little brothers cease being purchased from the hospital and become the seed growing under mother's heart. True, the fearful role of the teacher as the custodian of morality and proper behavior, outside the classroom as well, is gradually fading, thanks to the happy fact that teachers have come to count their working hours most punctiliously and are not prepared to contribute energy without additional remuneration. Parents, too, are nowadays inclined to yield much sooner than the parents of yesteryear, whether it's because *aliya* and what is permitted and what is forbidden in the Jewish State have affected their self-assurance, or because they are genuinely trying to be modern and progressive parents. As a result, the authorities descend upon us with claw and fang, disguised as the protective wings of father and mother, teacher and counselor.

Since ancient times it has been known to the medicine man, the priest, the land baron and the tyrant: knowledge breeds trouble—disobedience, disputed authority, challenged supremacy—and they have therefore preferred to have their flock remain innocent sheep. Democracy, of course, tends to complicate matters. In the enthused moment of its establishment, Israel may have proclaimed a democratic form of government, but later came the acid fruit: there's a Knesset, there's something of an Opposition, here and there the State Comptroller lurks, the budget is an open book, and the press insists on sticking its type slugs into everything. What can an absolute monarch possibly know about these complexities of life? His country's diplomatic emissaries are his personal representatives, responsible to him alone. His people may rejoice when and as diplomatic relations with a brother-potentate are successfully climaxed with the betrothal of the progeny of the two royal houses, or they may be summoned to arms when and as the negotiations collapse. Actually, no more than this is necessary. The people always rub the diplomats the wrong way, which dooms to failure any meeting of the minds between diplomats and the managers of public news media, if both camps are to remain loyal to their constituencies. In Israel, where affairs of state often coincide with security interests, the newspapers have a much more difficult time of it than they would in countries which restrict their tiffs to tariffs on apples and herring fishing rights. Inasmuch as in Israel today censorship of matters pertaining to the security of the state is inviolate (although these matters are not always dealt with rationally), there are some representatives of the people who try, here and there, to fashion magic carpets for themselves out of security's coattails. At some point, everything has to do with security: *aliya* and absorption and aid to developing countries and unemployment and recession and cutbacks and officials' residences. Silence is golden, and speech is tarnished.

The tendency to keep the public in the dark is mostly on the part of those who have advanced in years while guarding the information pipeline and have been drinking directly from the faucet. There is a committee of newspaper editors which receives information from Government sources on matters of prime importance (not always having to do with security), classified as being "off the record." Psychologically, this arrangement (invented by some clever devil) of divulging state secrets imbues the editor with a sense of equality with the captains of the ship of state, in return for which he is only too glad to withhold information from his readers.

There are many in positions of authority, national and local, who are still convinced that everything would be fine if only the press would stop interfering constantly. The question is not why is the pot so black but rather who put it on the window sill. It cannot be said that Israeli newspapermen always act as stalwart champions of justice, but if they have an ounce of true ambition and a touch of professional curiosity, they will invariably prefer uncovering new things rather than act as messenger boys, shuttling between the Government Printer and their own printing plant.

The "free newspaper" is a myth. A newspaper belongs to someone, and this someone—a political organization, as is the case with most of the newspapers in Israel, or a cooperative or an individual—has interests, more or less allegedly lofty. Unless his duties are limited to research on and publication of vegetable prices in the wholesale market, the newspaperman has his own opinions, foibles and prejudices, and these are reflected in what he writes, on what he elaborates and what he holds back. The copy editor who "checks" the information slants it *his* way. Long before the higher up censorship begins to function, there comes the self-imposed censorship: considerations of holding down the job, a career, working conditions, the strength of the opposition. Withal, Israel does have a free *press,* in that all the newspapers, political colorations and all, and despite their faults and shortcomings, provide in their aggregate a more or less accurate picture of the times in which we live.

Control of Israel's newspapers is difficult because the country has a superabundance of them (a dozen dailies in Hebrew and other dailies in ten languages). If the regime is as democractic as it regards itself to be, a Minister or his secretary cannot discharge his duty by picking up the phone and calling one editor; they have to talk to a dozen and inform, order, threaten, plead with or cajole, as necessity may dictate. Contact with the radio is much less complicated; only one line is called for. On paper, it is true, the broadcasting service is responsible to a public body and not to any Government ministry, and is, theoretically, above and beyond any partiality or partisanship, but it obviously serves, first and foremost, either the Government as a whole or its own policy-making bodies. As the experience of the British Broadcasting Company (the model for our own Kol Yisrael) has shown, much of the character of a radio service depends upon who is at its head. Hugh Green turned this mouthpiece of the Establishment, the old and pious Auntie BBC, ever neutral-smug-vacuous, into a broadcasting and TV service distinguished for its initiative and courage, equal to deprecating a Prime Minister and even taking a crack at the royal family. In line with the ancient Soviet joke, I'd like to ask: "*Nu,* so what? We can also criticize the British Prime Minister and wink at Prince Philip's expense," but then, the matter is not so simple. The Foreign Ministry has certain stipulations: re developing countries in Africa—*nihil nisi bonum;* re France—caution and watch the traffic signs; re Germany—please bear in mind that the situation is delicate; South Africa—truly a problem, when sentiments are torn between what is good for the Jews there and what is good for humanity. About China, so far, one may write whatever comes to mind.

TV telecasts and radio may be weighed in apothecary scales; the press may still report events in the political and security sectors in roundabout fashion, by quoting foreign newspapers, but when it comes to censorship of morals, the permissible latitude is far greater than what the old-timers could have imagined, even in their wildest Freudian dreams. Sex by the barrel, striptease by the bulk, "Kama Sutra" in Yiddish, "Fanny Hill" in Rumanian, "Who's Afraid of Virginia Woolf?" in popular Hebrew on the stage of the National Theatre. Let the young ones amuse themselves, and they will let their elders manage the affairs of state.

Morals censorship—of sex information, crime and brutality in pictures and print—usually adapts itself to the social climate in which it functions, proceeding somewhat belatedly behind the pace of progressiveness of its conservative elements. Twelve years ago the censor blue-penciled from the Danish art film, "Dita, Daughter of Adam," a scene depicting a naked female, photographed from a safe telescopic distance. Today we may see striptease on the screen fleshed from all over the world (essentially the basic items shown are always the same) and intercourse in all stages of sensuality—provided that one member of the Film and Plays Review Council or another, assigned to scrutinize this or that film, didn't get up that morning on his conservative side.

If there is any basis to the charge that film censorship is necessary for the prevention of perversion, then the members of the FPRC should be today, after several thousand reels of sex and crime, in a terrible state of moral turpitude. However, the last time I met the Council chairman he looked perfectly well-adjusted and morally impeccable. Obviously censors are hewn from different stuff than most of us.

I can still recall the good old days when the censor, in a move to win friends and influence people, would screen piquant film sequences which had been ruled out by his committee. Not since the days of austerity, when Zim ships used to distribute apples and cigarettes from foreign ports, was there such an outpouring of newsmen, educators, writers and public figures, plus their respective wives. The basis of morals censorship is that it's always intended for the other fellow, the weaker one, the vacillating one, the impressionable one. Its solemn duty is to protect the individual who, for some reason, is to be held incapable of taking care of himself, especially virtuous maidens and women of delicate soul. Yet if we assume that for any birth two are needed (in most cases, anyway), it is irrational that the facts of life should be less known to women than they are to men. Nevertheless, every argument about the subject always ends up with the infallible clincher: "But how would you like your daughter to . . . (go ahead, fill in the rest) . . . be photographed nude in a film?" (this facet of bare truth is already visible in Israel, or ". . . write a book about Lesbian love?" (it has already been done, in the *lingua sacra*), or ". . . reveal her sexual experiences to a pornographic magazine?" (we have a doozie of a one here, plus unlimited imports).

Censorship of pornographic literature functions here with admirable discretion. We have no display trials and there are no wholesale confiscations. "The Nude Lesbo" or "Garden of Desires" is not whisked off the shelves. Now in its second year, a committee of experts—psychologists, jurists, sociologists and others of cognate professions—is trying to determine just what constitutes indecent material, from the standpoint of local standards; Israeli law, dating back to the days of the British Mandate, is very unclear in this matter, and until the work of this committee is done and legislation deriving therefrom is enacted (years and years hence), Israeli newsstands will continue displaying nudes, the "Stalag" series, and other manifestations of permissible society. "Lady Chatterley's Lover" and "Tropic of Cancer" would have scored far more modest successes in Israel had their appearance not been blared forth with a fanfare of litigation and prohibition in England and the United States. Had the distribution of "Fanny Hill" been forbidden here, we would have gone about with the conviction that the Israeli reader had been deprived of a literary gem. Had the police declared war against Genet's works, their popularity in Israel would have zoomed to the seventh firmament. However, since they are sold uninhibitedly, and in the finest of bookshops to boot, they are held to be classics, to be perused by certified intellectuals only.

Pornography is a matter not so much of geography, as it is of time. Erotics evolve into classics. Rubens' plump females, who may in his day have been the stars of sensuality, will today excite none but the proprietor of a corset factory. Manet's "Breakfast on the Lawn," portraying men buttoned up to the neck in the company of nude females (it shook up Paris back in the 1890's), offers little that the Fourth Grade cannot view with equanimity.

The art of painting is currently above and beyond censorship. How else, when the difference between a phallic symbol and a telephone pole is revealed only unto psychiatrists? Abstract art has vindicated Henry Miller's contention of many years: pornography exists only in the mind of the viewer. Have you seen that disgusting work—that's right, the circle and the triangle? Nauseating!

In general, the blessings of abstract art are beyond compare. The Second Commandment clearly states, "Thou shalt not make unto thyself anything sculpted nor anything depicted," but at the time the Lord was unaware of the existence of Barbara Heppelworth or Caulder or Jackson Pollock. There was a time, in the early days of our community, when people refrained from placing statues in public spots throughout the land, except for a roaring lion or the seven-branched candelabrum. Today monuments abound everywhere and no one says boo, since the Bible has no comment to make on configurations of scrap iron displayed in public or on the exhibition of fashions in concrete. The Lord has a sense of indulgence, and the rabbinate is too busy with such issues as post-mortems—with real death, that is to say—rather than with abstract life.

Yet although the Lord has laid aside his blue pencil, his emissaries here on earth are guarding his interests like a battalion of Brink's. In matters pertaining to religion, censorship in Israel, official and arbitrary, supersedes even the most stringent Catholic countries. Italy's "The Bridal Canopy" and "Il Monsteri" have very glaring anti-clerical sequences, but can anyone conceive of an Israeli play, film or libretto which would present a rabbi in a ludicrous light, as a liar or a hypocrite? I dismiss the idea even as I am penning it.

But this particular phenomenon is not merely a reflection of the political coalition or of religious sensitivities. In every atheistic Jew there dwells the spirit of a father or a grandfather, of blessed memory, which would say to him: "*Nu, nu, nu!* They won't let you into heaven!" In the Beginning we were expelled from the Garden of Eden because we transgressed the local censorship laws; why should we unnecessarily run the risk of missing out at the End of Days as well?

Open House

The Fleshpots of Israel

THE LAST remaining strands which bind us to our faith are made of egg noodles. The Lord may have lost the battle to possess our sinful souls, but He has our stomachs in His sights: every *kneidl* is a cannon ball, every *kugel* is a projectile, every portion of *gefilte fish* is a blast. The Israeli freethinker is a split personality: the vocal cords are of the socialist, the intellectual and the atheist, but the taste buds are of the conservative and hidebound capitalist and the plain rotten bourgeois.

The religious parties may well be conducting their battles along the wrong lines. Instead of concerning themselves with postmortems (which haven't resurrected a single adherent for the religious camp) they should describe the horrible gastronomic void that would descend upon us if the Lord were to remove His presence from our kitchens: no jellied calves' feet and no meat-and-potato stew on the Sabbath (cholent); no fried *matza* and *kneidlach* on Passover; no *hamentashen* on Purim; no pancakes and jelly doughnuts on Chanukah, no *blintzes* and cheese cake on Shavuot. We would be left with the borrowed *hummous-tehina-schnitzel-chips* all year round.

Actually, all is not milk and honey in the realm of Jewish gastronomy. Kicking over the traces of Jewish tradition, the denial of the spiritual patrimony, the drive to imitate the alien—all these have left their mark. Only a few of what we call "Jewish dishes," that is, dishes prevalent among East European Jews, have taken hold in Israel, as though the sovereign nation, once it became ensconced on its own soil, rejected the food of the diaspora along with its other manifestations. But this is not the case, really. Only a few on the long list—*knishes,* gizzards, *lokshen, farfel,* plus the aforesaid—are suited to the Israeli climate and can make use of

193

local ingredients. And there are other factors: the disinclination on the part of the modern housewife to spend hours in the kitchen and to be guided by religious observance in dietary matters.

However, the stubborn love for life which is ingrained in the Jews is also evident in their foods as well, and every pot is a rampart. For instance, the gastronomic monstrosity called *cholent* has everything going against it: since the Sabbath is not universally observed, there is no need to prepare a dish capable of retaining its edibility after twenty hours of warming; the physicians keep condemning this morass of cholesterol; the dictators of fashion have set the styles to fit a matchstick and call it the ideal woman's figure; the gas oven is not intended for slow cooking; the Mediterranean heat prevalent during most of the year is certainly not conducive to the dish in question. And yet, despite everything, at the approach of Sabbath eve, people with pots in their hands begin queueing up at the few restaurants and meat markets smart enough to predicate their profits on the substantial setup of beans and stuffed derma.

There are still in our midst mothers, mothers-in-law, grandmothers and aunts who can prepare *cholent* at home, with their own hands, for which *cholent* lovers everywhere will be eternally grateful, but the generation of *cholent* women is rapidly vanishing. Perhaps here, too, the machine will take over, as with bread, noodles, jams and cookies once prepared by women at home. Huge industrial plants will produce *cholent* for the Sabbath (available in supermarket freezers), otherwise it will become, a generation hence, a piece of folklore, like the Queen of the Night and the Virgins of Israel. The way to a man's heart is no longer via his stomach, as it was in the days of pious Jewish women, and it also takes an inordinate depth of love, either for the husband or for the manifest destiny of the Jewish people, for a woman even to touch the serpentine pipeline of entrail and intestine, much less to clean and stuff it. The neck of a fowl may not upset the soul of the modern female as do the entrails, but the stuffed neck, as a dish, is not likely to stay around very long. Filling the neck of a chick can be quite frustrating; by the time you think one end is sewn up, all that remains at the other end is a hole. The *helzl* is at its best if it's of a fat duck or at least a hen which had enjoyed a full life, but the heroines in the yard die young.

No, our intestines do not have the fortitude of our progenitors, but several traditional dishes have nevertheless survived, in deserved tribute to the memory of our forefathers. If good old borscht did survive (though we call it *hamitza,* sour soup), it is not because the beet color is symbolic of the fighting socialism which has given us our leaders. Simply, beets are as cheap and plentiful here as they are in the Soviet Union, and borscht is easily prepared. In summer it makes a most refreshing drink; in winter, served hot with meat added, it is hearty but not heavy. Most important, it doesn't put you in a predicament: it's not like the souffle, where success hangs by a bubble. There is no other art form where the artist has greater license: the beet goes into the pot whole, in chunks, or grated, with or without cabbage (the latter can be quartered or shredded); the beet may be accompanied by lemon, vinegar or marinade, with or without potatoes, with mushrooms and/or tomatoes, carrots, marrow bones, beef, frankfurters, meatballs, sour cream, egg yolk—each woman according to her secret recipe. Borscht is like modern art; everything goes into it—except, perhaps, the kitchen sink.

Chicken soup has been on the menu from the very first day that a chicken, water and a pot fell into one and the same pair of hands. The Jewish version is known as "the golden soup," with egg noodles nestling on the bottom. To be in this category, the soup has to be fat, with large globules winking sagely like elusive amoeba; as such, it is the symbol of a well-to-do Jewish home. Today's chicken soup has less status and less fat and, especially, less chicken and more cubes, but perish any thought that would remove it from the Israeli menu, in restaurants, *kibbutzim,* army mess halls and the bosom of the family. Only once a year, on Yom Kippur eve, does the Israeli chicken soup revert to its former glory. The Germans evidently foresaw this eventuality. In the Middle Ages, the German *Jauche* meant "a liquid." As Yiddish *yoich,* chicken soup achieved its pinnacle of greatness, while in German it later came to mean sewage water. Now there's a bit of far-sighted anti-Semitism for you!

The future of *kreplach* (oversize ravioli) is now in the sink-or-swim stage. The issue is not the filling but the marketing. Shall we remain loyal to tradition and have *kreplach* boiled in the soup (on condition that they come packaged in plastic, ready to eat),

195

or shall we imitate the Gentiles and eat them as ravioli for the main dish? *Kreplach* (dough of eggs and flour, cut into squares and filled with meat, then folded over) were already known to the Greeks, who called them *catillos,* but before them, as may be imagined, came the Chinese and made wan ton for their soup when our ancestors were still dwelling in Mesopotamia. It is assumed that the Moors brought *kreplach* into Spain, whence they slithered all over Europe. Culinary savants have it that the Italian ravioli (with tomato sauce and grated Parmesan cheese) had its origins in the briny deep; chefs aboard Italian ships used leftovers from preceding meals to fill squares of dough, to which they fondly attached the name of *rabiola,* i.e., junk (we call food prepared in accord with this ingenious formula *kebab* or hamburger).

For some reason, the year 1960 witnessed an avalanche of ravioli in Israel. All the food processing plants seemed to have hit upon this brilliant idea simultaneously: canned ravioli in tomato sauce. For a while all Israel seemed to be watering at the mouth with the novelty, but as the advertising sages put it: you can fool people but not the digestive tract; soggy *kreplach* filled with matter defying investigation and lying limp in a pool of pink plasma is indeed a travesty on a time-honored and historic dish.

I've earnestly tried to get a clear answer to the pressing question as to whether there is a future for *gefilte* fish in Israel, with no success. Opinions are divided, and the fish themselves, being reticent about everything, were of no help. Why, really, do Jews insist on eating *gefilte* fish on the Sabbath? There is neither dictum nor decree for it. The Fourth Commandment ignores it altogether, and the dietary laws in the Bible make no specific reference to it. Of course, *there is* the verse: "And thou shalt call the Sabbath a joy"—and how can one enjoy the Sabbath without *gefilte* fish?

Let us expound further. Ever since Creation, fish has been a festival food of symbolic significance: fertility (one carp produces a million eggs), a remedy for the evil eye, sickness and weakness. The Catholics eat fish on fast days (a heavenly compromise) and on Friday, the day of Christ's death, which equates sorrow with abstention from eating meat, as Jews do during the "nine days" preceding the Fast of Tish'a B'Av. The supply of fish in the market was therefore at its peak toward the end of the week. The Christians bought fish for the sombre noon meal, while Jews bought it for the festive Sabbath Eve dinner. The well-to-do acquired the large variety, early in the day; the others waited for a more propitious hour, price-wise, and bought whatever was left. Since the latter category contained the small fry, odoriferously past its prime, the ingenious housewife would add onions, bread crumbs, eggs and pepper in order to camouflage the fact (this is strictly the Bondy interpretation of the origin; it does not necessarily preclude others).

With one fish to a sizable family (our progenitors managed quite well even without a Commission for Increased Birthrate), how many visible individual portions could possibly result? But with eggs and bread crumbs added, the portions became clearly discernible. What is more, the boneless chopped fish was safe for the elderly and the very young, who comprised a good part of the family. Some aver that the Jews stopped eating fish in its natural state, on the Sabbath, because the procedure involved labor, i.e., separating the meat from the bones. At any rate, the true origins of *gefilte* fish, together with the sauce that surrounds it, will no doubt remain a dark secret, until some archaeologist will discover a broken jar with a "Mother's Gefilte Fish" label on the spot where Moses smashed the tablets, whereupon we shall know that *gefilte* fish, like manna, came to us from heaven, directly.

In the American Jewish community, *gefilte* fish has become, along with circumcision and the bagel, the last vestige of the covenant between the Almighty and his Chosen People. Re the bagel: a battle has been raging, for the past half-decade, among philologists and folklore researchers regarding the name and origin of this item, which, like Saul Bellow, Sammy Davis Jr. and Arthur Schlesinger, has become the fort and fortress of American Jewry vis-a-vis the non-Jew (in New York alone 2,500,000 are consumed daily and four times that amount over the weekend). Version No. 1: the bagel originated in Austria, during the Turkish siege of Vienna, and got its name from *Bügel,* German for "stirrup," which is likewise rounded and void in the center. Version No. 2: back in 1606, sixty years before Vienna felt the terror of the Turk, the bagel was already being mentioned, in Yiddish, in connection with directives for *accouchement* and circumcision rites. The traditional, and most logical, version: Why is a bagel called a bagel? Because it has a hole in the center. Why does it have a hole in the center? Because otherwise it wouldn't be a bagel.

As far as mention of the bagel in Hebrew is concerned, we find a reference in the Tosefta (all the peoples of modern Europe were, at that time, gnawing at bones in their caves). But we must still ponder the question as to whether the Hebrew *ka'ach*, mentioned there, is really a bagel, though there is proof in the fact that the Arab word for bagel is etymologically similar. So much for the belabored bagel.

The choice of dishes for the Sabbath and the festivals, we find as we probe into history, was not accidental. Tradition here took the course of least resistance: the ingredients were readily available, the season was right, and so was the price. According to Jewish folklore, chopped eggs and onions comprise the first course on Sabbath Eve because the seven layers of the onion parallel the seven days of the week. This goes well with the practical aspect of the matter; the course can be prepared just before the advent of the Sabbath, on which preparation of food is forbidden. Also, eggs and onions are relatively inexpensive commodities, and eggs are especially good for beginning a meal.

The explanation for pancakes on Chanukah follows much the same line. Whence came the abundance of fat for the frying, in commemoration of the Maccabean miracle? December is the time when geese were killed for fat, put up in jars for the winter and the Passover, and the housewife, thrifty stalwart that she was, didn't mind allocating a spoonful or two for the pancakes. What would have happened, had Judah the Maccabee defeated the Syrian host in the summer? Friend, schmaltzy pancakes are much better than idle speculation.

Even the famed *hamentashen* of Purim, the "triangular ears" of Haman (he listened to everybody's advice, and that was his undoing), do not have a clear-cut pedigree. Wicked Haman may have entered the picture later, when the poppyseed-filled pockets of dough were already in existence. The Gentiles later called them "Judas Iscariot's Ears"—Judas being in their eyes no less a villain than Haman. Others believe that Haman's name became associated with the pastry because his name bears resemblance to the German *Mohn*, poppyseed, and *Mohntaschen* became "hamentashen."

All of the foregoing is by way of observing that one must have patience for everything in life, but especially in the culinary arts. A festival dish takes generations to evolve, and always on the sound aspects of reality. There is nothing that reacts less to directive and is influenced less by preaching than a holiday dish. A people can be ordered to pay taxes, fly flags and listen to propaganda, but not even a totalitarian regime can force people to cook according to ideology. It is a fact that to this very day there is no edible dish which symbolizes the rise of communism to power, although an ideological basis can be conjured up readily enough, from a long list headed by red borscht and chopped meat.

The dish came first, then the ideology. Man ate eggs in the spring when he was a tree-dweller, because that is when eggs are plentiful. And thus the egg became a symbol of spring festivals, Passover and Easter and everything else remotely connected with re-awakening nature.

It would be ridiculous to decree (as some zealous patriots actually attempted to do): "Ye shall eat mallow on Independence Day (vegetation of the field was all that Jewish Jerusalem had to eat, at one time, during the siege of 1948) and fowl stuffed with rice (ingathering of the exiles)." Even Moses didn't show such gastronomic arbitrariness. Besides, why mallow? Who knows what it looks like, or where it grows? Furthermore, why consider a festive meal for Independence Day in the first place? The occasion is for the outdoors—dancing in the streets or watching others dance, taking the youngsters to see the fireworks, watching the parade or going on a hike or attending a pageant of some kind. (But now, of course, we have television, enemy of the outdoors.)

If ever there will be traditional dishes for Independence Day, these will be sandwiches, roasted wieners or cold hamburgers, easily carried for hikes or parades. The ideological basis will follow: white cheese on pumpernickel—the black bread stands for our enemies, the white cheese for the purity of our arms, the green onion for the hope of the people to enjoy life, liberty and the pursuit of happiness.

Ah, Noah, Noah!

ARMIES AND alcohol have always gone off to the wars together and together have celebrated victories. One cannot possibly imagine Lord Nelson toasting the Trafalgar triumph with lemonade or General Zhukov celebrating the end of the drive on Berlin with a glass of orange juice in his hand. Folklore has steeped the profession in the axiom that great warriors are great guzzlers, and often expire with as much alcohol as blood in their veins—if not more, from Alexander the Great to Hemingway.

Behold the General Staff of the Israel Defense Forces at its first press conference after the victory in the Six Day War: what is it that the Chief-of-Staff is holding in his hand? A soft carbonated drink. Ingredients: sugar, artificial preservative, food coloring. His generals partake of the same. On ceremonious occasions, brigade reunions and commanders' sessions, the refreshment tables are stacked with bottles of lemonade, orangeade, grapefruit juice—just like kindergarten birthday parties. On the day you see drunken Israeli paratroopers lurching arm in arm out of bars, or meet inebriated Israeli Armored Corps officers trying to act sober, then we shall be a people like other peoples.

The Jewish soul within us rejects the very possibility of this ever coming about. Drunkenness has no place in the Jewish State—no humanity rolling in its own vomit in the gutters; no glassy-eyed youths groping along the wall for support; no toters of personal flasks on trains, their loutish heads rolling from side to side in rhythm with the train. The aversion to drunkenness has remained with us even after tradition has gone and Judaism has been converted from religion to nationality; deep internal repugnance and a feeling of shame comes over us when we see a man whose cup of intemperance runs over.

All this is the consequence of an ideological upbringing during the two millennia of exile. Our ancestors in the Promised Land drank quite freely, if we take the word of the most daring best-seller ever written. The propensity may not go back to Adam and Eve (although there are those who claim that the forbidden fruit was the grape; a ridiculous opinion, since grapes grow on the vine and not on a tree, but a case may be made for an apple sufficiently fermented to cause the effects of cider), but certainly to the Flood. Noah, as is stated, was indubitably a righteous man who found favor in the eyes of the Lord, but he found flavor in something totally different. From this starting point, the Bible is replete with tales of wine and banquets, and its verses tell of strong drink and inebriation, from Genesis to the Book of Esther. The spies sent by Moses to have a look around Canaan brought back a giant cluster of grapes to prove its fertility, and the solid citizen of those days was depicted as one who dwelt under his vine and his figtree (the latter probably serving as the recovery room). Is the vine merely symbolic? It does not have too much space beneath it nor is it as decorative as, let us say, ivy. Is it the grapes? Apples keep longer. Raisins? How many raisin cookies can one eat? Clearly it was because of the wine.

One can drink himself blind in congenial company, but anyone who is apprehensive about his surroundings and must be wary of them cannot risk becoming drunk. That is why Jews didn't go in for much drinking in the diaspora. However, our sages refrained from enacting prohibitions which no one could possibly observe, and they did not ban alcohol. People drank, moderately. They drank as part of a ritual. The Jewish religion does not forbid strong drink, as does Islam (a condition which merely intensified the production of that cure-all euphemistically called "medicinal brandy") and gave religion and alcohol a measure of respectable compatibility.

Here and there we may come across biblical sayings such as, "give wine to the bitter soul," but in drinking the accent is on the joyous occasions. The sages must have learned, from experience, that forgetfulness achieved with alcohol is of brief duration, and the resulting mood is twice as dark. He who drinks to drown out sorrow usually drinks alone, and there's nothing more depressing than to become drunk alone and undergo the effects in solitude.

201

Where there's joy and jubilation, there's good company and a happy occasion. *Lehayim,* everybody!

A Jew drinking in the family circle will not allow himself to overstep the bounds of sobriety. He wants to be the impeccable hero, at least in his children's eyes, which he may not be in real life. Even Gentiles who become drunk outside know that it is best to tiptoe into the house; being drunk is a condition to be in if you are with people whom you don't have to impress except with the volume you consume; with such people you can let your hair down all the way.

Drinking in the family circle used to have another obstacle. The bottles of home-made cherry liqueur were kept under lock and key, the latter kept by the woman of the house, who would bring up a bottle from the deep recesses of the closet only if the occasion called for it, then pour the precious liquid into small jiggers, known in Bar-Mitzvah parlance as "thimbles." So long as the stock of alcoholic beverages is in the hands of the house-wife—and the custodianship hasn't changed sexes for generations —there won't be such a thing as excessive drinking in the home. Housewives tend to look askance at bottles which empty too rapidly, regardless of whether the contents are oil or perfume or eggnog. That's why they replace the cork after every round, hoping that you take the hint.

The habit men have of drinking by themselves—if not on separate premises, as do the English and the French, then at least in a separate corner of the drawing room—may be the final phase left over from the good old days when women were women and knew their place; this is the final mark of rebellion against equal rights. Even in the most advanced, liberal and intelligent Tel Aviv social gatherings, there form, inside the first ten minutes, a women's section in one corner and a men's division in another. What draws the men together is not the opportunity to discuss the prospects of the new chemical combine or the fiscal policy of the Minister of Finance or the latest statements by Abdel Nasser. It is simply the desire to withdraw from within the radius of the spouse's watchful eye, the look she telegraphs when the third round approaches, and the frosty if gentle remark: "Don't forget, *dear.* You must leave for Jerusalem tomorrow, *early,"* delivered with the best smile of solicitous sociability. The wives of men who like to drink are very much like the wives of stamp collectors and other insane hobbyists; they suffer either in silence or on the upper octaves, but they do suffer, because money doesn't grow on trees and there's the little matter of health.

While objection to drunkenness is deeply engraved on our hearts, we are particularly offended by the sight of a drunken woman. All of us are in favor of equality for the sexes, but whereas a drunken male is a wretched sight, a Jewess who reeks of alcohol, whatever her moral standards, is a figure which stirs within us the indignation of thirty generations of rabbis. True, in films we see Audrey Hepburn and Shirley MacLain go into their cups looking very pretty and vivacious, without a blemish on either their charm or makeup; their noses do not redden, their eyes do not get that glassy stare, and their vocabulary does not outrage the censor. But there is certainly a gap between technicolor and red-nosed reality.

On the other hand, it doesn't make sense to train children, particularly daughters, to abstain from liquor altogether. An intelligent father who is capable of seeing what the future may bring forth (or, more precisely, who doesn't want to have his daughter bring forth, prematurely) will let his little girl have a taste here and a sampling there, a bit of sweet wine, some vermouth, a sip of beer. Drink, daughter, drink, so you may know enough not to fall victim to the first Don Juan with enough ingenuity to empty two glasses of champagne into your unsuspecting gullet.

In analyzing the stand against drunkenness, as one of the inherent traits—strong family ties and love for the book—once held as being characteristic of the Jew, there arises the question, whether this is a matter of natural and permanent immunity, even without social or religious taboos, or whether, from time to time, a retreading is necessary. If the younger generation of American Jews is any example, Jews also have cocktail sets, in their own environment. In Israel, certain changes in drinking patterns have doubtlessly taken place in the course of the past twenty years, just as modes of living in general have changed, and for the same reason: a rise in living standards, an imitation of western customs, a more hedonistic approach to life.

In the good old days, when the state was founded, the community was familiar with brandy, Alicante, port and Tokay wines, plus a variety of liqueurs described by misogynists as "ladies' drink." Then, suddenly, the land was inundated with hard liquor. Now even Mr. Zilbershpon's little grocery carries whiskey and gin, vermouth and arak, vodka and a dozen brands of brandy, with stars and mysterious insignia which, in France, attest to age and quality, but which, in Israel, have little to do with vintage and bouquet.

I think that the horizons of the world of liquor widened with the relaxation of Israel's boundaries. As soon as the Government began issuing exit permits and granting foreign currency allocations (really only twelve years ago), the Israelis discovered, especially at the bars aboard Zim liners, that there is such a thing as Liquor. In days of yore, when our host asked us, "What will you drink?" we said, "Whatever you're having" or "It doesn't matter." Then we discovered a likable liquor and said, "Courvoisier, no soda, no ice," or "Cherry Heering, please." Gradually the horizons expanded to take in Martel and Drambouie, curacao and rum, vodka and Tia Maria, and on to the mixes, Bloody Mary and Screwdriver, dry martinis and Manhattans and up to the rung of the professionals: Scotch.

Whiskey has been ousting brandy from every worthwhile Israeli position, owing either to the American influence or to its suitability, as some maintain, to the Israeli climate or to the status that it engenders. A new imbiber tends to speak, naively, of "whiskey"; imagine anyone mentioning a book, just like that, without reference to author or title. But as time and drinking go on he gets the idea and begins to distinguish between White Label and Red Label and Black Label, between Johnnie Walker and Black and White, up, up to Chevis Regal, Teachers and other names of renown (yet the conversation about comparative liquors among the professionals is no more interesting than the shop talk of contractors, lawyers, actors or journalists).

The problem of table wines is solved, in Israel, quite easily. Instead of going into a dither over the white wine vs. red with the veal, people have Vin Rose with everything, and all's well with the world. The moment that the experts begin with Chateau Neuf-de-Pope and Chateau Lafitte, a chateau here and a chateau there, it's best to sit back and let the boys have their fun. The dream of my life is to be there when a man, upon being proffered wine, for tasting, by the *sommelier,* would not murmur "Fine" but would gather up courage and say, "Not good enough. Take it back!" But I am afraid that, in Israel, the only result of such a daring step would be a dressing-down from the wine steward.

Yet despite everything, I have traveled the road in Israel from adolescence to maturity, but nowhere have I seen here a real drunk, except journalists from abroad. True, we have individuals who are known to be heavy drinkers—authors, artists, bohemians (everyone will be delighted to supply you with their names, and it will always be the same dozen). But I have yet to see genuine drunks reeling in the streets, in public places, at cocktail parties —and I have three pairs of glasses, none of them with rose-tinted lenses. Be that as it may, drunkenness is as yet no problem in Israel, a fact clearly indicated by its absence as a theme for authors and playwrights. When all is said and done, what is an Albee play, if not a hundred glasses of liquor strung together with snatches of dialogue? In this respect, our playwrights are being cheated; inebriety is even a better subject than a vanished marriage contract, and gives the actors an opportunity to disport themselves on the stage in true Stanislavsky tradition.

The Israeli songwriters, on the other hand, are not ready to resign themselves to this ignoble situation and to accede to the notion that they must give up the sadness of autumn because of the climate and the glee of drinking because of Jewish tradition. They keep producing tunes in the style of "Leaves are falling, autumn's here" or "Wine, wine, let's toast: *Lehayim.*" Generally, the songs about wine are the ones heard around boy scout campfires and the annual excursions of the Fifth and Sixth Grades to Beersheba and its environs, songs such as "When we die please bury us in the wine cellars of Rishon Letzion" (what's wrong with the Eliaz wine cellars in Binyamina as burial vaults?). However, tunes and liquor should be kept apart; it's a shame to mix good alcohol with poor tunes.

A national beverage, like a national diet, must necessarily exercise a telling influence on the character of the people. Vodka drinkers are different from beer drinkers, and wine drinkers are not like tequila drinkers. I may be prejudiced, but I cannot associate beer with thought or intellect. Perhaps it's because, in my mind's eye, I can still see the Czech taverns on Sundays, heavy with the smell of beer, and the white coasters under the glass pitchers on which the tavern keeper penciled one line after another, a line for every liter. True, my grandmother used to drink beer, unusual for grandmothers in well-to-do bourgeois families. Invariably, on my way from the tavern, tankard in hand, I would lick a bit off the creamy foam, more as a matter of principle than of pleasure. But despite my love for her and for Tonda Masaryk (nephew of Thomas Masaryk and the first brewer in the Abir brewery in Netanya and the embodiment of a good heart), I associate beer with something crude, for the masses, good with anecdotes and buttock-pinching, hunting songs and brass bands. You would hardly imagine four philosophers bent over tankards of beer and contemplating the mysteries of life and death, as did the Chinese poet Lee Po and his comrades, over glasses of wine.

Wine enjoys a much better image. "Wine gladdeneth the heart of man"; wine is song, wine is maidens in sheer dresses, wine is Francois Villon, wine is Italy, signora, amore, wine is a philosophical approach to life, culture and good taste—as long as you keep your mind clear of the Spanish laborers and their wine-skins on a train ride of hundreds of miles, drinking, sleeping, burping, or of the stout and sated Viennese, practicing pseudo-Gemütlichkeit over glasses of Heuriger.

The Mediterranean region, however, was a grape-growing region long before the advent of the Hebrews, to say nothing of the Moslems, so that if a national beverage is in order, let it be wine, unless we introduce an innovation into history and establish a culture steeped in orange juice or carbonated lemonade. After all, the first evidence of the Israeli presence in the territories taken during the Six Day War was neither Israeli flags nor signs in Hebrew, but hundreds of Arab soft drink stands, selling made-in-Israel soft drinks like Tempo, Cristal, Tassas, to quench the thirst of the tourists.

No Place Like Home

THE AVERAGE Israeli labors twenty years to acquire and pay for an apartment, ten more to finance housing for his growing children, leaving him barely enough time to save for a plot for his interred bones. Our best years are buried beneath floor tile, and our hearts are poured in concrete. And we stay put, therefore, unlike the La Ronde cycle: dwelling, furniture, decor—no more room; dwelling, furniture, decor—everything's old and worn; dwelling, furniture, decor—public auction of the estate of the late . . .

What sets the Israeli apart from other house-bearing snails is the cost of financing—the high interest rate, the linked mortgages, the short-term loans, and having to be the owner, whether it is a house or an apartment. Only the very poor, or the very rich, or the very astute when it comes to making money work for them, live in rented quarters and pay a high rental without key money (this being money paid to Tenant A in Landlord B's building by prospective Tenant C in return for taking over A's apartment; Landlord B gets from one-third to one-half of the sum, depending on the length of A's tenure).

For this average Israeli, his home determines and is the expression of his way of life. A home is reason enough to move to another locality, to change jobs, to oblige the housewife to take on an outside job. The size of the dwelling also dictates the number of offspring. We are slaves to wood and cement, handmaids to glass and china, and we are proud of our glinting chains.

Anyone who devotes so much to his own home is bound to pay little attention to building for the public weal. We are not interested in public edifices. This is the province of the municipality, a local council, the Government. The Greeks spent their days in public places—in the forum, on the court esplanade, in temples, in the

207

agora (reserved for male freemen only; women and slaves keep out). In comparison with their magnificent public buildings, their private residences were rather plain, built as an afterthought, and today not even their ruins are extant. With the Jew, however, ever since the destruction of the Second Commonwealth, the motto, paraphrased, has been "a man's home is his temple." The Jew seeks a domicile which will protect him, give him cause to be proud, point up his status, be his retreat. The home is the bastion, the fortress. For all he cares, public buildings could be made of cardboard or, to comply with fire regulations, of asbestos.

Israel's cities are running riot with people changing homes. This one has taken a beating in the exchange and is licking his wounds, that one has made the change and his brain is still spinning from the multiple transaction procedures, a third one is about to make the change and is frantically scraping the down payment together. Then there are those who are poised for the plunge the moment that conditions will permit it, as well as those who cannot make the move at this particular time, much as they would want to, and must perforce content themselves with enclosing a porch or adding blinds. Those who have the feeling that "this is it; we shall neither remodel nor renovate, and we shall not leave it until the pallbearers come," are the rich, the elderly, the very tired, or the brand-new owner imbued with illusions about himself and his household.

When the hour for moving tolls, there also comes a moment of truth: you look at the walls, scraped and scratched by the furniture that once stood there . . . the sunken tiles around the sink . . . the paint peeling off the doors . . . the rust stains in the bathtub and, outside, the furniture stacked on the sidewalk—bare, unprotected, despondent, lonely, every stain and nick exposed to the illuminating glare of the sun; the open crates packed with worn housewares, used cartons crammed with shapeless bundles of clothing, and you stare in amazement: is it for this that I toiled, on this that I lavished my years and strength, my money, my pride? A dismantled home is like the body of the sunbird; the feathers are the same, but the beauty was in the living spirit.

Paint does wonders to convert the grave of old dreams into a new dwelling. New people move in, with new dreams for this fine, beautiful spacious domicile. And we, suffused with the smell of lime and fresh enamel, admiring the smooth tile and the gleaming faucets and the virginity of a new home, forget all memories of the past. Here everything will be different, wonderful, perfect. Moving into a new home is like standing under the wedding canopy; the heart is full of dreams.

Selecting a home may be a fateful step, but it is often taken out of considerations of secondary importance. People may decide on a certain dwelling because of the large colored bathroom tile, the stainless steel sink, aluminum shutters, formica cabinets—minor items which lose their importance as soon as the novelty wears off. They neither add anything to our self-satisfaction nor do they detract from it, except for the envy we feel if, in comparison with what others have, ours come off second best.

The mode of life in our home is set without our being aware of it. A large drawing room, which one enters straight from the stairwell and which is surrounded by bedroom cubicles, is not a matter of taste or fashion; it is an essential shift in the role of the home. The long dark corridor of the once-upon-a-time home was not an object of beauty, but it was a sort of bulwark against intruders, a strainer for unwelcome visitors. Every room had its purpose, its identity, and in their aggregate it was a home designed for the dwellers therein. Later, in the early days of the state, came the square foyer, also a deterrent but much more amiable; one could not burst in upon the interior, but a discreet peek was technically possible. Once beyond the foyer and the clothes alcove was the drawing room, open for inspection. Now all of our possessions, our taste, our habits, our claim to pride are on display. The living room is intended primarily for guests. Its generous proportions come at the expense of the other rooms, and the household exists in a squeeze in order that the guests may be graciously accommodated, whether the visits are daily or only once a month. This may be an outgrowth of the vital Oriental concept of hospitality (and indeed, compared with English, French, Italian and other western homes, ours are open to strangers). More likely, this reflects the influence of the American way of life and its close correlation of home and status and the emphasis on what meets the eye. The drawing room, into which most of the money goes, is not to be confused with the term "living room"; the drawing room is out of bounds to youngsters, to disorder, to work. Someone may drop in, at any moment; the home has to confine itself to the bedrooms.

Civilization marches through our home without our being aware of it, like the hero of Molière who suddenly discovered that he had been talking prose all his life. We accept the fact that the large dining table in the center of the room, with the numerous chairs surrounding it and the light fixture directly above it, are passé. Never did we ask: "Who said so?" or "How was this decided?" We merely went out and bought the low coffee table plus a sofa with an easy chair at each end, without realizing that a style of living had gone with the times. For the large dining table in the center of the main room was born in the days when illumination was expensive and the entire family used to gather about the sole fixture, overhead—the women with their handwork and the others with their reading or homework. In those days food cost a great deal and receiving an invitation to dinner was like receiving a gift; women used to worry about their cooking as they do today about their figures. A large table was the setting for either a meal or animated conversation, a face-to-face rapprochement, togetherness, as it is called today. Scattered chairs create aloofness, interruptions, fragments. The repast has been replaced by the snack, and the cook has been eased out by the hostess.

The urban home has remained basically the same as when it was built, probably because *homo urbanis* hasn't changed much. The size of the homes owned by the plain citizen, whether in ancient Mesopotamia or Hazor or Hellas or Chaucer's London, ranged—according to archaeologists—from sixty-five to somewhat more than a hundred square yards (homes of the truly affluent measured twice as much, and the manors of the nobility were in a class by themselves). These are the exact dimensions of most of the housing units in Israel. The housing authorities who built immigrant units in the first years of the state, spread over thirty square yards, knew very well that they were putting up nothing more than cages.

Room dimensions are also changing, just a trifle. Ceiling height is a man vertically placed plus some air space; a ceiling lower than that causes claustrophobia, and one higher invites an inferiority complex and colds. Bedroom width is a man horizontally placed surrounded by a modest marginal strip. A man will build his bedroom small, though the drawing room may be huge, perhaps because even in his sleep he must sense the protection of its four hugging walls against lions and wolves, thieves or cats, all in accord with the period and the locality. The poor French monarchs who had to sleep in the halls of Versailles didn't fail to build for themselves intimate pavilions and small hunting lodges, where they could sleep like human beings. There is no loneliness deeper than that of a man sleeping alone in a chamber a hundred yards square. Small wonder that, when they did have to sleep in Versailles, the French sovereigns had to make use of endless concubines; someone had to warm the canopied bed.

In the realm of slumber, we in Israel are in the vortex of a revolution of which Marx, under his featherbed, never dreamed. First, the very existence of the bedroom: most of the members of the old-time community, in the city as well as in the *kibbutz,* were wont to sleep in the living room, first on iron bedsteads which, in their daytime camouflage of brown-and-black spreads, became settees, and later on corner sofas which opened up and folded back in a variety of patterns. A separate bedroom insinuated pampering and sex and other defects of bourgeoisie. Today even the most vociferous *kibbutznik* deems it proper to sleep in an official bedroom, as soon as he receives his unit in the new housing section for old-timers. Getting used to sleeping double is a more difficult matter. There's the climate (too warm), culture (reading disturbs the spouse who wants to sleep), diligence (what if one spouse has to get up early?). Even if these hurdles are cleared, the parties involved still cling tooth and nail to the last symbol of individuality (if that's what is bothering them): separate sheets and separate blankets. Till death do us part is fine, but there's a limit to everything.

Every housing innovation, every technical achievement, every change in style is initiated by the well-to-do; by the time that these filter down to the masses, a new cycle is already in operation. Whoever has the means for it, seeks to have what others do not. We have gone through the days of massive "European" furniture, of straw stools and round brass tables of Oriental design; we had a period of blond furniture of bleached wood and bookshelves on posts; there were the stages of formica and teakwood, which

211

in turn gave way to latter-day antiques in colonial style or one of the several French Louis series. In the offing we may have futuristic furniture of fiberglass and aluminum, footless and cornerless. Fortunately, only a few can afford the services of an interior decorator or a change of furniture whenever a style goes the way of all styles. Most people hold on to the old furniture, adding a piece or two with every innovation. In the course of the years the dwelling becomes a conglomeration of mish-mash, something from the austerity years and a touch of the Scandinavian, a bit of the Oriental and a breath of the rural, a drop of America and a pinch of Chinese. There's very little Israeli that our homes have in common, other than African statuettes, Chinese prints and Murano ashtrays. An Israeli dwelling can be identified by the potted philodendron in one corner of the drawing room; the light, well-scrubbed and polished floor tiles (the result of cascades of water and the latest of floor detergents, plus a vigorous swishing of the mop); the shower and the smudgy wash cabinet behind the bathtub (a structural ineptitude); the aforementioned sofa and two chairs and a painting overhead, marking the area as the focal point in the room; signs of constant remodeling; bedding being aired on the porch; light and air throughout the home.

There should be a definite correlation between a man and his furniture. At times you do sense it, as in the home of an old-time couple: polished dark furniture, embroidered coverlets on the seats of the armchairs, family photographs on the walls; or, as in the home of an artist in an old Arab house, arches, Eastern trappings, a rug-covered sofa; or, as in the home of an elderly author, bookcases along the walls and writing desk covered with papers; or a room in a *kibbutz* with its light furniture, striped drapes on the windows, a large bowl of fruit on the table.

Had we in this country wanted to create a uniquely Israeli style of home furnishings, we would have found ourselves a thousand years too late. National styles no longer simply sprout, in this world of modern communications. If our logic were to take its cue from our eagerness to imitate the West, we would dispose of much of our furniture, have a built-in closet in every room (blank side to the bedroom, partly open to the drawing room). A dining nook, a sitting nook, beds, a work table, carpeting, floor lamps—

period. All those end tables, tea carts, liquor bars, shelves for the doll display, flower pot stands, souvenir showcases—out! One readily envisages all this, for the homes of others.

The desire to collect and display souvenirs has apparently come down to us from the days when a journey to a resort was a major and unforgettable event, and a visit to a foreign country was an adventure to be forever cherished, when every color reproduction merited an exhibit and every visit to the photographer went into the diary, when every plate was precious and every vase a legacy. An Indian doll in Fenimore Cooper's chamber had some meaning, but an Indian doll made of Japanese plastic in Hong Kong, which a friend picked up in Naples and made of it a gift to us in Ramat Gan is a bit out of character. We buy, get and keep them all, albeit without any sentimental attachment: the Queen's Guard in a fur hat of nylon, cigarette cases embossed with the Eiffel Tower in gold, Lassie depicted on German china, a tile with a leaning Tower of Pisa, a pseudo-Grecian vase purchased just before the ship left Piraeus, a whittled African antelope brought in by a seaman, a Viking warrior picked up for a minor monarch's ransom, a Chinese (People's Republic) print showing Robin Redbreast perched on a bough of cherries in blossom, a turtle fashioned out of shells, a donkey made out of rope. Artistically they are just so much trash. They collect dust. They create work. But to throw them away would still be very painful. Difficult, too. An insult to the donor. Perhaps we should settle for a niche for souvenirs in every Israeli home, drawn over with a curtain like the Holy Ark which only the housewife may pull aside and look—and then only to assuage the soul.

Mini, Daughter of Figleaf

ISRAEL'S WOMENFOLK, blessed with a healthy sense of self-preservation, have withstood all and sundry attempts to have a national attire foisted on their figures, by way of a Greek-like toga, a Yemenite blouse or a Bedouin cloak, as plotted by fertile fashion designers with a penchant for the patriotic. In these modern days, when Japanese women are no longer versed in the art of draping themselves in kimonos and Spanish girls put on their lace dresses only when the interests of tourism are involved, when the whole world is, from the standpoint of fashion, one big, more or less happy family, there is little room or hope for national sartorial individualism. In this respect, too, Israel arrived on the scene much too late.

The distinctiveness in the fashion style of Israeli women is not in what they wear as in what they omit: stockings in the summer; hats for the sake of beauty (the straw morning cloche is for protection from the sun); long evening gowns (except in the case of Tel Avivian hostesses with international illusions); gloves (these they carry, wrinkled and worn, in their palms). In contrast with the West, there is relatively little difference in dress between the various social strata and classes. Throughout the length and breadth of the land (we no longer phrase the area, from "Dan-to-Beer-Sheba" or the like; defining boundaries can easily get us into trouble), in city or village, in *kibbutz* and *moshav,* in the north and in the south—it's the same simple summer cotton.

The dress distinctions between the newcomers from the various diasporas are gradually vanishing. Only the elderly women continue wearing the traditional community garb, embroidered pantaloons or fringed kerchiefs. There may be a few more pearls, more peroxide blondes among those from east of the Oder-

Neisse, a bit more stress on the utilitarian, the good-for-at-least-another-year among the Yeckis, a bit more satin, lurex and conservative styles among the North Africans, somewhat more chic among the Hungarians from the big cities. But the differences are not ingrained and are not unique with any age bracket. From the viewpoint of dress, the integration of the ingathered is complete.

Only in B'nai Brak and in the religious quarters of Jerusalem does one come across something in the way of native fashion: the small hats of laced straw, the light suits and flower-print dresses. Wide in the skirt, with round collar and long sleeves, the dresses bear an unmistakable label: "Fashioned with the Grace of the Lord." The pious women who still wear hair-pieces owe a debt to their secular sisters: ever since wigs came into vogue in the modern world, the situation in the religious camp improved beyond compare. No longer is this area dominated by the uniform wig of reddish hair, crimped and lifeless, which shouted its identity from afar; now one sees well-tended hairdos of shining hair in natural color, wonderful to behold.

Fashions prevalent among the pious Jewesses of Meah Shearim are also fashions of sorts, albeit of a much earlier period. There is no evidence that Mother Rachel, when first seen by Jacob near the well, was wearing a long pleated skirt, a blouse with long sleeves plus black wool stockings, or that Prophetess Miriam wore a knitted hat which her own hands had fashioned. Needless to say, fashions as such were not handed down from Mount Sinai. There was a time, two or three hundred years ago, when present Meah Shearim styles were no more than the latest rage, like the disc dresses of Paco Rabane, but in a society placed on guard by distinctive external influences, they became a religious tradition.

Ideological conservativism always vests itself with conservative attire; this holds true for Catholic church dogma or the principles of the proletariat alike. Female veterans of the labor settlements wrapped their ideology in their favorite clothes—laced shoes, blue suits and white blouses with the round Bezalel Art School brooches—to safeguard it from harm. It is not by chance that the major changes in *kibbutz* attire came along with the revolution in many other economic patterns of the modern *kibbutz*.

Morality is, generally, fashion behind the times. The woman

215

who, five long years ago, protested against the skirt which reached only down to the knee has in the meantime shortened her own skirt by a good few inches, and is now being upset by the thigh-high mini and the transparent blouse. I well recall that faithful, dedicated cashier in the Workers' Kitchen in Haifa who, in the year 1950 C.E., barred me from contact with the vegetarian liver and fried fish fillet because I was wearing a dress with a tiny aperture at the neck, which she denounced as a plunging neckline unbecoming to a member of the Histadrut. In general it may be assumed that the attire currently regarded as unsuitable for a Member of Knesset or a consultant in a Government office, or a secretary in the Ministry of Welfare or a daughter of a *moshav* (depending on the vantage point from which the critics are firing) will suit the women in question, with no aspersions cast, three years later, when fashions will have moved on to more modern pastures.

One of the polls, which have lately descended upon us like starlings upon an apricot tree, indicates that the M.K.'s most in the public eye at present are David Ben Gurion, Shimon Peres, Uri Avneri and Shulamit Aloni. It is worth noting that, in addition to their different spiritual contexts, each of them is distinctive in his or her personal appearance. The poll proves that one should perhaps take a longer view of the short dress. One cannot claim that Ben Gurion is the darling of Saville Row, but there is still something about him which will never allow him to overstep the narrow boundary line separating individualistic appearance from the ridiculous, even when he puts on his old army pants, his ancient battle-dress and turtleneck sweater. In the last respect, Ben Gurion antedated his generation and wore the polo neckwear long before Tony Armstrong-Jones or Richard Burton ever heard about the Left-Wing Zionist Party.

Menahem Begin always maintains the meticulous appearance of a Polish nobleman (we who, before coming to Israel, knew the leader of the nationalist underground only from what we read about him, expected to see a duplicate of Che Guevara). Here and there in the Knesset we come upon members of the rightist sector or the moderate religionists attired in the dress of successful business men, but the majority of public servants and appointees consists of a long array of wide trousers hanging like burlap,

216

baggy, cuffs flapping in the breeze, and light shirts in various stages of creasing, draped over paunches in various stages of protrusion. Just you wait, honorable sirs, until the TV cameras come edging up to you! It will be one mad, headlong rush to the tailor to press those clothes while the steam is still hot.

The illustrated world press carries breathtaking accounts and depictions of changes taking place in the realm of men's wear, showing John Lennon in a floral jacket or Lord Harlech in a mauve ruffled shirt. But in Israel everyone dresses as he always has; this country—young, dynamic and developing—is conservative at heart, as proven by the results of the national elections from their inception to this day. Only two marginal groups are inclined toward colorful innovations in dress: engineers and young artists who studied abroad and proudly wear the sartorial insignia of the outside world, and working boys of sixteen or seventeen who live it up during the short span between compulsory education and compulsory military service, as they dream about the great life ahead.

Not all of the ancient fashions still abide with us. Gone from the Israeli scene are the knee-length "Zalman" shorts (which are attempting a comeback in the guise of Bermudas). Also gone are the British Army knee-length socks; gone are the white summer linen suits so beloved by the old-timers; gone are the pith helmets worn by the British officers, jungle explorers and Solel-Boneh construction foremen. Trouser cuffs shrank gradually, the amount of shoulder padding became less heroic, the jacket was shortened, Terylene replaced wool and Dacron succeeded poplin. Otherwise, however, the changes have been few, certainly not to be compared with the revolution which took place simultaneously in women's wear. Ziama, Sascha, Munya can attire themselves in what they wore thirty years ago without attracting undue attention (at most, people will smile at their excessive sentimentality), but if Manya, Tanya or Zinya were to appear in what they wore in those unforgettable best years, they would be followed by mobs of kids, eager to see a show.

Israeli cartoonists still persist in personifying Israel as that pert lad in shorts, open sandals and *tembel* dunce cap, in complete disregard of the fact that shorts are nowadays worn only by kids of primary school age and a few nature lovers; the status of the *tembel* cap is not what it used to be, either—as soon as it became a Zionist symbol, distributed free of charge by El Al Airlines and tourist agencies to their customers, the Israelis began to shun it. After all, what Israeli can afford to be mistaken for an American tourist?

Israeli males posing in newspaper ads as prototypes of some ideal man are dressed a) in dark suit and tie (if the paper were to exude aromas, one would detect the unmistakable fragrance of aftershave lotion) to go with copy suggesting confidence and trust, and b) colorful shirts and tight jeans, if the impress is to be the vigor of youth and zest. The sole *tembel* cap which appears in current commercial promotion belongs to the touseled head of "Tal," trademark of the farm produce from western Galilee settlements, personifying the man of soil and toil, as he offers the fruits of his labor to the expert taste of the men in the dark suits.

There was a time when the Israeli male would acquire his one and only suit in deference to a wedding or some other formal occasion—dark blue or brown, double-breasted and square-shouldered. Today the suit is standard socialist equipment, and none but the genuine snob would allow himself to be seen at the Mann Auditorium in a handknit sweater. There also used to be quite a cult in the attitude of the old community toward the necktie, as though it were the strangling symbol of capitalism, of the exploitation of the working masses, and of degeneracy, while long white underwear with drawstrings at the ankles was the foundation of the pioneer image. But in reality the necktie should not be regarded with such hostility; like Yiddish, it has no future to begin with. The management of a tourist hostelry which demands that a guest put on a tie for dinner is as much behind the times as the Israeli Minister who insists on not wearing one as a matter of principle. If he can lower his ideological standards enough to ride in an official limousine driven by a private chauffeur, he can also make peace with half a yard of silk around the neck, after all, it's not a noose.

The Female Image, Revised

CONCEPTS OF the beautiful female change only superficially and in the less important details: a few pounds more, a few pounds less, but basically they are focused on the same strategic points—eyes, legs, lips, breasts, thighs. Only the priority varies with the times.

Inasmuch as all the depictions of the biblical beauties were consumed in the conflagration which destroyed the Temple, we must rely on written delineations exclusively, which confirm that the principles have not changed; only the analogies are different. There is less of a likeness to livestock; no modern Solomon would dare compare his beloved to Pharaoh's mare and her hair to a flock of goats (even if they did come from Gilead), her teeth to a herd fresh up from the water hole; she wouldn't know what he was talking about, anyway. Dove's eyes no longer constitute the superlative compliment, and the twin progeny of the gazelle has also dropped in the popular poll rating. Today's beloved prefers to be likened to foodstuffs and dry goods: almond eyes of chocolate brown or olive black; coffee-hued skin and lips like raspberries, cheeks like peaches and hair like silk, a nose like a button and breasts like apples.

True, the biblical paean to the woman of valor declares that charm is deceitful and beauty is vain, but it is quite obvious that the author of Proverbs wrote the critique under the watchful eye of one of his official wives (one not given to deceit or vanity), or that he had passed the age of sexual endeavor and was substituting less tangible values. The fact remains that, elsewhere in the Bible, the physical description of the maiden is given first. Jacob's readiness to work fourteen years, as a farmhand without fringe benefits, in return for Rachel stemmed not from her skill at milking goats, cooking pottage or ironing shirts of many colors, but simply because she was comely and shapely, while Leah had a sty in her eye.

Down the generations, good mothers have been consoling their not altogether attractive daughters with the line that beauty isn't everything, that soul and character count for much more (a fact with which any male will concur, *after* he has taken unto himself for a wife the choicest morsel in the neighborhood). Beauty enjoys the singular advantage of being visible: immediately, on the spot, on the dance floor and the beach, at the lunch counter and in the bus, while the sweet soul resides in the innermost depths, and by the time that reveals itself in its undisputed glory, all the young men have gone off with the others.

Feminine beauty has a definite market value, like building plots, gold coins and oil stocks. A pretty girl, unless she is stupid beyond toleration, can command top price on the matrimonial exchange: a successful architect, a manufacturer, a millionaire's heir, an American tourist. How did Esther win the favor of Ahasuerus— by her ability to recite Psalms or bake a yeast cake? She was simply prettier than the others, and reacted favorably to the beauty treatment of the day (six months' anointment in myrrh and six months with perfume, rather overdone, according to modern cosmetology).

Once upon a time a king's ransom, or at least substantial affluence, was needed to promote a maiden's beauty (or even keep her clean) but today all of us are in the upper class. Soap and water, cosmetics, oils, bras, hairdos, everything's within reach, more for some and less for others. True, past generations managed to have real beauties, shepherdesses and flax spinners as pure and refreshing as nature had made them, but their beauty faded quickly, what with a shorter life span, for one thing. Secondly, it is not the beauties who require these additives of pulchritude but the ordinary daughters of Eve, who didn't come off the press in perfect shape.

There is this difference between absolute beauty—beyond question, stunning, breathtaking, the kind of beauty that floors men and leaves women feeling helpless—and relative beauty, i.e., charm, an attractiveness which draws attention to the positive features and away from the defects. When we emerged from the quarantine in Auschwitz—hair cropped short, dressed in rags, frightened—Lotte was there. Lotte, the class beauty from our primary school, slim, large brown eyes, beautiful as a goddess in an old gray sweater. Willi, the German camp commandant, spied her immediately and later ran away from Auschwitz, just to be near her when she was deported and protect her from harm. There's the power of beauty for you, for Lotte was as stupid as the day is long and never earned a decent grade in school.

Nowadays, the supply and variety of cosmetics a girl has, if she hearkens to women's magazines and their advice columns, would have made Cleopatra green with envy (according to an ancient coin bearing her likeness, Cleo was rather ugly, but she either had other attractions or she exploited the shadows of the pyramids to prevent Julius Caesar from seeing with whom he was having the pleasure): eyebrow pencil, shadow in various hues for daytime and evening, mascara, liquid eye color, brushes, rouge, lipstick in a dozen shades, facial milk, liquid base, powder, lacquer of various tints, spray, day cream and night cream, plus a few other items in jars, packets or tubes. To paraphrase Winston Churchill: "Never have so many owed so little to so much."

Those of us who grew up with the spirit of socialist Zionism (it forbade cosmetics on ideological grounds, something that had to do with women's rights and the purity of the struggle) used to dab our cheeks with two spots of rouge—Santa Rosa plum purple—and rub them with a handkerchief, or touch a lipstick to our lips, so faint that our counselor couldn't notice it. We felt as daring as the women who attach false lashes to their own or paint gold stars on their eyelids, and the results were almost identical: appearances didn't improve very much, but our self-confidence skyrocketed. And here we have one of the ironclad rules of the beauty cult: let a girl consider herself pretty, and others will begin believing her.

Our contemporary Israeli girls are without doubt outwardly prettier than ever before. They give more thought to their dress, they visit the hairdresser, they are much more adept at emphasizing their good points, they take better care of their figures and even succeed, notwithstanding the Mediterranean legacy, in keeping slim and having almost shapely legs. One can see this on the lawns of Kibbutz Mishmar Haemek as well as on the Ashkelon beach, at the California restaurant as well as on the concourse of the Hebrew University in Jerusalem. But, the prettier they get by universal standards, the less Israeli do they become. The world is moving in the direction of standardization, in concepts of beauty as in everything else, and national distinctiveness is going by the board.

When one examines the periodic pageants of beauties from north, south, east and west, arrayed for the Battle of Miami Beach, the resemblance of one to the other is like drops of heavy water. Only the Japanese and the Africans provide a positive identification of their origin, and even they try to tone down the distinguishing national characteristics as much as possible. Modern technology is no incentive for the emergence of a national-type beauty. Gone are the Israeli girls of tanned face, long brown tresses and eyes courageously flashing.

There is something akin to this fact in the tendency of the impresarios of the Israeli beauty queen contests to change those names of candidates which give away something of the candidate's personality, Ora Jamili, Vivian del Bianca, Michal Harrison, to standard names which signify nothing: Ora Vered or Aviva Israeli. These have an Israeli sound and conform with international requirements, so that any Anglo-Saxon M.C. would have no difficulty in saying, "It's now my pleasure to present to you Queen Name-short-and-snappy, a former soldier," without cracking a denture.

The Israeli Defense Forces might be able to do without the women in its ranks, but they are indispensable to the Foreign Ministry, the Tourism Ministry, the United Jewish Appeal, the film-makers and other purveyors of the Israeli image. The Israeli woman soldier is the greatest discovery around these parts since the Bible. Whom else could the TV crews have photographed during those long days of waiting in May of 1967 before the Six Day War broke out? What else could the illustrated magazines have featured on their front covers? What can the ambitious Israeli starlets use to cover up their deficiencies in acting, singing and moving about if not the Sten gun they once handled in boot training? And yet, a woman who in the course of years managed to gain weight as well as knowledge, and became immersed in a world of formica and rubber foam and shopping and endless housekeeping, if she had served in her younger years in Palmach, Irgun or the British Army or the Israeli Army—something will always set her apart from the ordinary housewife: a spark of alertness, a bit of inner pride, like an iron ration for the day when self-confidence begins to totter, the capacity to stand the long months when the husband or son is in the armed forces, and to live with the fear that death is lurking about.

There was a time, when the Israeli beauty queen contests first blossomed forth, that a maiden from a good Zionist home had to have a good portion of daring in order to be a candidate for such unrefined entertainment. The seventeen years since then have seen a radical change come about in the attitude toward beauty on display, beauty as a life's career. Mothers and daughters alike now bend their best energies toward attaining the dazzling status of international pulchritude.

The first steps are quite unostentatious: preliminary titles, beauty queen of the Mediterranean cruise ship, Queen of Netanya Beach, the Sophia Loren of the Craftsmen's Guild, the Brigitte Bardot of Holon. Then comes the assault on the walls of Jericho, trumpets blaring—the Queen of the Water Festival, Cover Girl for *Haolam Hazeh* Magazine, an entry into the gossip columns (the reciprocal relations between the gossip columnists and the glamor girls is a fine example of idyllic symbiosis in nature), then the final hurdle: the Beauty Queen Contest, attended by the most marvelous things in life—being photographed with Paul Newman, appearing in the pages of the *Daily Mirror,* a bit part in a German film, and eventually perhaps to win the hot breath of a salami manufacturer.

A questionnaire circulated today among eighth and ninth grade girls in Israel's urban public schools (I still hold out some hope for the *kibbutz*) as to what they would like to be if all roads were really open to them, would doubtlessly indicate that most of them have their hearts set on modeling, airline hostessing, movie stardom, pop singing or any other feminine careers which, judging from what the women's magazines and weekend supplements say, would impress them as being the apex of happiness. But compared with the number of Israeli girls who set out for international stardom, the number of those who did make it is infinitesimal. Like blinded butterflies, though, drawn to the neon, these girls cannot see, in their dreams, either Haya Hararit (who turned

223

Ben Hur's head with her bottomless decolletage and has since dis-appeared into the depths of London) or Aliza Gur (who had herself photographed from every conceivable angle and approach in a vain effort to conquer Hollywood) or Ziva Rodan (the protege of photographers, now bemoaning her wrinkles). The one whom these hopefuls see is Dalia Lavi, who went from calendar girl for Tambour Paints to international stardom, strewing her own path with the hearts of noblemen and stage directors, to the pinnacle of being introduced to the Queen of England and playing opposite Peter O'Toole, and dressed in the finest French haute couture for her homecoming. A hundred models display locally made knits or promote the qualities of Velveta soap, but there's only one Alma Ben-Porat to gaze at them from the pages of *Vogue* and *Officiel,* wrapped in the creations of Cardin and Balenciaga.

The more modest among the starry-eyed store away the dreams of world conquest and get down to more practical aspects of life: finding a husband who will give them everything—jewels, furs, a white sports car, global travel, a ranch-type home set in a garden, all in return for the little he gets. When our first brave daughters went forth on world conquest, they stated, repeatedly and genuinely, that no young men anywhere could match ours. In time, however, they learned to appreciate the qualities of the men abroad as well. And indeed, the diaspora is not bad at all, if you view it through several carats. The wedding takes place in the glamorous setting of the Hilton or the Sheraton. The bride is positively ravishing in her long gown of stiff white. The bridegroom kisses her passionately for the benefit of the popping cameras. Then comes the rude awakening: marriage to the owner of a Chicago zipper plant or to the son of Baltimore's fashion king entails matrimonial rigors, duties, pregnancies, moods, in-laws. There's morning, afternoon, night.

The splendored wedding, the multitude of guests, the long white dress are the signs of changing times. For her wedding Mother put on her simple Sabbath dress (or, if she lived in the *kibbutz* and was already in an advanced state of pregnancy, her future husband and a stand-in friend appeared before the rabbi). Well, Mother was old-fashioned. These are modern times, Ma, and equality for women is not a must. A few Israeli girls still want to learn how to parachute, how to drive a tractor or be an officer in the merchant marine, but they are the isolated cases; the general inclination is to let the men do what looks to be a man's job. Gone are the days when pioneer women fought for the right to wield the spade and hoe in the orange groves alongside the men. Despite the equality granted by law (except in personal matters; this, being in the hands of the rabbinate, forms the last remaining bastion of the husband-male), to get the same wages for the same work, and perhaps because of this, there is a general retreat from the captured positions. It was a tough struggle that was waged by the mothers and grandmothers who lent a ready ear to Comrade Lenin: "We shall liberate the woman from her loutish and degrading servitude, from the solitude of the kitchen and the smelliness of the nursery." The kitchen may be equipped with the latest electrical appliances, but in principle the woman is back where she started. The change is apparent in the *kibbutzim* as well; more than two-thirds of the female members are engaged in doing the work that women have always done, in the kitchen, laundry, clothes stockroom, taking care of the babies, teaching school. Agriculture is the male domain. Also gone are the days when a female member of the labor movement, glorying in the attainments of her sex, used to call her husband "my comrade" or "my fellow" or simply by the family name, as a way of circumventing the usage of *ba'al,* the Hebrew term for husband, which insinuates proprietor, master, owner, and connotes the subjugation of woman.

Yes, we have a woman serving as Prime Minister (and since Golda Meir is clever, people say she has a man's head on her shoulders). There are eight women judges on the lower bench (none in the Supreme Court). There are women members of the Knesset (one of them a deputy speaker) but Golda is the sole Cabinet member of the fair sex. Women are to be found in the diplomatic corps, but only one holds the rank of ambassador. On the surface all fields are open to her, but here, as elsewhere, a woman must be a Belgian workhorse to carry a professional career, a family, a home, and most career women give in, somewhere along the line. Once a woman, always a drudge.

Despite the gratifying fact that Israel's women comprise one-third of the labor force, men account for an infinitesimal percentage of culinary help, and this is often confined to uncorking bottles of brandy and charging the seltzer siphons with gas cartridges. Ladies, those s.o.b.'s granted us equal rights, so that we should choke on them. You want creative work, personality, a professional career? Suffer!

In his heart, the Israeli male carries around the character of the region; he is the proprietor of a Mediterranean harem, who likes to keep his women on the go between sink and bed, ready to fulfill every whim and command: shine shoes or soap a back, sew on a button or stuff the derma, all depending on tradition and origin. However, inasmuch as "he who finds a wife finds goodness," and inasmuch as he who enjoys two salaries finds even more than that, the Israeli male forgoes some of his demands and suffers, *nebich,* in silence.

The Males Among Us

THANKS TO the outcome of the Six Day War, the global reputation of the Israeli male soared to superman heights, and this he finds most difficult to maintain in his private life. Actually, the sole item that does distinguish the Israeli civilian male from his counterparts elsewhere on earth is his passport. As for all other attributes, each of our males carries on according to his personal capacity. The verdict regarding "the Israeli male" handed down by hostesses, starlets and glamor girls from abroad has him as being either bold or timid, too active or insufficiently so. However, without questioning their professional expertise, how can these judges successfully delineate the Israeli male when women with university degrees, certified social scientists and veteran newspaper women find it difficult to describe him? Apparently, one can talk about the Israeli male if one doesn't see (in her mind's eye only, of course) too many of them: Mr. Silbermintz (groceries and delicatessen) and Yehuda Zahavi (poet and essayist), Reb Zlotnitsky (Collector of Contributions for the Mermelstein Orphanage), and Jo-Jo, the electric banjo strummer—each one an Israeli male and yet not adding up to THE Israeli male.

The popular conception abroad views the Israeli male as a Zahal officer or at least a First Sergeant: brave, daring, tall and robust, poised and self-assured, with powerful arms and a prominent chin. However, as I hold a march-past, in my mind's eye, of all the Zahal officers known to me, plus the photographs of the men cited for valor (whose deeds bespeak their courage), I doubt whether more than one out of ten would fit the description. They look like all the others: thin or stout, creeping towards baldness or with short legs. If you insist on going by appearances, dearie, you will wind up swooning in the arms of a PX attendant.

227

To the women of the world, of the East and of the West, the current prototype of the Israeli male is Moshe Dayan, not because of his deeds or duties, but because—well, he looks *different* from the others, in a way that the manufacturers of Hathaway shirts knew how to exploit 15 years ago. Abba Eban and Pinhas Sapir were never in the running, for nature decreed it otherwise: spectacles and a bald head are no match for a black patch over the left eye.

In most countries, there is the kind of adoration given to an image, rather than to an individual, this image being movie stardom, the microphone, nobility. In Israel we have no nobility; even "Prince" is just another family name. As for movie stars, the most famous one today is Haim Topol, and few will argue that maidens are likely to swoon in his presence; he is also undone by the satirical roles he plays, for humor does not go hand in gauntlet with the valorous knight. On the Hebrew stage, the Great Lover type hasn't been seen for years, and actors currently portraying Romeo or Marc Antony, in the measure that the Hebrew theatre still goes in for such characters, would hardly be the wishful targets of young girls' dreams, except, perhaps, Oded Kotler. Among the crooners, only Arik Einstein and Yehoram Gaon approximate the description of the handsome male. Things are also changing with the advent of television, and the feminine audience of Kol Yisrael Radio are in for disillusion when the deep male voice is revealed to them cut down by nature to a modest size.

Generally, the Israeli male suffers from a mistaken identification with the "Israeli braggart," the only prototype that bears the "made-in-Israel" mark on his forehead—he of the raucous voice, crude behavior, of blatant exterior Don Juannish self-assurance steeped in illusion and of a lack of self-confidence expressed by the determination to make an impression.

When you talk about men, the conversation naturally veers toward women. This is to be expected; the appellation of "male" is in place only when juxtaposed with "female," otherwise one can talk, theoretically, about persons and personalities, rather than males. In Israel we have a confluence of two currents of thought, when it comes to men's attitudes toward their legitimate wives: one school holds that the female is the male's peer, as preached by pioneer socialism; the other, reflecting the Oriental school, regards the woman as the custodian of home and hearth. In respect to the latter, we have achieved an admirable measure of integration: all the Israeli men, whether they come from the East or the West, love to have their meals served to them right under their noses and, awaiting their pleasure, a ready and comfortable bed and/or a soft lounge chair (in which respect they are no different from the women). But whereas an Oriental male may still exercise some authority in the matter by virtue of his being a male, in European and other western families he must be able to augment his virility with other inducements—gifts or cash, for instance.

The man-woman relationship does not involve competition on the vocational or professional levels; in this area there has actually been some retrogression from the days when working mothers took over the labor supply market. The contention is restricted mainly to the specific influence of the woman on the management of family affairs. Listen to radio advertising or glance at the newspapers: blades, shirts, beer, suits, all male accessories, buy it for him, give it to him, as though he were an infant incapable of deciding whether to use Eddison blades or let his beard grow. All the building contractors will tell you that it's the woman who makes the decisions, who nags and pushes and turns on the screws when selecting an apartment, even though this step will be sapping the energy of the male for years to come.

At one time the automobile was held to be the realm of the male and was selected to suit his taste. Today the family car involves a dialogue, and driving itself is no great indication of virility, despite the delusions of some old-fashioned drivers, not when an 18-year-old maiden with a pert hairdo, a traffic cop by calling, can stop you and hand you a summons. Also, in other countries, familiarity with the vintage of wines and liquors is held to be a male domain, but in Israel the wine or brandy is picked up in the supermarket by the housewife, along with the olives, mayonnaise and steel wool, and she is the one who decides which wine goes well with the veal roast she is preparing for the guests, also of her choice.

When it comes to vocational training, our Ministry of Education is still guided by Europe of the Middle Ages, when the women spun flax and the men went hunting in the forest: the girls are taught to baste embroidered aprons and weave belts for pleated skirts (the kind that Polish maidens once wore when they used to frolic in the meadow), and the boys are taught the secrets of glueing cartons together or cutting animals out of wooden board. Not only is this division of the sexes outmoded; éven its backwardness is outmoded. Even the most robust male should know how to sew on a button, and the most feminine female would be much better off if she could take care of a short circuit, glue a leg on to a chair or change a tire.

Even the most ardent advocates of the Israeli male are unlikely to accuse him of being the perfect gentleman (discounting the brief period of courtship, which can lift a man to superhuman levels): he has no manners, he plods ahead into the elevator, he misses no opportunity of not giving up his seat on the bus, he does not help a woman with her coat nor does he open the car door for her (except in the aforementioned impression-making period). Perhaps this is how it should be, for here the men are repaying the women in their own coin: you want equal rights— then suffer the disabilities! No coddling. If the truth be told, manners are not a matter of sex and are not merely a male obligation. If the Israeli women had manners they would rear a generation of sons who would know how to behave towards a girl, an elderly woman, a man, a woman, a child, a dog. Brashness, like murder, begins at home.

The status of the Israeli male in society is subject to two factors: in one direction, there is a tendency to curb his rights, by virtue of the nature of the consumers' society in America, which we imitate, consciously or unintentionally; in the other direction, his status is elevated by the peculiar situation in which Israel finds itself today. In a locality subject to warfare the first instinct is for security, and the worth of the protector goes up. It was natural for the men who remained behind on the home front, when the major mobilization took place in May 1967, to have felt old, useless and inferior. With no aspersion on their patriotism, it can be said that the desire to be where the men were provided sufficient reason for their despondency.

From a certain viewpoint, Zahal is the alternative, in Israel, to the clubs, pubs, bistros and executive luncheons; it provides a substitute for the English or American stags and smokers. Feminine company, though charming, has its drawbacks: one must behave, keep up appearances, practice reserve. This is when the women in the vicinity are young. The company of mature women, particularly if they happen to be clever, imposes the aura of Big Sister covering up for you, in the best instance, or of prim Mother. In either case, male company is much more preferable. Zahal, custodian of the last male preserve, fortifies the unit spirit, even when the men are employed in the PX's. You will note that, in times of tranquillity, the servicewoman is allowed to shine forth in all her smart glory, but when the country is in a life-and-death struggle, she is left behind. The cameramen want her next to the mortar, Uzi in hand, but Zahal likes her in the background. The Six Day War went by the book of the past century, despite the 'Mirages and the AMX's: the women waited at the threshold for the men to come back from the fighting. Yet, after his return to her, there is an alcove inside him to which entrance to women is strictly forbidden.

Murder Begins at Home

ONCE A MURDER becomes a statistic it loses its horror. The human being, slain by his brother, is gone from the scene; the fear and the hatred fade away, and so does the sense of finality of the act, leaving nothing in its aftermath, neither restitution nor atonement. Only the statistic remains, and it has nothing to do with either Cain or Abel.

Statistically, we in Israel make a fairly good showing, i.e., there's no reason for undue concern. To put it otherwise, compared with other nations, the incidence of murder in Israel is comparatively low—one murder per year per 100,000 inhabitants. The significance of this computation, if there is any at all, is that two Haifa residents will meet with a violent end this year, aside from the dozen who will die in traffic accidents. Perhaps; you can't really depend on figures.

Even as a statistic and a determinant of our rating among the nations (we secretly hope that we *are* different), murder is a slippery item. It is difficult to classify, to sort into categories, like dead butterflies in a cardboard box. The police are very good at maintaining the murder files, where they lay to rest the corpse of every victim of violence, including those slain by Arab infiltrators (actually these do not belong in our analysis of Murder Israeli Style, since the perpetrators are not ours). The total number of killings hit its peak at the height of the *fedayeen* activity on the eve of the Sinai campaign (73, in 1956), and dropped in times of comparative peace. In 1964, only four cases of murder originated from the other side of the border. This situation has changed considerably by Arab terrorist infiltration since the Six Day War.

Having deducted, from the annual total, the murders committed by infiltrators, we are left with a more or less set figure: twenty to thirty cases a year; interestingly enough, this figure has remained constant, despite the increase in the size of our populace. In the early years of the state, the police used to classify murder cases according to nationality, Jews separately and minorities separately. Later, in deference to the concept of equality, this procedure was dropped. But I, in putting together, as the police do, an identifying kit of our Jewish murderer (whose very existence has not been accepted for generations), shall practice discrimination and disregard the incidence of murder among the minorities (this accounts for one-fourth to one-third of the total, and they differ from Jewish cases in motivation; blood vengeance and family honor are still matters of consequence). And so we are left with ten to twenty purely Jewish murders per year, but the conclusions are still not clear. Homicide is homicide, according to that particular section of the law, but the murderer is not always a killer, as we look at it. The father is afraid that he is afflicted with heart disease; he shoots his wife, his children, himself, and his name goes down on the police blotter as a murderer. An elderly dentist anesthesizes his mentally disturbed daughter and puts an end to his own life; statistically, this, too, goes down as murder. These we remove from our list—all these heads of families who, in a dark moment of despair, took their children along with them, and thus died twice.

We shall also remove the mothers—there were three or four of them—who did away with their incurably afflicted children, in body or spirit. The list also notes a dozen teenage girls who found themselves pregnant before society was prepared to acknowledge their motherhood (they had neither the sense nor the time for an abortion, which can still be performed in Israel without undue difficulty, in a hospital, paid for by the Sick Fund); they gave birth out in the field and in toilets, alone or in the presence of infuriated female kinfolk, then strangled the infant in its first breath and buried the body in the dunes or wrapped it in paper and threw it into the trash can—only to have the small bundles testify against them, post-mortem. We shall not count them either.

This leaves us with some 200 genuine murderers, from 1948 through 1966, an eerie procession of misery, of afflicted souls and duped lovers, wrathful husbands and irritated neighbors, young

233

and old and bespectacled and paunchy—just like a queue when you're waiting for the clinic to open. Very few among them have the killer image—the tough ones whose faces betray their inner violence, those who murdered for money, premeditated and coldly calculated.

The Israeli murderer commits the crime usually inside the home. No place is so prone to murder as the family retreat, and no occupation is as hazardous as being a married woman. Again and again, the same details, the same scene. A man comes into the police station, his hands stained red, and tells the officer on duty: I murdered my wife. Husbands tend to use the knife; rarely do they throttle or use a blunt instrument. The motivation—other than the buildup of the hostility which at times enter every home —is always uniform: injured male pride; the woman in question (the mistress, the common wife, the fiancee) had threatened to leave him, or she had left him and refused to come back, or she had deceived him, or told him the child wasn't his (she may not have told him, but he suspected, and she may not have cheated, but he was afraid she was going to). The plot has other variations. One man lit mourning candles near the body, before going to the police; others wait for the police to arrive. Ages differ; the impulse is there even at 66. The occupations—watchman, beggar, textile worker, kibbutz member.

Murder is one of the last remaining functions where the division of the sexes is glaringly evident. Women are usually the victims, rather than the perpetrators of murder, but the gentleness of the feminine soul is not the reason; ask anyone who ever saw the monster into which the weaker sex can be transformed under prison or concentration camp conditions. She may experience the impulse to commit murder, but there are barriers between the impulse and the act; the children, physical weakness, fear. There were only two cases of the wife slaying the husband; in both, the circumstances were not clear and the sentence was light. When a woman commits murder, the act carries greater logic: she kills not the one whom she wants to keep from straying but the one who is seducing him to stray—her rival.

Murder motivated by factors other than emotion, rare among Jews in general, does not exist at all among Jewesses. This may stem from the fact that Jewish women still live mostly within the bounds of their home and are not placed in the path of many temptations (an anti-feminist may even claim that planning a crime on the level of the Great Train Robbery in England calls for the mind of a genius, not to be found among women). But quite a different reason suggests itself: a young girl of a more or less passable appearance who dreams of all the good things in life does not have to resort to robbery to acquire them. The bed is more to the point and far less risky. The mistress of a wealthy elderly gentleman can get more from him than a masked bandit.

The annals of murder in Israel reflect the history of the land. Each period has its own particular brand. During the first years of the state, most cases were a reverberation of the War of Independence: two soldiers killed four Arab women to avenge the death of their cousin in the fighting; an old man was shot to death in the act of stealing a rug from an abandoned Arab house in Safed. Count Bernadotte was assassinated: "On the date of September the 17th, 1948, at 5:00 o'clock in the afternoon, Count Bernadotte left the Farm School adjoining the former palace of the High Commissioner in Jerusalem, with his entourage"—so begins the police announcement, which does not distinguish between prince and pauper; "several suspects were arrested and released for lack of evidence"—to this day.

Mass immigration, homelessness, wandering: Emil Tieffenborn, 41, married Esther Lernman, 26, as a formality which enabled her to get out of the Soviet Union. He traveled with her to Poland, then to Sweden and on to Israel, and when she didn't want to live with him any longer, he bound her to himself, eternally, in the Zerifin Immigrant Home. *Shanty-towns, tents, congestion, unemployment, poverty, dismay:* the Shar'abi children quarreled with the Ashaul kids, in Sha'ar Haaliyah; the mothers joined in and the fathers took a hand: one dead, five wounded. In the Mancy transit camp an altercation breaks out between Iraqi and Kurdish immigrants, someone picks up a rock. In the Tel-Adashim camp grocery, Daniel Rosenbach got into an argument with the cashier over an error in the addition; one grabbed a stone, the other went for a knife.

Era of austerity: all because of the then precious commodity: food ration stamps. Three men tried to rob the stamp stacks in the building of the Food Controller in Jaffa, shot the guard and

235

didn't have time to take anything. *The housing shortage:* the small room in Stanton Street, Lower Haifa, meant enough to David Salomon to kill his landlady when she asked him to move. The apportionment of key money was enough to induce a war-crippled veteran to enlist his two friends in doing away with Shmuel Ben-Zion, an affluent real estate man in Jerusalem.

The outward motivation seems so miserable, so trivial, so senseless compared with the severe and decisive act itself. Over what were people murdered in Israel? Over a bunch of radishes which a man from Kfar Nachman's transit camp pulled out of his neighbor's patch; over trash cans which a grocer in Ramat-Gan's Hapodim Street wanted to place under the window of a neighbor; over rolls and pastry that both the grocer and the restaurant owner were selling, next to each other in Peretz Street; over the roof across a balcony which cast a shadow over a neighbor's window. Worthless, miserable murders, dagger-like exclamation points after a sentence of lives of suffering, wanderings, instability, a battle for small things, over a job and a small room.

The immigrants became acclimated, and circumstances did improve. A murder now involves a respectable IL. 160,000 loan. And we are already on the way to becoming a people like other peoples: we've had the first Jewish murder over sports—the fellow was interfering with the soccer game, his neighbor said, when arrested.

Those who hailed the appearance of the first Jewish prostitute on the streets of Tel Aviv (this made us as good as the rest of the globe) had to consider one of the consequences: the first murder of a prostitute by her procurer, the kind of murder which Jews of pre-war Europe considered to be strictly a non-Jewish incidence, plausible only among the residents of Moldavanka in Isaac Babel's stories. Since then several prostitutes have come to a similar end —liquidated by their procurers when they threatened to leave them. At times the shepherd of the prostitute is also the husband, by address or legally, and he either gives himself up to the police, with the same "I've murdered my wife," or he lets the law have the privilege of finding him.

Three cases of murder had a homosexual background, one in a cave on the Carmel slope, where a Haifa newspaper vendor lived with his two young friends, and the other in the home of a decorator, age 67. In the sphere of homosexuality, integration with the Mediterranean region's notorious traditions is still in its infancy.

Family honor is still a motive for murder among Jews as well, in the transitory generation of Israel's new society: a father stabs his daughter for having conceived out of wedlock; another kills his because he suspected her of going out with men (the postmortem showed that she was still a virgin). Relations between Jewesses and Arabs, a phenomenon with which we shall have to make increasing peace in the future, have in the meantime claimed a victim among the Jewish girls: Rina Dali, 19, was set afire, alive, in her parents' home, while in the next room the family sat in judgment.

Not even the kibbutz, rampart against many of life's problems, is immune to the ravages of infatuation. Only a few murders have taken place in the kibbutzim—and all on account of love. A Neve Or girl shot her lover because she was afraid he was going to leave her, and a woman of Kibbutz Amir killed her rival of Kfar Gileadi. A South American immigrant in Mesillot killed his wife's lover. An exception was the case of Abigail Solomon, 29, of India, whose strangled body was found at the edge of Kibbutz Giv'at Brenner; the act stemmed from motives (blood venegeance and secret symbols) far removed from collective settlements, and the kibbutz locale was purely incidental.

Some places and addresses go well with murder, from the vantage point of the armchair spectator. Cafe Esperanza, in the seafront slums of Old Haifa (two drunks argue whether the cafe radio should be tuned in to *Kol Yisrael* or the Arabic station; one dies). A tavern in the old town of Ramle, the old Arab quarter in Jaffa behind the port, the Hatikva section in Tel Aviv—dilapidated houses, tin shacks, poverty, congestion, filth, crime-breeding soil; all are locales for mayhem. But murder can invade, by mistake, serene sections with private homes and well-kept gardens: Ramot Hashavim, Ramat Hasharon, Nahariya, Neveh Sha'anan. And how could a father have murdered his family on Ani Ma'amin ("I Believe") Street?

If the murderer is not a husband or a lover or a father or a son (several sons liquidated their mothers because they refused to give them money or nagged them), then chances are that he is demented. Without becoming entangled in the judicial maze as to what

237

constitutes responsibility for actions and the famous McNaughton ruling (quoted at great length by every neophyte attorney) and the extent of the murderer's sanity as indicated in the course of the act itself, we find that quite a few of the murders in Israel were committed by mentally disturbed individuals, people who had been under doctor's care or had been released or escaped from mental institutions, prior to the act: Soldier Peter Stein, 23, climbed the Gan-Yavne water tower and shot the first three people in his sights; Yitzhak Resnik, the tourist from Argentina who came to Israel because his mental state "had improved," stabbed a classmate in the Hebrew course and, two years later, did the same to the chef of the institution to which he had been committed; smiling Zalman Mandelbroit, an Ata Textiles employee, shot his foreman, and Victor Nizan murdered little Rahel Levin near the Hiriya transit camp. Of three little girls murdered in Israel since its inception—a very small number, compared with what is going on all over the world—two met their death at the hands of the demented.

Murder, as such, no longer upsets the Israeli public. New immigrants are no longer shown the "special attraction" of earlier days: Danoch's padlocked store in the Yemenite Quarter. He was the first Israeli sentenced to death on a murder charge (the death sentence has since been abolished and Danoch was set free, long ago). Murder today must present several fringe facets in order to hold the headlines for more than a day. Added notoriety must involve one or more known personalities, or a romantic background or a good deal of the mysterious or perverse, or be tied in with a robbery—perhaps all of these combined.

The first murder in Israel which contained all the elements which turn mere violence into a notorious episode was the Meir Park murder. Today, the storm which that act precipitated, twenty years ago, would be regarded as rather puerile. We have achieved sophistication even where murder is concerned.

Two *cause celebre*'s in the young state were those of 16-year-old Maggie, mother of an out-of-wedlock son, murdered by her lover, and an Israeli Army sergeant's murder of Mira of Kibbutz Kinneret; guides in the Tiberias area still point out the dilapidated hut on the shore of the Sea of Galilee where the act took place. The murderers have since been released, as have most of those convicted of the crime in the '50's. At least, in abolishing the death penalty, we have unfettered ourselves from the Middle Ages and no longer adhere to the biblical doctrine of a tooth for a tooth, an eye for an eye, and often a life for a life (although some commentators interpret the doctrine in a more liberal fashion: *not more* than an eye for the loss of an eye).

A life sentence usually ends up as 24 years' imprisonment, then it drops to 18 and sometimes 12 or even eight years, what with presidential amnesties and one-third off for good behavior. As you study the sentences meted out in murder trials you are repeatedly impressed with the fact that our judges and Presidents are indeed progeny of the compassionate, and this consoles us when we contemplate the rigors of bureaucracy in other spheres.

The sympathy aroused by passion murders does not hold for murder committed in the act of robbery. The amounts for which men kill are so pitifully small! Abraham Chapnick shot Siman-Tov, the watchman, for IL 200 (even though, in 1952, this was equivalent to today's IL 1,000). Real estate broker Nadler was murdered for IL 400. To get hold of Aharon "Archick's" IL 440, a Bat-Yam murder gang put a sleeping drug into his tea and finished him off with an axe. Rafi Blitz, who fired into the crowd in his frantic getaway from the Zafon Theatre, didn't have time to grab a single coin from the box office. The two bandits who became frightened at the sound of a window shutter being lowered, shot the manager of Bank Leumi in Beersheba and ran away empty-handed. Albert Politi struck a ragpicker over the head, on King George Street in Tel Aviv, over a bundle of old clothes, then went to the police with a story about some young man having sold him the telltale bundle. Thanks to American films and British detective fiction, we have come to understand—if not to accept—murder over millions as part of life—over property, valuable collections, a sizable legacy, yet there is something about these petty murders that makes us uncomfortable.

Only one case of murder involved a mysterious legacy: Yaacov Yossef, a dealer in real estate and foreign currency and a loan shark besides, was found murdered, near the Netanya Highway. Prior to his death he had revealed to his cronies that he was expecting an attempt on his life because of a large legacy awaiting him in the United States (whence he had come in 1934); the

239

person who was to transfer the legacy to him was likely to kill him in order to keep the money for himself. Hundreds of individuals were interrogated, but neither legacy (if one ever existed) nor murderer (there certainly was one or more) was ever found.

The incidence of real killers is relatively small. We assume that Jews, as a people, are averse to violence and crime, despite the outstanding Jewish-by-birth members of some of America's gangs. But it is also possible that geography has something to do with it; there is no such thing as an easy getaway across the border, and ports and airports can be watched with greater efficiency than the open highway. A robbery with murder involved sets the entire little country in motion. Falling into Arab hands is not much better than surrendering to the police. The greater intellects go for ill-gotten gains via the wider areas of forgery or embezzlement, then take off before the law gets wise to them. Statistics show that, in these areas, we are holding our own with the rest of the world.

One circumstance may really set the Israeli institution of murder apart from the others: the neighbors. They are everywhere. They are easily awakened by loud voices; they are suspicious of a door locked too long; they note that the lottery ticket dealer on Bank Street didn't open his store at the regular hour. The neighbors saw the accused leave his house, very much upset. The Israeli neighbor is alert to everything that goes on all around him. Walls are thin, the hallways narrow, the windows many. The Israeli neighbor is always on the watch.

The Public Problem of Privacy

EVERY MAN is king in his own home; pity, then, that the monarchy has long since been abolished among the Jewish people in Israel. Our home is not our castle. It is a glass cage, a railroad station, a tracking room. It is not George Orwell's ruthless Big Brother who is watching us. This role is being carried out, no less efficiently, by the devoted husband, the faithful wife, the worried parents, good neighbors, friends, acquaintances, people within the radius of a more or less reasonable perimeter, colleagues *in situ,* the press, the radio. Only an infinitesimal few, and for a snatch of time only, get to know the meaning of genuine privacy, and invariably they do not know enough to appreciate it.

Or to put it in another way: your home may indeed be your castle, but your castle is not your own. The rest of the family shares it, in close quarters between thin walls. The same two or three rooms do double and triple duty; they are the dining room, living room, guest room, den, bedroom, recreation room, music room. Actually, the parents have one room and the children the other, with a built-in closet for all. There is no such thing as knocking on a door before entering. The door, if there is one to begin with, is open anyway.

The housewife alone gets to know the meaning of privacy in the family home—and this only at given times, usually in the morning when the others go off to work or school. For a brief hour she can do whatever her heart desires: scrutinize her figure in the mirror, nibble from the box of chocolates (if the scrutiny is not too discouraging), try a new hairdo or run through the reducing exercises. She alone can enjoy the carefree feeling that only a locked door can give. She is usually also the sole member of the family who has a specific place where to hide things, behind the stack of sheets in the linen compartment or back of the canned stuff on the kitchen shelf. The others—the husband and children —don't have a single nook, in this de luxe apartment (three exposures, central hot water system, formica cupboard in the kitchen) to hide their secrets from prying eyes: the bug collection, the confidential diary or the bundle of old love letters, a bit of mad money or a photograph of a love long gone. Mama puts things in order, Mama empties pockets and arranges drawers, good Mama is into everything.

You do get to enjoy some privacy in a tub of hot water, behind a closed door (locking it is not always permissible; people have been known to faint in bathrooms), free to examine the woeful rotundity of your figure or the state of your toenails, or just let your mind wander—until a worried voice is heard through the door: "Are you all right?"

Only the toilet, being separate from the cubicle housing the tub or shower, remains as the last stronghold of complete privacy for *homo familias*. Here the door does have a lock, although the key may have been removed for the sake of the children's safety. Here the head of the family can isolate himself, without upsetting anyone. But the time is not unlimited; after all, others are waiting for their turn.

The most formidable threat to a man's privacy is the modern, pseudo-American Israeli style of construction: the large guest room, into which a stranger stumbles straight from the threshold of the main entrance, and the miniature bedrooms (but then, how much room *should* a bed take)? The guest-living room is where all the other family activities take place (as charmingly depicted in color by the family magazines: the father is reading, the mother is embroidering, the sons are playing, the daughter is writing, all in the warm glow of the delightfully designed floor lamp)—one apartment next to the other, buildings side by side, one balcony opposite its neighbor, the walls are thin and the windows are large. You cannot even quarrel sincerely with your own legitimate wife without an informal audience of the neighbors. They know everything: the degree of your hospitality, your listening habits, furniture style and the length of your underwear, the rug pattern and the sparkle of your pots. The greatest Israeli invention of the century, after the *sherut* (taxi-jitney), is the

242

balcony shutter enclosure. For years Tel Aviv lived out on the open balcony—ate there, relaxed, slept, spat out pumpkin seed shells and fed orange peels to the earth below. On the day that the shutter appeared, the balcony became an additional room; people suddenly discovered that in Israel, too, one can live indoors without injury to body and soul.

Any old-timer will recount the good old days when doors were kept unlocked to enable friends to drop in whenever they pleased. The doors are locked now, but this is no deterrent. People simply ring the doorbell. *Shalom,* we're here. This is a legacy of the open Russian heart and the Russian home, always filled with relatives, friends, neighbors. The Israeli home is always in a state of emergency against neighbors dropping in, for a moment; the children's pals, who pop in at the most inconvenient times; the guest who arrives without prior notice, invariably when the apartment is upside down, the husband is unshaven, the kids are sick, the refrigerator is out of order and all that's in the larder is an assortment of soggy bagels.

The Israeli way of life is simply incompatible with privacy. Why do most people in Israel live in apartment complexes, if not to be helpful to each other? To the neighbor you represent two lemons, while she to you is a package of margarine; you keep an eye on her sleeping baby, and she will pay the delivery man for your gas tank; you may use her telephone, and on your way there bring along the vacuum cleaner. Now, when you first live among the English you feel very much depressed: it's unnerving to live alongside people for months and not know anything about them, other than their names (and at times not even this), to feel that you can moan and groan until the walls tremble—and no one will come in to ask you what the matter is. On the other hand, you soon get to appreciate the convenience of not having unannounced callers. These, if any, are visiting Israelis.

One can be on good terms with a Frenchman and yet not cross his threshold. The Italian invites to his home none but the members of his family. The Israeli invites home, indiscriminately, strangers as well as acquaintances, people he has bumped into quite casually. In general he is proud of his home and its appointments, the living room and its ornaments, all obtained through hard work; he is also eager to hear what is going on elsewhere in the world, so that he may come to the conclusion that he has it better, despite everything. For him, to acquire friends for Israel is a commandment, a national obligation.

An open house has to be just that—not merely the large living room designed primarily for guests but everything: kitchen, bathroom, bedroom, built-in clothes closet. The guests wish to see and the host wishes to show. After all, the spread for the bed had been purchased specifically to impress visitors (and the painting above it to arouse their envy). All we need is that exponent of female efficiency, that European invention of the preceding century, the concierge, who looks to the orderliness of the home, distributes the mail and keeps the front door shut, who knows who's in and who's out, who stayed overnight and who brought the flowers, who bought a new piece of furniture and who sold her old fur coat. In Israel, with no such institution in existence, the neighbors fill the role (except for the orderliness bit).

The private life of the Israeli is broken into so often that you sometimes wonder how he manages to do his bit for the natural increase of the population. Bill collectors, tradesmen and fund-raisers pay their visits in person. The mail brings postcard appeals to your generosity, raffle tickets, greeting cards from charitable institutions or reminders of a variety of anniversaries. You didn't ask for all this and you are not obliged to accept it, but inertia prevents your sending it back. Now add to the personal visitations the poll takers who simply must know whether you prefer pea soup or how your refrigerator is holding up, nor can you overlook the emissaries of organizations who have come to ask you to be one of their pillars. Then there's the record player in the next apartment, featuring Petula Clark when you're really in the mood for Marlene Dietrich.

Everything in life being relative, sensitivity over privacy is no exception. If you've been pampered and have read too many articles about personal freedom; if you have secessionist tendencies and for some reason prefer seclusion to the company of your well-wishers, then you are bound to feel that too many people are sticking their nose into your business. But if you were ever privileged to live in a totalitarian state, you will appreciate all those wonderful little things that you can do in privacy and un-disturbed: to read whatever book you're up to reading, including pornography or the Russian press; to listen to any radio broad-cast within hearing, including the Arab enemies and defamers of your state; to discuss the oversights of the Government, with your children listening; to arouse the envy of the neighbors, if this makes life sweeter for you; to wear shorts or a flowing robe, according to your means and your personal taste; to bring forth progeny, in whatever number you wish and in tune with your mood; to talk on the telephone and have no fear of wiretapping.

Israel has few firms engaged in gathering data for commercial use, nor are we in any immediate danger of getting a central information pool, as they have in the United States. Israel's population registry asks for the family name, parents' names, date and place of birth, personal status and citizenship, address and occupation—as is the case in most countries—plus some data peculiar to Israel: date of immigration, nationality and, especially, religion, an item which most countries regard as being strictly personal and of no possible interest to the authorities (elsewhere Jews have been the first to rise up against its being recorded in government files).

Our elections are absolutely private and secret. The ballots are kept out of reach and the envelope is sealed. But by the time you reach the polling booth, the entire country knows for whom you'll be voting. This is all right, if you don't care whether the world knows it or not, especially if yours is the right vote for the right party; but what if you're one of those oddballs who think that their party affiliation is their own private affair? As long as it's only a minor party hack who drops around and wants to know if "you're one of us," you can stick to principle (if it doesn't jeopardize your job) and tell him that it's the business of none but yourself. But how are you going to handle a Committeeman, a friend in the Movement, who pays a visit to talk about things in general and the quality of your brandy in particular, then says, in afterthought: "Someone has told me that you intend voting for those skunks. You aren't, are you?" This is one of those leading questions which fetters you regardless of the answer you manage to give. And why should you have to justify yourself when the matter is essentially between you and your set opinions?

In some countries it is considered an intrusion on privacy to ask a man about his income. We think that it would be well-nigh

impossible to break the ice at a gathering of men if we were not
to open with the friendly question: "And how much do you earn?"
In Israel, furthermore, this item cannot be kept secret indefinitely.
Those on salary are given away by their rating and scale, and the
monetary calculation can be done quite easily. Where a member
of the free professions is concerned, the determinant is his mode
of living: if he employs a full-time maid, drives a 1500 cc car,
and goes abroad every year, then he must be good for at least a
net two thousand Israel Pounds per month. After all, since when
are financial matters considered to be a person's private domain?
Most of the money goes to the Treasury, anyway, and the Treasury
belongs to the public—so why all the secrecy?

Pregnancy, no matter how much you want to keep it private, is
bound to come forward in time. Illness becomes public at once.
In some way, via somebody (another hospital inmate, a friend of
the nurse, the wife of the clerk at the information desk, an acquaintance of your friend's confidante), everyone knows immediately what ails your bones, kidneys, liver or gall bladder, what
limb or organ is in danger and which one is not, whether you'll
survive or not. Some people love to talk about their illnesses and
others hold this to be their private affair, but opinion flowing
around them all will have them out of this world even when they
are still very much alive.

Every individual has the right to protect himself against willful
intrusion on his personal life, his home and his correspondence
—so says the Human Rights Convention, to which Israel is also a
signatory. However, the Convention abides in Geneva, and we are
here; the Convention deals with legalities, and we deal with
reality. An Israeli citizen may write to anyone he wishes, and no
one will know the contents of the envelope except the writer, the
recipient and the censor (for perfectly justified reasons of security);
he may receive as many letters as he desires, and the only other
person who will read them will be his wife (for just as perfectly
justified reasons of security). If she does not open the letter before
it gets to you, she puts the envelope down before you with the
significant facial expression: "So, a letter for you!"—to which
there is little you can say except: "You can read it." Of course,
you can have the letters go to your place of business, and the
secretary will play the role of your wife, with equal efficiency.

It should be noted, with some regret, that, in so small a country as Israel, it's impossible to keep a secret very long, especially in the Establishment, and even more so when it concerns him and her. We have no secluded love-nests in the hills where a boss can while away a few days with his secretary. There are no hunting lodges in a forest, or intimate inns on little-known beaches. There is no place where you can be sure that some exuberant acquaintance won't come up and beam jovially: "What are *you* doing around these parts?" One may be able to keep a romance from one's legitimate wife, or from one's husband; they are usually the last to know, or the last who want to know. But there can be no secrets from neighbors, colleagues, office receptionists, relatives and friends. To succeed in maintaining a love affair in Israel, one has to be an ex-member of the underground.

We thirst for privacy especially when we want to hold one to a secret, but by that time privacy has slipped away. We must seek to achieve it when our actions are still as white as the snows of the Lebanon, when anyone is welcome to know our deeds, associations and net worth. Privacy demands sacrifice—not to expose your heart, not to seek confidants, not to be sought after by the press, not to appear on any radio programs and run the risk of being asked personal questions, not to be friendly with neighbors. All of which poses the question as to whether privacy is worth the sacrifice.

In the Land of Canine

THERE'S NOTHING in Jewish law, to be sure, which forbids a man to keep a dog, but there's no encouragement for it, either. The canine image, as depicted in Holy Writ, is not particularly sympathetic: the biblical dog, if he is not obligingly holding back his tongue, is licking the blood of our enemies or feasting on the fallen or returning to his vomit, or, under the best of all circumstances, is dead. Small wonder that the pious Jew has always kept his distance from the dog; the nations among whom Israel sojourned were steeped in animal-worship—cats and dogs and cranes and peacocks—and it was natural that the Chosen People should keep away, as much as possible, from animals which were not co-opted for providing a livelihood, and to reject the animal as the subject and object of human love.

Life in the diaspora only served to widen the gap between the Jew and the dog. The cramped style of living in the ghettos was not conducive to the maintenance of pets of any kind, and even if the room were there, the tendency was not. The dog was associated with the Gentile: the patron, the superintendent, the officer, the governor. Dogs accompanied the representatives of these men of authority as they made their rounds, and they were set by their masters, more than once, upon the wearers of the long cloaks. Moreover, strict adherence to the tenets of the Law precluded keeping a dog in the house. How would one go about explaining to the pooch that the spare ribs dug up from the Gentile's back yard were not compatible with Jewish dietary laws? And how should the dog be impressed with the fact that chasing rats on the Sabbath is unbecoming to a Jewish animal, who should be resting in accordance with the Fourth Commandment? And what should one do with a dog seen eating bread on Passover? And how long must a dog wait, after a carnivorous meal, before he can switch to dairy foods? Be that as it may, pious Jews always bore an antipathy toward dogs. As Dr. Chaim Weizmann once expressed it, if a Jew loves a dog, then either the dog isn't much of a dog or the Jew isn't much of a Jew.

The early Jewish settlers in the Land of Israel adhered to the tradition of their forbears. Under Turkish rule, Jews kept dogs only for purposes of sheep herding or protecting life and property. Urban canines, pets and toy dogs came to the country in the company of the German immigration. And indeed, for many years one of the synonyms of a Yecki was "dog-on-a-leash." A doctor, a pair of glasses and a dog would go out for a Sabbath stroll, and the old-timers shrugged: "That's for Gentiles."

Association with a dog always indicated the measure of his Jewish owner's free-thinking and assimilation in the general population. Dogs were owned by Jews of Vienna, Moscow and Prague, but nowhere in greater numbers than in Berlin. Inasmuch as the Germans loved dogs—disciplined dogs who obeyed their masters to the letter—and since German Jews admired the culture of the land and strove whichever way to be part thereof, they also went in for dogs and learned to like them. The Yeckis brought along with them Doberman pinschers, wolfhounds and dachshunds. The British of Mandate days, lovers of dogs by nationality, imported terriers and setters and boxers and cocker spaniels. But the true canine population explosion began only with the establishment of the state, when the immigrants from Europe brought either dogs (the poolies, quadruped balls of tight woolen yarn, are the Hungarian contribution; the Pekingese came with the Rumanians and the toy poodles with the French) or an emotional fondness for dogs, whom they acquired, from local stock, as soon as they could afford it. Along with golf, prostitution, beauty queens, underwater fishing, hunting and passion murders, Israel's registered 20,000 canines give proof that we are on our way to joining the family of decadent nations.

Dog fashions all over the world keep changing, as do clothing and furniture. Where are the lazy fat mopsies that decorated every bourgeois home as late as the end of the last century? Where have you strayed, O small black and brown pinschers so adored by the generation of World War One? Gone is the Golden

Age of the terriers, and the glory of the dachshund has faded
away. We in Israel are lagging a bit behind the new universal dog
fashions; we are still in the era of the small French poodle, when
elsewhere it is the Chihuahua that is the latest rage. We have just
begun to take in the vanguard of canine aristocracy—the Afghan
hound, but it doesn't take much to develop this breed: he, she
and two months of pregnancy, plus the fortitude to survive the
rigors of Israeli life.

There is a definite correlation between the rise in the canine
population and the rise in Israeli living standards, reflected not
only in the choice of breeds but in the very maintenance of a dog
on the premises. The upkeep of a dog, as that of a child or a
mistress, costs money. In a modest home, assuming that the dog
is willing to exist on pot luck, his cost of upkeep—counting
immunization, license, spraying and other pleasures—comes to
some fifteen or twenty Pounds a month. But if nothing's too good
for the beast, and he simply must be given a hairdo, hairwash
and medical examination at frequent intervals, his monthly
upkeep may run higher than a welfare allocation for an entire
family. And if a healthy dog is expensive to maintain, an indis-
posed canine can cost twice as much. There is as yet no Sick
Fund, in Israel, for dogs; perhaps no consensus has been reached
as whether separate funds should be set up for Labor Federation
dogs, National Party dogs, or General Zionist dogs.

Our lack of dog cemeteries is even more deplorable, although
we are not surprised—not when we see what goes on at the Tel
Aviv regional cemetery in Holon: beggars rattling their poor
boxes, bulldozers leveling additional parcels, funeral corteges
awaiting their turn at the Purification Building. If this is what
human beings can expect as they are laid to their eternal rest,
what can await a dog? Only he who has lost a dog, his compan-
ion of many years whom he loved and to whom he became
attached, and who now has to throw its body, wrapped in a sack
or plain paper, into the garbage container or to put it into a suit-
case and ride far beyond the city limits and find a spot where he
can legally bury it—only he knows how hard it is to say, Here
Lies My Dog.

Some Jews are all for maintaining dogs for practical use: sheep-
dogs and watchdogs and police dogs and seeing-eye dogs and

dogs needed for a livelihood, but a dog to no purpose repels, irritates and frightens them. The trouble is that dogs can readily distinguish those who are afraid of them and those who are afraid of Virginia Woolf, and they react accordingly, baring their teeth and acting as though they had no reassuring bark at all; they know you for what you are, you miserable dog-hater!

Many of us in Israel resent dog owners because they are too devoted to their pets—as though only human beings should merit the care and worry and love that they show to the four-legged creatures. And yet, in many cases, the love which a dog receives from its owner is the love that others, humans, had rejected. The lonely man who lives with a dog is not lonesome. At least he has someone to greet him at the door, someone waiting to be caressed, someone who needs care and affection. As long as the Jew was alone and pious, he spoke with God; now that his piety is practically gone, he talks to his dog (or to his psychiatrist, if he is very wealthy or is a member of a *kibbutz*).

Some people simply don't have the kind of home where a dog can be comfortably quartered. Others have no time for dogs, and still others have no feeling for dog-keeping. Not everyone is capable of dashing along the boulevard, tied to a dog, and stopping, in full view of his amused neighbors, at every third tree in order to enable his charge to select the precise spot where to answer nature's call; nor can everyone talk to a dog as if it were a human being: "Come on home, Lucky, right now!" A person has to overcome a certain something before he can become a dog owner—the fear of appearing ridiculous to others, of becoming sentimental in public, of being observed in his loneliness or of losing his dignity. There are men who just won't empty a garbage pail, and others who wouldn't wheel a stroller even if their male heir is in it. And there are those who won't be seen on the street with a dog.

Fortunately for the species, border incidents and the Six Day War have shown that the dog is an efficient yet inexpensive defensive weapon (and canine embargoes are not yet in style). This has increased the demand for dogs and has eased the plight of the inhibited, who are ready to state their love of country in public but who will acknowledge their love for dogs only deep in their innermost heart.

Nowhere in the world do dogs speak as many languages as they do here in Israel. Our dogs speak German and French and English and Hungarian and Rumanian and Czech and Russian and Polish and even Yiddish. Some dogs speak Hebrew plus one foreign language. A Jewish dog has a talent for tongues. Also, the language obviously influences a dog's character. A Yiddish-speaking cur cannot possibly palm himself off as the peer of the elegant French-speaking pooch, and a Polish-speaking dog is of necessity more flustered than his English-speaking colleague. Two instances give away a man's origin: when he counts his money aloud and when he speaks to his dog.

Dogs with owners of diaspora origin usually have foreign names: Waldi is invariably a dachshund, Bobi is a pinscher. Blackie fits a setter and Bebe is a Pekingese. Rex and Hector identify boxers, and Lassie, to be sure, is a collie. Dogs who reside in a purely Hebrew environment, being second or third generation in the land, sport truly Hebrew names: Uzi (strong), Amitz (brave), Abir (noble), Barak (lightning), Ziv (bright), Gil (joy), Hetz (arrow). Names such as Sh'hori (Blackie) and Humi (Brownie) are usually reserved for dogs of unintelligible breed. Those who preach co-existence in the region will be happy to know that we have our local strain, the Canaanite, but he, like the natives, tends to be wild and cannot be easily disciplined.

Around The Clock

Holidays and Their Problems

THE UNDERLYING problem that Israel's numerous holidays and festivals pose to the average non-religious Israeli is for him to find an ideological basis for the welcome fact that schools and business premises are closed, without getting the Lord into the picture. Some holidays—Passover, Purim, Tu Bishevat (Arbor Day) and Chanukah—readily lend themselves to a national-historical-pastoral interpretation. Others, such as Shavuot (Pentecost) and Succot (Tabernacles), are still without secular sanction, while a few—Rosh Hashanah (New Year) and Yom Kippur (Day of Atonement)—are exclusively in the shelter of the wings of the Almighty.

This drawback of the High Holy Days could be overcome more easily if they would have some tangible symbolic expression, such as the masquerades of Purim, the *matza* on Passover, and the candle-lighting on Chanukah, which lend the aura of tradition to any Jewish home proud of its liberalism. But all that we have for Rosh Hashanah, and even more for Yom Kippur, is prayers (mostly penitential) and listings of transgressions—matters of significance, perhaps, to the observant and the pious, but rather unworkable from the botanical-archeological-rational approach. Many individuals who have no compunctions about eating non-kosher food all year round tend to fast, more or less, on Yom Kippur, with no logical reason or explanation for this annual attack of religiosity (it is understood that the memory of the parents, blessed be their rest, has something to do with it) other than the lame excuse that it would not be fair to excite the appetite of the neighbors with the aroma of fried onions or the fragrance of coffee—not when they are being flagellated with fasting.

On Succot, there's nothing wrong with decorating the balcony

255

with colorful paper chains and Japanese lanterns and eating out-doors around the Italian-style wrought-iron table. Now with Old Jerusalem liberated, we may include a jaunt to Jerusalem and a visit to the Rockefeller Museum, a stroll through the alleys of the market place and a snack of *hummous* with sharp relishes. All the other Succot trappings—the Four Elements (palm, myrtle, willow and citron), Hoshanah Rabba (climax of the holiday), Shmini Atzeret and Simchat Torah (expression of love for the Law)—are too involved and legalistically encumbered to explain to the family in detail. It is much more convenient to consider Succot as the Harvest Festival, which lends itself to rejoicing because the grape harvest was not too abundant to cause a drop in prices and because the apple harvest is safely stored under refrigeration, until prices go up. Any other presentation of Succot cannot hope to escape the theological queries of the inquisitive youngsters.

"Round and round, without a stop, on Chanukah spins and whirls the top." Now this is a holiday to our progressive taste! The Maccabean revolt does credit to nationalism; the *menorah*, designed by an avant-garde artist, is a marvelous item of decor for the home; lighted candles are always esthetic, jelly doughnuts are delicious (unless they are cold and dry), and the miracle of the seven-day extension can be explained most rationally—the oil that the Maccabees used was highly concentrated. In short, had we not been endowed with the Chanukah holiday we would have had to invent it, if for no other reason than to provide our emissaries abroad with an adequate counterattraction to Christmas.

The customs of the Gentiles are a great help to Jews-by-national-ity-only, ranging from the cascade of greeting cards sent to friend and foe on Rosh Hashanah, to Bar Mitzvah parties in rented halls with a dance band, an M.C. and an invariably dreary meal. It's too bad that Sylvester (New Year's Eve) Night sounds so un-Jewish; readily celebrated in Israel, it would gain greater accept-ance by Jewish tradition if it were called Michael Night or Joseph Night, perfectly good Christian saints with perfectly good Jewish names.

"Tu Bishevat is here, the New Year of the Trees." We go out to plant trees in a grove in memory of a departed soul, unless it pours and the event is postponed until further notice. As long as the curious youngsters do not ask who set the date of Tu (the 15th of the month) Bishevat, instead of the 23rd of Sivan, it's possible to survive the holiday without any acute problem of ignorance.

Now Purim, you see, was never a problem. The author of the Book of Esther was considerate enough of the non-religious public not to mention therein the name of the divinity at all. The tale of Queen Esther is of questionable educational value, if we choose to delve into her ambitions and tactics, but, as sages and communists maintain, the end justifies the means. The main thing is, that when the smoke lifted, the Jews "rejoiced and were merry." There are masquerades, loud but mild carousing, *hamentashen* parties, and there's not a soul in Israel—be he an atheist, an uncompromising blasphemer, or merely a new immigrant with a shallow Jewish background—who would find it problematical to celebrate Purim, unless he is one of those unfortunate creatures who always feels worst when all around them there is gaiety and laughter.

Passover—the Festival of Spring, of Freedom, of the Exodus from Egypt—lacks not for historical symbolism. Even the *Haggadah* (the Recitation) is quite practical, if we delete such boring segments as "The Merciful One shall be King" or "The breath of every living thing shall praise Thy name" and substitute snatches of Bialik's poetry and a bit from "Happiness and joy and cheer, for spring and Passover are here," the way the *kibbutz* version has it. Actually, this night is sufficiently distinguished from all other nights in that the entire family, and all the members of the *kibbutz,* are together for the whole evening, once a year; there are *matzot* and *matza balls* (distinguishing the Passover menu from all other menus); there are the four cups of wine which one is bidden to drink; there is the *afikoman,* the half-*matza* hidden early in the ceremony and later discovered by the children and given up in return for prizes. Every man and his Passover; every Seder according to its own version.

Lag Baomer needs no Jewish scholarship to explain it, despite the misleading title which refers to some complicated reckoning of time during which one may not wed. The important thing is that the youngsters light bonfires, bake potatoes, sit around, stare open-mouthed into the tongues of flame and stay up late with the glowing embers. Lag Baomer has nothing to worry about, regardless in whose honor the bonfires are lit—Rabbi Akiba, Rabbi Simeon Bar-Yochai or Bar Kochba, even though the last mentioned has an advantage over his competitors; one can relate more readily to his rebellion against the Romans (135 C.E.), without getting involved with miracles.

Shavuot, on the other hand, poses a problem for any urbanite who owes an explanation of the holiday to his progeny. As the Festival of First Fruits, Shavuot is custom-tailored to the *kibbutzim,* where goats bleat and lambs gambol and hay is stacked and girls dance barefoot on the lawn and underfoot is the latest crop of infants, but the urbanites just cannot cope with the gross demands of the Festival, in the fashion that the uncouth tillers of the soil do it, and their very being rebels against the outdated substitute custom of bringing early fruits to the edifice of the Jewish National Fund in town, which, in the eyes of the secular set, is even on a lower level than the rabbinate. Shavuot as the festival commemorating the giving of the Torah at Mount Sinai has other problems: on the one hand, we love the Bible and have no complaint about commemorating its date of publication, but we do entertain some doubt as to the author's copyright, and until the matter is clarified by the scholarly among the members of the Israel Association of Authors and Composers we shall hold our compliance and enthusiasm in abeyance.

Man needs festivals to ease the mundaneness of the year. They are the milestones, the gulps of air as we swim with the current of time, the defined seasons for golden dreams and rosy planning, and not even the members of the League Against Religious Coercion would dream of giving up any of them because of ideological reservations. After all, the man who is not blessed with offspring can celebrate the holidays in his own fashion—sleeping, drinking, hunting, underwater fishing, gorge himself with food or detective stories or do anything he wants, without any ideological content intruding. But he who has contributed to the continuity of the nation must make an effort in the direction of "Jewish living," so that at least his children should have what to say, in later years, when they appear on the "My Father's House" broadcast. Always, as I listen to this program, I almost expect the hero to rear back and cry out: "My father's house was terrible: my parents were uninteresting and I was glad when I got out"—as so often happens in real life. But the chances of such individuals appearing on this program are nil, not when they are lacking the necessary ingredients: memories of a snowy-white Sabbath tablecloth and of candlelight reflected in the glowing faces of the gathering—things that belong to the world of the solid citizen. Only a rebel, a revolutionary, a fighter for sexual freedom tends to come from a father's house bare of the warm festival atmosphere.

All of these problems have their source in the Sabbath. Even if we overlook the unreasonable divine demand to refrain from driving, swimming or football on the ordained Day of Rest, we cannot shunt the Sabbath aside as though it is not of our own creation, or eat, on Sabbath Eve, the same tomato salad-egg-buttered bread-yogurt of the rest of the week, and to read the same skimpy format newspaper. We must do something to mark the Sabbath from the ordinary day, and the easiest and most proven method is a hot meal on the Sabbath, preferably with soup and at least one traditionally Jewish course, before the family scatters for get-togethers with classmates, the old gang, the friends. In these confused times of reducing diets it is not love but religion that tests man's intestinal fortitude, and there it blossoms forth, in the form of chopped liver on *chalah, cholent, gefilte* fish, honeycake. Out of this delight in food, out of this pantheon of Jewish gastronomics there may one day emerge a revival of the faith, God willing—and religious political parties notwithstanding.

Nor is contemporary literature doing anything to ease the Sabbath struggle within us. Yehuda Leib Peretz, Hayim Nachman Bialik and the other instructive writers whose works nourished the Israeli in his youth, describe, most charmingly, the familial and idyllic Sabbath: candles, chants and melodies, synagogue worship, fish, miracles bringing Sabbath cheer to the homes of the poor, and these tales sank deeply into his consciousness, to the point that he could feel that this would be the legacy he would leave to his children, long after National Insurance will have defrayed, at least partly, the cost of his funeral. Had our authors appended, to the biblical accounts for school children, a few stories extolling the beauty of the Sabbath as spent in bed (for purposes of overtime sleeping and reading only) or in a bathtub bubbling with fragrant foam, or in listening to the radio and/or watching television (telecast from Egypt), or in going through the Saturday supplements of the dailies and the foreign magazines, or in a swim at Herzliah Beach or a hike through Galilee, they would have spared us the repeated feeling of discomfiture because we, charged with the task of increasing the population physically, are not doing enough for our Jewish roots, which, when all has been said and done, constitute the sole authentic excuse for our presence in this region.

It is true that the Sabbath is a Jewish discovery, but we, the returnees to Zion without a skullcap, have come to it via the Sunday Sabbath of the Gentiles—not the Gentiles of Scotland or Ireland, who observe the Sunday Sabbath with all its strictures, but those who had divested themselves of the burdens of religion and go on picnics instead of to church, and sing of love and the lonely rider instead of hymns, and go to football games instead of perusing Holy Writ. The negative attitude of the new immigrant toward the Sabbath, Israeli Style, is a dependable criterion of his integration as well as the improvement of his material situation: the more acceptable that the Israeli Sabbath appears to him, the better off he is materially. Now that he has a comfortable home and a car or a Vespa or money for cabs and a season pass for the swimming pool and transportation to the beach, it is quite easy to accept the Israeli Sabbath as something that is as it should be. But if you dwell in cramped quarters without a single tree in the neighborhood and you're dying for a bit of greenery and quiet, and the per capita cost of transportation by cab is a matter which must be weighed most seriously, there is much resentment against the laws of the Sabbath, which seem to operate against the interests of the poor.

And yet, Sabbath need have no fear of losing its grip in the Israeli republic; no evil will befall it. Firstly, it needs no legislation to protect it, although its guardians claim it does; secondly, no one, not even a senior socialist, would dare lay a hand on the status quo with regard to public transportation and other Sabbath decrees, in the *kibbutz* or in the elegant suburbs—not when we can mitigate the situation with cars, air-conditioning, annual trips to Switzerland or Scandinavia, as our public emissaries are wont to do. Furthermore, we have no complete dedication to secularism.

Like the American Jew who demands *kashrut* in Israel (even though back home he indulges in lobster, shrimp, frogs' legs and other abominable food), because someone has to see to it that the tenets of the faith are observed—and he himself is incapable of doing it—so do most liberals still harbor the sentiment that it's actually desirable to have about 20 per cent of the population take the Sabbath seriously, as it deserves, attend the synagogue and be familiar with all the prayers. Someone has to keep an open line to the Throne of Glory. You can never tell; we may yet need its Occupant to put in a good word for us.

Recreation Israeli Style

ANYONE PLANNING to make a study of what the Israelis do in their
spare time should be forewarned: ordinarily the Israelis have no
time to spare, i.e., their leisure time is merely a euphemism. Their
lives are actually packed with things that have to be done, regardless. We must obviously paint the railing and take care of the
correspondence, wash the car and put the stamp album in order,
read the paper or take the kids on a trip, do the crossword puzzle,
visit the Segals or for God's sake, we can't put off any longer
inviting Dworkin and that wife of his and what about the alumni
meeting. Very few things are done for the sheer enjoyment of it,
and these have to contend with prohibitions and inhibitions or
reasons of health. Labor and toil are no longer extolled as the
core of our existence, but we have discovered that it takes all of
a man's strength, concentration and perseverance—his entire
being—to carry out all the things lumped together under "recreation," as perhaps it should be: if we already let our hair down and
relax, there should be a "must" attached to it.

Israeli recreational habits naturally vary according to age,
schooling, finances and the season. In the summer they center
about the water cult, salty and/or polluted, impregnated with
people or chlorine; in winter we become fire-worshippers, looking
for warmth and the hearth, and finding it in brandy and smoulder-
ing eyes. But there are some forms of entertainment which all
Israelis share, no matter what their status is and regardless of
origin or accent. At the very top of this category is the revered
and sanctified Sabbath afternoon nap. The streets and roads are
all but deserted, the byways are desolate, in the villages not a
sound is heard along the shady lanes, and in the *kibbutz* not a
leaf trembles. All Israel is immersed in the sweet slumber of the

Seventh Day, resting along with the Creator from two-thirty to four, at which time there wafts heavenward a fragrant aroma of an offering never tendered in ancient Jerusalem—the redolent odor of His People enjoying coffee and cake.

Last year, a survey conducted by the Applied Social Research Institute to determine how the populace spends its leisure time in the country indicated that the bulk of the citizenry prefers to spend its free time at home, evenings and on the Sabbath, rather than out of it, whether by natural inclination or religious restrictions or financial embarrassment. But, aside from all other considerations, the simple fact is that the Israeli loves his dwelling (acquired with so much effort), his furniture, everything in it; he is attached to his home because, as a Jew, he is close to his family and his home is his shield and shelter, the core of his existence and the promise of continuity. This is where he eats, drinks, sleeps, reads his newspaper, listens to the radio or watches television, chats with his friends, discusses politics, plays with the youngsters, looks out of the window or from the balcony to see what is transpiring outside—*nu,* what better can life offer?

Anywhere else, reading the newspaper is regarded as leisure time activity, but in Israel this is a *must.* How can one *not* read a newspaper? What other subject of conversation can he possibly share with others? What else can take up his thoughts? In serene Switzerland, perhaps, a citizen may or may not glance through his newspaper, and the meadows will still remain green, but here, with fate hanging in the balance day by day, with not one day passing by without furnishing some misgivings to clutch at one's heart, when something is always bound to happen—a fire at the airport or grenades at the central bus depot, shelling at the Suez or demonstrations in Nablus, peace feelers in London or disaster at sea—in this small country, no individual can afford to be detached from daily events and live for himself alone.

For this reason, listening to the newscasts is a distinct civic duty, almost a religious obligation, and the time signal of Kol Yisrael, announcing the hour of seven, morning and evening, is heard throughout the land: the entire nation has its ear to the radio. Beyond, over and above the facts and their details, we must also get to the very bottom of things, to understand how they evolved, what the Russians are cooking up and what the Arabs are plotting, what the Americans are contemplating and what China is scheming. For this, we tune in on the commentaries: "This Day" and "This Evening" programs, plus the "Week's Roundup" on Saturdays. No, this is certainly not a matter of leisure time; this is partnership with destiny.

The Friday (Sabbath) editions descend on us with pages upon pages of symposia, round tables discussions, travelogues about the Himalayas and news about the progress of science in cancer research. We devour everything—less as recreation than as a bad habit, but also moved by a sense of duty and fair play: people did write, a newspaper did print, and you did pay for the paper. Should you then cast it all aside, skip over it, ignore it? Someone did take the trouble to write; read it, stupid, at least the first few paragraphs—if nothing else, it will enable you to put the paper aside with a clear conscience. Consider, then, the time consumed in reading, each and every day, one or two newspapers, in listening to four or five newscasts plus the commentaries thereon, and in viewing the thrice-weekly television documentaries, and you will realize that the Israeli is engaged, at least three hours a day, in ferreting out the answers to a simple question: "So what's new?" It really knocks you out, bringing up this country.

Findings of social behavior surveys indicate that the most popular item of recreation, outside the home, is the movie theater: 85 per cent of the populace attend movies regularly; some 51 million tickets are sold annually, in a population of less than three millions. Deduct from this number the ultra-Orthodox Jews who regard the movies as an abomination, the Arab women of the old school who feel that their place is at the hearth, the youngsters whom we take along only when there is no alternative, and you will find that every Israeli sees at least 25 films a year, and pays for the privilege. If we would add the *kibbutzniks,* who view at least one film a week, the army camps, the cultural circles and the youth clubs, where movies are shown free of charge, the total can be doubled and still be authentic.

Why do Israelis attend movies more often, as statistics show, than any other people on earth? True, we still do not have full-scale TV entertainment, which can take up an entire evening all by itself, but even before the Age of Television descended on the world, the number of cinema lovers here was far above the global average. People go to the movies to escape tension and to relax; they go to the movies because, like all Jews, they go for all kinds of culture in a big way; they go because their own country is so small, and movies reflect the glitter of the big wide world; the young people go because they have few places where they can get together; the masses go because the movies provide the sole outside entertainment which costs little and can be shown everywhere, in the most isolated outposts; people steeped in cultures of other countries find in the movies things they loved back in their lands of origin. Also, the movies fulfill at least two basic needs at one and the same time: conviviality as well as the privacy of darkness. All this adds up to three little words: *we love movies.* It's as simple as that. And we do not discriminate; everything goes, to the tune of 430 films a year—Ingmar Bergmann and the late Walt Disney, Francois Truffaut, Antonioni, westerns, musicals, even Israeli films—and every film is, as advertised, unforgettable, spectacular, thrilling, provoking, revolutionary, the greatest love story ever put on the screen, the most epoch-making historical spectacular, not to be missed. The cinema, too, is a must.

Night clubs, on the other hand, are held by the Israeli solid citizenry to be an "alien gratification," in existence primarily for tourists and the glitter set, the glamour girls and the bachelors who squire them around or meet them on the premises, and the men with shady occupations who obviously don't have to get up in the morning and go to work. Obviously, this is not the place for the average man with an average purse—unless he is entertaining tourists. Besides, what male in his right mind and in the company of his legitimate spouse is likely to spend ten Pounds on two miniscule drinks? And that is only the beginning. As for the spouse, her thoughts on the subject are of the kind to make the evening a total loss: the fifty Pounds we are spending would buy me a new pair of shoes, or a sweater for Orit and jeans for Opher. Chances are, therefore, that the pair won't ever get to the night club. And what is there really to see in all those striptease joints? Always the same thing. The discotheques and discobeat clubs, featuring The Churchills, The Jacks, The Snobs, The Lions, The Princes and The Lords, recent graduates from development towns and the big city fringes, are mainly for young people, out for a good time before going into the army. And who in the mature thirties would gather up enough nerve to come up to the portals and then be greeted with: "Watcha doin' here, Grandpa?"

There was a time when Jews were considered to be cafe habitues by nature, even the exponents of this medium of recreation, but in Israel the coffee houses have been disappearing from the scene and are being replaced by steak joints and milk bars and other centers of gluttony. Gone are the black-tie waiters, the solid marbletop tables, the Yecki proprietors, the folks who once frequented the cafes as an emotional outlet. Business is still being transacted in the current versions of the coffee shops and tea is still drunk there; it is customary to seek shelter there from a sudden shower, and a cup of coffee is good either before the show or after it. But the mood of dignity, the prestige and the culture are gone. That's how it is throughout the world, except in the people's republics in eastern Europe, where one finds the last of the truly bourgeois coffee houses. The "Ballad of the Sad Cafe," in Hebrew translation, ends with a deep "Oy!"

About a third of those polled about their recreational habits and outlets mentioned a hobby: creative arts, such as music, painting, sports, cooking or girls, and collecting hobbies, the latter being almost exclusively in the domain of the males, partly because women have no time for such foolishness, what with the picking up they have to do after their husbands leave. They also dislike spending all that money, and, above all, they see only the practical side of things: three bells put up in esthetically strategic spots in the home are decorative, but who needs a closetful of a hundred and fifty small carillons? The same goes for figures of elephants, placards, conches, butterflies, Chanukah candelabra, old glass, stamps, pipes, religious items—each a dependable dust collector. One needs the simplicity of a child to be a true collector, for the moment he brings himself to ask the question: "Suppose I have the full collection, so what?"—all the magic will fade away. Collections as a hobby may be suitable for an English manor, but they are in total contradiction of housing conditions in Israel. Between a dining nook and space for a hobby, the decision is obvious.

As to music, it is difficult to estimate the number of music lovers in Israel. What is exciting modern music for one is cacophony for another. Hassidic melodies, so delightful for one ear, will evoke "shut-off-that-thing-immediately" from the owner of another. Furthermore, it is difficult to tell how many of the thirty-six thousand regular subscribers to the Israel Philharmonic concerts (doubtlessly a world record) come for the music and how many for the bon ton. It is thought that at least one out of every five Israelis is interested in one facet of music or another, ranging from opera to jazz, but there is obviously a vast difference between the seasoned music lovers who are able to solve the music quizzes and are willing to brave the rain to hear a Buxtahude work performed by the Chamber Ensemble, and the bulk of the music lovers, who prefer to listen to a solid Beethoven symphony or snatches from opera sung by Franco Corelli, as they talk, eat, read or wash the dishes.

Sports are divided, as entertainment, between active and passive categories, and these are again sub-divided; either for the glory in it, or for health and figure, the latter denoting a monthly income of a thousand Pounds and over, age forty and over, and weight of 185 lbs. and over. One may incidentally enjoy the exercise while performing the duty, but joy is not the main incentive. Country clubs of status are few in Israel, and membership is still a matter of being able to afford the fees and dues. Membership in the Caesaria Golf Club, the only one of its kind in Israel, is still regarded as being reserved for people afflicted with the Anglo-Saxon cult—and the sufferers are certainly not of the poorer class; tennis, on the other hand, once the sport of the selective few, is growing numerically but losing ground socially. If the *kibbutzniks* are playing tennis and Labor's departed stalwarts nevertheless remain unmoved in their eternal abodes, then the game is obviously not an expression of the rotten bourgeoisie. (Sports undergo the same vicissitudes as do other human activities: low ebb and high tide. In Europe of yesterday, billiards was the game of merchant princes and famous physicians, who played bedecked with a heavy gold chain stretched across an equally impressive paunch; today, in Israel, it is a game for idlers and young men with nothing better to do). Athletic meets or sports competitions hold little attraction as such, even for spectators. An ordinary contest draws a hundred onlookers with difficulty, and of these, ninety are in all likelihood relatives of the participants. Swimming, with natural and other facilities being what they are—either in the surf, under the watchful eye and whistle of the lifeguard, or in a swimming pool so crowded that the water is all but invisible—may be included in the categories of workouts for the war effort or of superstitious considerations, but certainly not as a sport. Fencing, underwater fishing, sailing, horseback riding—each has its handful of devotees, but all of them together will not fill one soccer field.

Soccer! This is actually the one sport which belongs in the category of Israeli mass entertainment. On an ordinary Saturday, some 120,000 fans attend games featuring 260 adult teams; on a tournament or league championship Saturday, the number climbs to 200,000. These, plus the thousands who attend junior league jousts, plus the players themselves (these cannot very well be dispensed with), the referees and the physicians who treat them for bruises after the game, and the bagel and Eskimo Pie vendors in the stands, bring the total to approximately one-tenth of the population. Were it not for Sabbath prohibitions, the number would be even higher; the desire is there, however, judging from the children in skullcaps one sees, while driving along the highways on Saturdays, kicking a ball around; God is mighty, but soccer has greater drawing power, and who can tell—perhaps He, too, looks on from the Throne of Glory as his children disport themselves in this fashion.

The reasons for the popularity of soccer in Israel need no elaborate explanation. It's an ideal game, really: it affords two or three hours away from the womenfolk; for every twenty-two madmen embroiled in a struggle over a ball that costs no more than 100 Pounds, there are thousands who sit and watch in comparative tranquility. After all, with beef prices so high, Israel couldn't possibly have bullfighting as its national sport, and baseball still lacks both players and spectators. Hockey is out for climatic reasons, and cricket demands the kind of patience that no one but an Englishman possesses. Soccer also serves many Israeli citizens as a link with the culture of soccer which they knew in their youth. And as a clincher for soccer's supremacy, let it be noted that soccer has made a more significant contribution to the integration of the ingathered than have all of the ideological seminars and all of the inspired speakers of the past century.

All Israel's A Stage

In the number of inhabitants, the entire State of Israel is no larger than a medium American metropolis like Philadelphia or Baltimore. But even if we assume that one Israeli is equal to anyone else (this is hypothetical and for the sake of comparison only), the situation in the realm of theatre is out of all proportion. Israel's theatre audiences total three million spectators per annum, drawn from a Jewish population of two and a half million, and this includes women, children, the aged, those whose mother tongue is Kurdish, Croatian, or Portuguese with a South American accent. In a single week one may view in Israel, according to the latest count on my own fingers, twenty-five plays in Hebrew, three in Yiddish and one in English, among them (in translation) two works by Shakespeare, one by Ibsen, one Gogol, a Molière, an Albee, a Pirandello, to mention only the greats.

It all began with *Habimah,* the first Hebrew troupe since the ensemble organized by Miriam, sister of Moses and Aaron, on the East Bank of the Sea of Reeds; then came the workers' theatre, *Ohel.*When the *Cameri* (Chamber) Theatre joined them, twenty years later, the very earth shook with excitement. But it is the same with theatres as with children: the more that are begotten, the less is the fuss made over them. Today the score stands at a dozen theatre troupes, four of them on thespian heights and the others in a constant state of shuffle and reshuffle—split-ups, mergers, premature births and sudden deaths.

The Hebrew theatre has come up with an economic marvel: at one time every Hebrew theatre was deep in catastrophic financial trouble, and the actors went around hungry; today every Hebrew theatre is still deep in catastrophic financial trouble, but the actors themselves are basking in prosperity. No actor is either un-

269

employed or on the waiting list; neophyte performers are grabbed up as soon as they graduate from a drama school or are discharged from the military entertainment troupes, half-, third-, and tenth-baked, just so as to fill the role calling for someone, anyone, to say "Kiss me, beloved" or "Yes, Inspector!"

The fact that we have some sixty plays performed in the course of one year, with every theatre busy, is indicative that the Israelis have use for them. Nor is this the result of prosperity in the land. Here, take Switzerland as an example: money is like dirt there, yet all that Zurich can offer is one *Schauspielhaus* and two small troupes. A person is not drawn to the theatre only when he is well-off; ask any soldier on the front, or any former inmate of a concentration camp (we were ready to run so many risks, in Theresienstadt, to forgo so much, just to put on and see a play). To anyone who likes the taste, theatre is like brandy: there's nothing like it when you are in a good mood, and nothing more comforting when the blues have you in their grip; if you have the money, there's no reason for abstinence, and if you're poor, what else in life can provide a few illusions for so little?

One is hard put to evaluate the full effects of the odd Israeli custom of distributing a few hundred complimentary tickets (doubles) to any premiere, as a means of increasing the theatre's popularity. At first glance, this custom would seem to indicate that ours is a panhandling public, or it may be a sort of masochism and naivete on the part of the theatres themselves. Ninety-nine percent of the invitees can well afford to pay the full price of the tickets. Furthermore, these are not the people who come to the theatre for the sake of enjoyment but rather out of some sense of obligation; they sigh under this cultural burden and tend to be a hostile audience until the actors provide sufficient reason for them to feel otherwise. The theatres assume that, if the recipients of the Annie Oakleys, who set the financial and/or the social tone in the community, can be induced to frequent the theatre—whether by invitation or payment is immaterial—thousands of their neighbors and acquaintances and underlings (those below the complimentary level) are bound to follow in their wake, at full price; thus would they also be able to converse, if and when called upon, about Cheestakov or Harold Pinter.

There was a time when Israelis would gather, in the evening, around an assortment of saltsticks, watermelons and seltzer bottles to discuss authors and literature: *King of Flesh and Blood* or *Yevgeny Onegyn* in Hebrew translation. Today's talk, fortified with whiskey-and-soda, cocktail wieners and iced coffee, centers on the performances and the actors—unless the security situation is tight, as so often happens, whereupon all discussion veers towards politics.

The major advantage that the theatre enjoys, relative to the other performing arts, is that it's so easy for anyone to become expert at it. Now, in order to be able to render an intelligent opinion of a painting (particularly if the one we are discussing consists of three brown lines on a background of yellow) one must have, if not knowledge, at least nerve or crass hypocrisy. Similarly, if one is called upon to comment on the warmth in Oistrakh's tone, he should not be embarrassed by having to conclude, first, whether the instrument involved is a piano or a cello, aside from the requirement to live through a two-hour concert without falling asleep. The theatre, on the other hand, is wide open. All one needs to have to see people ambling across the stage is a pair of eyes, and if he furthermore has ears he can hear them conversing; this makes him a connoisseur of the theatre and, if destiny calls, a critic, orally or in writing.

The actors, directors and others in the theatre are the standard-bearers of a millennia-old tradition, going back to the sacrificial rites; as the rams and goats of those days, they now bear the sins of society. There is no other profession so prone to criticism, so vulnerable, so enthusiastically attacked—and without effective defense. The dream of every actor, comes the Messiah, is to sit together with two or three friends (if he has that many left at the End of Days) and take apart his critics.

And yet, despite all the prattling of the average Israeli critic, any actor who responds to the question: *"Nu,* have you read what they said about you last Friday in *Haaretz?* with "No, I haven't had a chance to read the papers," is but continuing to act after working hours. We have not yet attained the situation on Broadway, where the criticism of one man can cremate a play into which a fortune had been invested. Still, even here, woe to the performance on which the critics zero in—unless the item is an entertaining comedy, in which case it is beyond their reach, and

271

the crowds keep streaming to see it regardless of whether they had condemned it to perdition or not.

The status of an actor in Israeli society, also an inheritance from the dim past, vacillates between two extremes: he is either on top of Olympus, exalted as no laurel-wreathed hero can hope to be, the close friend of monarchs, ministers and millionaires, or else he is the target of continuous carping and criticism, the prey of every gossip columnist and aspiring cub reporter, shunned by proper society. But whereas elsewhere an actor may be admired professionally yet banned socially, in Israel the exact opposite is true. Analyzing each of the actors on the Hebrew stage today from the professional viewpoint, we can make mincemeat of every one of them, but socially the actor is the lion. Every good bourgeois likes to have a few actors and actresses in his circle of friends, colleagues and house guests. We, whose true features are known only to the hairdresser or the cosmetician, find it very pleasant to sit with an actor in a Dizengoff Street cafe and bask in the warmth of the acclaim which he draws. Needless to say, this attachment carries tremendous weight with the kiddies; Yossi Banai's autograph is worth twenty of Nobel Prize for Literature laureate S. Y. Agnon, and a phone conversation with Yehoram Gaon can be overshadowed only by calls from at least thirty Knesset members.

However, the adulation given to performers on the legitimate stage (they never appear as "entertainers" or in films) is not what it was when we were young—when we were prepared to wait, hours on end, in the line at the box office to get S.R.O. tickets, and then stand somewhere up in the third balcony, under the roof, sweating and elbowing to see, from the craziest angles, what was going on, far below, on the stage, yet sensing the sound of the Muse's flapping wings (as depicted on the Iron Curtain, with long hair and gossamer veils covering the strategic areas, floating, with no regard for gravity, through fanciful vegetation). S.R.O. in Israel is rare, if it exists at all; admission is relatively less expensive than to any other form of entertainment—the equivalent of three dollars will get you the best seat in the house. The lines at the box office are much shorter; people no longer stand at the stage exit waiting for their gods to appear, in the flesh, and flowers are sent to actresses usually by relatives or the respective husbands.

We are quite conservative, as young nations go. Let the theatre be what it's supposed to be, without the element of experimentation. The absurd theatre must be vulgar, as well, if it hopes to make an impression. Classics are always good, especially Shakespeare; all the high school students must take in something as cultural as that. Plays geared to the entire family, from Grandma Yocheved to little Iris ("Solomon the King and Shlomi the Cobbler," "Peter Pan") are sure-fire hits. The little man pitted against the world, in all variations of the struggle ("Schweik," "The Overcoat"), will always find a sympathetic ear. A tender love story is solid box office stuff, provided that the heroes in the plot are not of retirement age (of late the Hebrew theatre has chalked up some notable gains in this area; at least our heroines do have shapely figures). We adore doting mothers, particularly when they are portrayed by Hanna Rovina. Whatever proved to be a hit on Broadway and the West End is bound to repeat its success here, mainly on the merits garnered abroad. God and religious issues invite trouble, unless they are presented with entertaining humor. The Holocaust is still the Holocaust. Jewishness has been doing well of late, now that the early pioneers are no longer ashamed of it.

In certain quarters one hears moanings about the dearth of original Israeli plays; numerically, however, the record is good. Since the establishment of the state we have had close to 130 original plays, a total far beyond the wildest dreams of Honduras or Madagascar. But even if only two or three deserve to be left to posterity, we should be satisfied, seeing that all that remained of Dr. Herzl, the playwright, is the State of Israel.

Where Has All the Money Gone?

THOSE AMONG us with many years behind them but of sound memory, who still recall those distant days when our currency was worth three dollars for every Israeli Pound, have grown to meet every price rise like a swimmer breasting the waves: we shut our eyes, lower our heads, and wait for the crest to break. We remember the days when *falafel-in-peetah* cost five *grush*; now we pay half a Pound (50 *grush*) therefor, and we shall overcome even when it will cost five Pounds. Nothing about inflation would surprise us any more; what is likely to confound us is some sign of monetary stability.

It is for this reason that we showed such nervousness in those brief spans of prosperity—when the income tax rate was cut and salaries went up, more contributions for workmen's compensation were set aside and we suddenly found ourselves not overdrawn at the bank nor in debt to the grocer, with a balanced housekeeping budget, as though we were not in our own milieu. We were well aware that such a situation was abnormal and unnatural; it couldn't go on. Now, the Lord be praised, we are far more at ease: taxes have gone up, prices are rising, indebtedness is bound to rise, everyone is predicting the worst, and we are feeling very much at home. To us, Israel is more than just sunny skies and laundry drying in the brightness and the smell of orange blossoms and camels tethered near the housing projects and there is sand in your shoes and a steak in your *peetah*. Israel also means a fatalistic approach to fiscal problems, summed up as: one way or another, things will work out.

From this standpoint, our position is infinitely more favorable than that of our forebears. We have already partaken of the Tree of Knowledge, and the fall from grace is already behind us. We harbor no more illusions: not toward money, not toward securities, not toward economic stability, not toward the goodness of thrift. We still save, still buy bonds, still maintain our life insurance —since it's man's nature to be concerned, despite everything, about his children and his old age—but we no longer enjoy the complete faith that all this will safeguard against the onslaught of evil times. We had seen our parents, in the Old Country, hoarding pennies and shillings and zlotys and putting them aside: dowry for the daughters and schooling for the sons, sustenance for old age, and they did it with complete faith and full trust such as we ourselves will never know, and lost it all.

For this reason we find it difficult to impart a sense of thriftiness to our children. We say, out of sheer habit, just to have the impression sink in, superficially: "Money doesn't grow on trees. You have to take care of your things. Can't you see how hard we have to work to earn the money? What—again a half Pound for a notebook? You bought one just two days ago!" At times we feel put out by the short shrift that our heirs make of what we had earned with the sweat of our brow or with the tortures of boredom or complete lack of interest in our job. But deep down a small voice keeps insisting: "So what? Is it really that important? Let it burn a hole in his pocket. No one ever became rich by saving. Nor is our generation the one to do the preaching."

Jews, the world has long maintained, love money. In this they differ in no way from the Gentiles; the Dutch, Swiss, French, Greeks, Czechs all love money, passionately. Not as a means but as the end. The miser who burrows through his hoard of gold coins for the pleasure of physical contact with the precious metal is not one of ours. It is not the money itself that Jews love but the things that it can buy.

The image of the Jew as a usurer, the dealer in money to stockpile his own hoard, emerged from the soil of Germany, England (prior to the expulsion in the thirteenth century) and other countries throughout Christendom of the Middle Ages. The Catholic Church forbade the faithful to lend money at interest, under threat of hell's fires and an unmarked grave, but the rulers in those days, precisely as their counterparts today, were in frequent need of urgent loans to tide over a war or to maintain the royal pomp. Inasmuch as the Jew was already doomed to purgatory and most occupations were closed to him besides, he was utilized by dukes, counts and kings, just as we use banks today. For these gentlemen, dealing with the Jewish lender had one tremendous advantage over the bank: the lender enjoyed no governmental protection. The borrower repaid the debt, if he was in the proper mood; if not, he cast the lender into the dungeon and struck the transaction from the records.

The Jewish claim that money could take care of everything grew out of sheer optimism; Jews *hoped* that it could—and it did, to a considerable extent, but not always and not in all cases. Money came in handy when one had to ransom his life from the oppressor, when one had to get a residence permit, a trading license, exemption from military service in Czarist Russia. Money could *not* buy Gentile love, but it did make headway toward winning an outward show of respect, a benign smile, a greeting, a strip of the sidewalk.

To Jews, having money has always conjured up preceding impoverished generations. Money was therefore never taken for granted. Jews loved to talk about it and to display signs of its presence. A Jew with money wanted the good life that went with it: a beautiful home, beautiful furnishings, a beautiful wife (the three, according to the sages, broaden man's sensibilities; and if the wife is not beautiful to begin with, a happy ending can be achieved through furs and diamonds). He also wanted a front pew in the synagogue, status in the community, fine husbands for the daughters and choice economic pursuits for the sons, right down to the fine plot in the cemetery. Today Jewish millionaires, unlike their secluded and unpublicized non-Jewish counterparts, are not ashamed of displaying their wealth; they enjoy the large art collections and the ostentatious homes that their money has brought them.

The Rothschilds, whom the world regards as the Jewish monetary symbol, are not typical of their people at all, except for the strong family ties and their attitude toward Israel. Jewish money is generally much more volatile, here today and gone tomorrow. Financial empires built in one generation are toppled in the next by war, revolution, confiscation, expulsion. Jewish dynasties are founded on spiritual treasures. In this respect the House of Rothschild is much more akin to the noble houses of the English and the Italians, whose prime security is not threatened by any changes in the regime; the silver collection on the first storey may disappear, or the Gobelin tapestries looted on the second, but the edifice itself remains.

What is more, Jews respect money rather than love it. Anyone who claims that to him money is of no interest is either free of any responsibility and lives only for himself, or exists at the expense of others, or has all kinds of money, or is simply a hypocrite. Even the *kibbutznik,* who receives according to his needs, is not immune to the sweet taste of money, precisely because, in his case, the money he receives is for those small personal luxuries that add luster to life. Even in the *kibbutz* family there is quite a bit of fiscal calculation: should we buy a painting or a talking doll or a bottle of brandy or take a trip? How about saving the vacation money and buying an electric iron?

The value of money changes, not necessarily according to the exchange rate, but according to the intensity of the desire which it would fulfill. If you are a youngster, and all that you are thinking about, at the moment, is a stick of gum, then ten *grush* is a fortune. And if you are dragging yourself along the city streets and are dying for a glass of beer but don't have one because for the *lira* you can buy a thousand and one things of greater urgency, you get to hate the whole world, regardless of the fact that it's only one Pound. He who has ever felt the impotence, the humiliation, the grief, the hatred that can be caused by a *lira* that isn't there, will ever be aware of the real worth of money. No, not to be rich— just to feel sure that you can spend the bill without a twinge of conscience.

This is perhaps why Jews are inclined to be spendthrifts: most of them can still recall the days of revolution and war and upheaval and unemployment. That is why they really enjoy spending money impulsively, on something silly, something they really do not need.

And all preaching on behalf of thrift notwithstanding, the experience of four devaluations in twenty years suggests to us that indebtedness is better than thrift, as a simple calculation will show. In 1948, one Israeli *lira* = $3.00; in 1968, one Israeli *lira* = 28c, until the next devaluation.

In Pursuit of Honor

THE ROMANS were satisfied with bread and entertainment, but we, given a slab of bread and a slice of honor, would ask for nothing more. We need honor as a tire needs air, here in Israel of all places, where social stratification is as yet undefined and customs are not ingrained and all of us are still hovering between earth and firmament. Honor is the vindication of our identity, our existence, our way of life. All of us put in a better appearance in the looking-glass of honor.

Unlike beauty or an ear for music, honor is not sufficient unto itself. It must always have others in attendance, to dispense it. But the glory-seeker needs more than simply people around him; he must have a rating. Honor is a comparative matter. Where everyone is the equal of everyone else, there is no such thing. Honor was born out of inequality and bred in a differential of brains, property, status, power. One does not glorify the man whom he regards as being his equal—and justly so.

The trouble is that honor is not distributed according to coupons nor by merit or logic. Everyone is after just that slice of honor, or a larger slice, without any definite system and without fixed laws. Honor is dispensed with logic, orderliness and equity only in the realm of the King of Glory or by his representatives on earth; whoever jostles nearest to the Throne of Glory rates highest in the public eye. A *tzaddik,* an erudite Torah scholar, a Hassidic rabbi and an Exilarch are close to the Kingdom of Heaven, just as a nobleman, the court counselor and the royal chamberlain are close to the mortal throne. They have the major portion of honor, and this rubs off on those in their vicinity, so that a bit remains for them, and so on down to the last beggar in the line, who can gain honor only from other beggars because of his lucrative territory or his ingenuity in procuring alms.

It is for this reason that peoples, the Jews among them, have attached such importance to the family tree. A scion of the Schneierson dynasty or a Hager or a Twersky inherits a bit of honor at birth, and if he furthermore becomes a scholar and is filled with knowledge, his glory will endure forever. And even if he is a *tzaddik* and shuns honor, it shall overtake him, since he is unfamiliar with the sport and cannot outrun it. We secularists, however, are pioneers, cleaving our way toward honor, with neither compass nor tradition to guide us, simply by instinct and perseverance. A republic is not a monarchy, and a President or a Prime Minister is not a king, certainly not in a country as small as ours, where too many of us have known the high office holders in their green salad days, when Shazar was Rubashov, and Eshkol was Shkolnick, Sapir was Kozlowsky and Ben Gurion answered to the name of Green, as managers of Kupat Holim Health Insurance branches or Labor Bureau clerks; we ate with them, took trips with them, worked and argued with them. True, one's honor is enhanced when one has, in his circle of friends, several Cabinet Ministers and Knesset members, but this in itself does not guarantee permanence. Honor should be assured by more solid factors than by an association with office holders whom the first Government crisis may sweep away like chaff in the wind.

A family tree does not mean much—unless the family name is Rothschild. We secularists do not possess the long memory of the traditionalists. Who amongst us would remember the names of the early Zionists if there were no main streets named for them, and even then Nordau, Pinsker, or Ussishkin do not conjure up any familial images, except for the dyed-in-the-wool Zionists. The honor that a well-schooled son once imparted to his family has lost much of its glamor. There was a time when the impact of the Torah scholar was felt even by the untutored, but nowadays the greatest scientist in the field of magneto-structure or the diseases of the Legosterum can be appreciated only by experts in those fields. This appreciation can be measured by titles (doctor, professor), but these are not in themselves sufficient to induce Israelis to accord a scientist king-size glory; expertise in any field of scientific research will engender a feeling of respect on the part of the populace only if the scientist is also endowed with the secret of manipulating communications media (i.e., publicity).

THE ISRAELIS

Purity of heart, modesty, unselfishness, compassion and all similar noble traits have no bearing on the accordance of honor. On the contrary, modesty is the outstanding foe of honor. How can we pay homage to a man who isn't even known? If he insists on being modest, let him at least be known as the most modest man in town.

There being no Central Honors Dissemination Institute in our midst, we must rely on contests: Bible quizzes, Beauty Queen and Kitchen Queen competitions, contests centering on familiarity with the land or with the works of Sholem Aleichem. All these are useful in filling the void of Honor in a republic without a nobility. "Sir" is indubitably a more desirable title than "Bible Champ," but "Bible Champ" is infinitely better than nothing. The pragmatists among us—people without vision—keep protesting against the proliferation of prizes and demanding that they be reduced in number but, on the other hand, upped in value. This is an unrealistic approach. The Kugel Prize and the Bublick Award, the Religious Erudition Citation and the Ramat Gan Municipal Award in Juvenile Literature and the Mother-of-the-Year Award tend to slake but little of our thirst for honor; still, the prizes number far less than the inhabitants of Israel though they are a blessing not only to those who win them but also to all others involved: they enhance the prestige of the donors, the distributors, the judges.

Honor is a compound of family and status and respect and prestige, and its expressions vary in keeping with time and place. Today the peak of Mt. Glory is publicity. Who is most esteemed? He who picks up the telephone and says: "This is . . ." and no one on the other end of the line says: "And who, pray tell me, are you?" The Esteemed One is written up in the papers and interviewed on the air. When he enters a restaurant the waiter hurries to ready a table for him, and when he presents his papers to the customs official, he gets them back with a salute: "My respects, sir."

It is clearly not nice to pursue honor. It is known that honor eludeth him who pursueth it. But with a little bit of luck and a lot of stick-to-itiveness it can be caught, if only by the coattails. After all, those who work the communications media do not have a Geiger counter by which to locate a person worthy of being honored. They should be guided a little. They who seek honor shouldn't wait until some interviewer wakes up, on a clear day, and, with no better prospect in the wind, writes an article about them. The interviewer's attention should be drawn, delicately and tactfully, through a friend: "Say, I got an exceptionally good subject for you. I really don't know whether he'll go along—he's very modest and hates newspapermen—but I'll do my darndest." Inasmuch as many people do hate newspapermen, but love publicity, they will also be carrying with them a photograph, quite by accident, in case an article about them should unexpectedly emerge.

Since there doesn't exist an acknowledged honor-gauge in Israel, such as the Legion of Honor or titles like *Hofrat* and *Kreisrat,* other distinguishing symbols must be found to denote the Esteemed One. And these exist: the way people greet him, with a slight bow and without the "how-goes-it?" addendum; the way he is introduced to others, on those rare occasions when introduction is necessary in the first place: without elucidation, without the minutiae of occupation or profession. No one would think of saying: "Please meet Aharon Meskin. As you may know, he is a veteran actor in the Habimah Theatre," or, "You've heard, of course, of Ben Gurion; the former Prime Minister of Israel, you know."

A true honor barometer is The Invitation: to the weddings of Cabinet Ministers' daughters, to theatre premieres (not above Row Fifteen), to gala concerts featuring foreign artists, to official cocktail parties in the company of the diplomatic corps, receptions at embassies and festive dinners in honor of guests from abroad. Of course, an invitation in itself is not enough; the seating is also a determinant. Seated next or close to the guest of honor, a Cabinet minister, an ambassador—and you've arrived. But if the seating card plunks you down at the end of the table, near the waiters' thoroughfare, or, Heaven forbid, near the door leading to the comfort premises, friend, you have a long way to go on the road to honor. At cocktail parties, with no seating to determine priorities conclusively, the invitee must take the matter of honor into his own hands. He who takes his honor achievement seriously should never get to the affair during the first half-hour, with only a handful present to witness his entrance; on the other hand, he should beware of coming but fifteen minutes before the party is scheduled to break up, else he will find the tables bare and the glad hand of the hostess rather moist. "We Shall Be the First" was a marvelous song for the pioneers, but nowadays we prefer to be among the last. Anyone who courted disaster and was the first to arrive learned his lesson and now gets there much later. The party clock thus keeps pushing farther. In Tel Aviv and its environs the earliest is ten-thirty, and there's still a long night ahead. If you find that you must please your baby-sitter, who obviously wants you out of the house, the thing to do is to sit in your darkened car, somewhere near the host's residence, and wait patiently until the mainstream of the invitees has flowed in. There's money to be made in operating a service to supply early comers, who would save the first guests the embarrassment of barging in on empty chairs and having to say, in feeble consternation, "I do hope we're not the first ones!"

There was a time when the very fact of being an old-timer in this country provided at least half of the honor requirements of the population, but today this fact can bring forth acclaim only from the tourists on their first visit (those who still tend to become emotional over Jewish stevedores and tomato growers), new immigrants still laboring to find their way in the maze, and our well-wishers among the people of the earth. True, a certain amount of honor is still attached to being native-born, but the recent crop cannot expect the portion of the old-timers, who, as they announced the gladsome tidings of their birthplace, could depend on thrilled oohs and aahs to follow. As the native-born increase in number, their portion of honor becomes more and more meager. After all, what is so important about being a third-generation Frenchman? Only an immigrant Jew would regard it that way.

The lion's share of the honor rising out of the existence of the State is derived not by its residents but those who glory in it, from overseas. Take away from the Zionist movement the self-esteem which it accords to its adherents, and it will lose its magic. Zionism distributes honors on two counts: firstly, it provides honor for the leadership, the long list of title-holders: chairmen and presidents and treasurers and secretaries, locally, regionally and nationally, in the lands of their sojourn. Secondly, it gives its fruit on the soil of Israel itself. To obtain honor from Gentiles calls for either outstanding personality or a great deal of money, but in Israel one can obtain, for an investment of a paltry few tens of thousands (really a small sum by other international standards) what would demand millions elsewhere: meetings with the heads of the nation, official receptions, Ph.D.'s *honoris causa*, a donor's shiny plaque on a building. For Jewish tourists, the slogan should not be "Follow the Sun" (which they can do in Costa del Sol and the Bahamas) but "Go for Glory" or "Come and Be Honored."

The money comes first, then the honors. When a tycoon no longer shows any interest in big deals and begins setting up foundations and distributing funds to good causes, he evidently has enough money and is now in the honor market. If in monarchal, hidebound England one can acquire a minor title or at least a few initials after one's name, in return for financial largesse, why should we discriminate against the millionaires? We have no Sirs, Lords or Dukes, but how about a little village in your name? This is incontrovertible evidence of generosity.

When you come to think of it, the rich of today are not in the enviable position of their forebears of yesterday. When Patriarch Jacob wended his way home from Haran with cattle and maid-servants and other servants and camels and donkeys, everyone could see the wealth and honor he had accumulated in the course of his employment by father-in-law Laban. But the contemporary millionaire keeps his stocks and bonds in a safe deposit box, either here or in Switzerland or in America. He would have to hang up a few originals by French impressionists if he wants others to believe him.

Yes, the days when cattle and camels and sons constituted a man's wealth are gone. Today the sweaters are of Orlon instead of sheep's wool; camels shuttle tourists around, and the number of sons does not necessarily lend glory to the parents. Jacob with his twelve sons would today be a social oddity, if not a downright welfare case. With all our loyalty to the community and its growth, we realize that society looks askance at progenitors who produce more than four offspring. As for daughters, whose chastity was once the halo of family honor, only the old-fashioned among the Orientals would think of avenging an intrusion on the family honor. We, the progressive parents, build the honor of our home on foundations less fragile than a daughter's maidenhead: a private home on a half-acre plot, teakwood furniture, electrical appliances, in short, things modern.

Concepts of honor also change. Indebtedness used to be a blot on a man's honor. Today, as a man's debts mount, so does his honor; it signifies that he is a dynamic, ambitious individual who knows how to work with other people's money. Only he who is bound hand and foot by archaic illusions would nowadays say "I don't owe a cent" and expect a pat on the back for it.

Honor is a creature unbridled by criteria. It doesn't always choose to follow the talented. And it is right. Suffice it to say that a man is talented; why honor, to boot? Honor should be primarily for those whom nature has not thus favored. A talented poet should be contented with writing poetry. A less talented poet might be chairman of the Association. A simple computation based on the number of photographs in which he appears, on festive occasions, plus the number of addresses he has delivered at anniversary banquets, plus positions held in all sorts of undertakings, will add up to the number of years since he has last written anything worthwhile.

Tribal, dynastic and encampment honors no longer entice us. These have been replaced by organizations. Every Society, every Association, every chartered non-profit Corporation: Bride's Aid Society, the Israel Music Lovers Society, the Spinka Hassidim Brotherhood provide, in addition to their functional value, a backbone, a crutch, self-confidence enough for innumerable honor seekers, founders and honorary presidents, chairmen and treasurers, honorary secretaries (as distinguished from paid secretaries without honor). Whoever seeks only a bit of glory remains faithful to the small societies. Whoever strives for greater glory cleaves his way to the big time of good causes: Ilan, B'nai Brith, Working Mothers, Maccabi—the stepping stones to the biggest pedestal of all—the Knesset. And, unless they no longer grace the world of the living, that's where they are today.

Live and Labor

THE BRITISH have been taking it for granted, for many generations, that a scion of a good family, a product of Oxford or Cambridge, is capable (thanks to this special background) of filling successfully any post whatsoever, be it politics, the military or administration, with no necessity for other training for the vocation. Similarly, in the Land of Israel it was once held that a genuine pioneer, a man of the Labor *aliya*, would do well at anything—farming or managing a plant owned by the Labor Federation, building highways or representing national institutions abroad, writing for the labor press or riding a horse on guard duty, as the need may be, without any vocational training, simply because he had the compass of ideology charting his way.

The pioneer tilling the people's soil was the ideal of the new society and even he who did not engage directly in plowing and planting (the Movement assigned him to other duties and consequently he couldn't contract malaria at the Kinneret nor fructify the wasteland), he, too, was aware that a home in the city or a desk in an office was a crying shame and a poor substitute for the real life on the collective farm. True, a few vital professional occupations, such as medicine and teaching, were unavoidable; the doctor and the teacher were therefore made welcome in the labor settlements, even though it was obvious that their hands would never grasp a hoe. Still, it was understood that they practiced their professions in the spirit of pioneer motivation, on behalf of the People of Israel generally and of the returnees to Zion in particular, to heal those who were draining the marshes of all kinds of malaria or to influence city youth to go back to the farm. Professionalism was suspect; it was tolerated only when it was absolutely necessary.

285

The "Labor Federation wage structure," as it was once called, faithfully reflected this criterion: every laborer was entitled to the same basic wage, regardless of level or skill, plus increments based on seniority and family size. The old-timers took great pride in pointing out to the newcomers that the factory manager or the newspaper editor earned less than the fellow with the teacart, inasmuch as the latter had fathered eight children, all of whom had to eat. This was a praiseworthy approach to the equality of the laborer, based on the End of Days, but it made no sense at all to those of Israel's citizenry who came here without the pioneering background, and in the course of time they grew to be the majority.

Israel is now nearing the Age of Professionalism. Specific schooling is necessary for specific duties. Only Israeli army generals still wear the halo of "our men can do anything"; when they leave military service, they are made secretary-generals of ministries, administrators of mines and ports, with the faint hope that they will succeed in dissipating civilian confusion by applying the principles of military discipline. Even in the *kibbutzim,* where members exchanged duties as a matter of traditional ideology, most of the members are now assigned to permanent responsibilities, whether it is turkey breeding or bookkeeping, with a few months' service in the dining room to assuage everyone's feelings of fair play. The current struggle between the young and the old over who is going to manage Labor Federation enterprises is not merely a contention between the generations. It is chiefly a struggle between men of the Labor Movement and the professionally-trained, between those who hold ideological fervor to be the first and foremost requirement, with skills and know-how tagging behind, and those who give these skills and know-how top priority, to which one may append, if and when necessary, the ideological touch.

To date there has been no official revision of the Ideal Israeli Society, and it can be assumed that it is still the farmer who is tilling his soil—despite crop surpluses and all the talk about the need to reduce the ratio of farmers in the population—and the construction worker who is building up the country. Factually, however, ever since the mass *aliya* of the 'fifties, this ideal has been expressed in two diverse categories: on the one hand, we have people, chiefly among the older settlers, who live and breathe labor ideology but whose style of living smacks strongly of the bourgeoisie; on the other hand there is a deep stratum of people who arrived after the rise of the state and who never knew the Labor Movement (especially the newcomers from the Afro-Asian countries) who are laboring in industry and farming highway construction, who never regard their work as an expression of conviction but rather as the dictate of reality. Very few people are likely to declare, proudly: "I am a laborer"; proudly they might say: "I am a member of the Labor Movement," and if they do say "I'm a laborer," it's without any undue pride. Today labor as a class is a matter of circumstance rather than of ideology. Just as the Rumanian or Moroccan immigrants used to say, whenever they thought that their origin lacked prestige, "I am from Buco- vina" or "I am from Southern France," so are manual workers likely to say now, "I'm a foreman" or "I specialize in textile finishing," without giving his job the coating of ideology. The various labor parties have been in power ever since the founding of the state; their adherents account for about 60 per cent of the electorate, yet most Israelis, on the basis of their viewpoints and way of life, belong to the middle-class, a designation much more respectable than the pardon-the-expression "bourgeois" or its worse derivative, "petit-bourgeois." Among the progeny of the Labor Movement veterans, other than the "generation of continu- ity" in the *kibbutzim* and *moshavim,* an infinitesimal few are laborers or regard themselves as laborers. They are professionals, with some emotional affinity, more or less genuine, toward socialistic ideals, here and there.

Yet, despite the approximation of professional standards to western norms, with men of science and research heading the list, there are, nevertheless, certain differences that set Israel apart. Money still isn't everything: an El Al pilot earns four times the salary of a combat pilot, yet the status of the latter is much loftier, especially since the Six Day War. The *kibbutz* man still enjoys higher esteem than the private farmer, and the manager of a Labor Federation enterprise is still more highly regarded than the manager of a private plant, unless the latter is also a mil- lionaire. On the other hand, nowhere else in the world is the position of the rabbi as lowly as it is in Israel, among all except

the twenty per cent of the population which constitutes the religious community.

On the whole, occupations once regarded as being strictly
Jewish—tailoring, shoemaking, watch repairing and furriery,
while not in decline as far as status goes—are simply not part of
the accepted Israeli system. To the Israelis, these occupations are
a throwback to the older generation, to the Jewish past, and the
new generation keeps away from them. Young people who do
turn to the crafts prefer modern technology, mechanics, aeronautics, machine tooling, electronics. The bell has been tolling for the
small-time artisan, the fellow who repairs what the machine has
fashioned, working in an alcove, a basement or a tiny store, with
equipment consisting of a work bench, a chair, a shelf, a transistor
and time—mainly time to repair shoes about to fall apart, sew a
patch on to a pair of pants, hold long chats with the customers
or just sit in the doorway and watch others hurry by. The age
when people had time is no more. Of all the occupations in the
past only hairdressing has been rehabilitated, in consequence of
global fashions, but the practitioners are no longer called barbers;
they are "hair stylists," with an upsweep of French names like
Leon, Armand, Francois.

The teaching profession has undergone some change in Israel.
In the early settlement period, the great men in our midst, the
writers and the thinkers, did not hesitate to engage in teaching,
but in the course of time, teaching changed from a mission to a
means of livelihood. The males gradually withdrew from the
profession (except in the *kibbutz* and the religious schools, where
teaching still fills a definite ideological role), and the primary
schools became the domain of women teachers. Today teaching
is altogether a feminine profession, suited particularly for married
women with families, because in this profession pregnancy can be
coordinated with the summer vacation. The influx of pupils in the
wake of mass immigrations lowered the standards in the teacher
market, so that the mediocre high school student, with nothing
better in sight, could always apply to a teachers' institute and be
accepted. But now that *aliya* is a trickle and a surplus of teachers
is in the offing, and as the Ministry of Education raises teaching
standards and the modernization of the late lamented Russian-
Prussian systems is in the air, perhaps we shall yet hear a woman

288

declare, "My husband is a teacher," with the same pride that she now says, "My husband is an architect."

The decline in power of ideology, in Israeli life, is manifested by the low rating of the party worker's position. Once upon a time only the elite in the ranks of the Labor Movement were chosen to fill representative posts, and their status was commensurate with it. Today the appellation "party worker" is almost an insult, implying either hopeless ineptitude and pompousness or intrigue and crude bossism. Only in the development towns has the party worker retained positive social status, chiefly because he is still in the position of doling out the gravy, but if an urban party hack wishes to maintain worthy status, he must go into party work as a profession, and right at the top: as adviser to the minister or as his ghost writer, a political secretary or the executive secretary to the party (but never on the local level). He would also do well to have another job, just in case.

Some professions and occupations rise and fall with the vicissitudes of time. Time hath given and time taketh away. During the days of austerity, in the early 1950's, butchers and textile dealers enjoyed a prestige unheard of in Mandate days, but prosperity knocked out the props from under their status. There was a time when the members of a transport cooperative enjoyed the pioneer status of Negev settlers; later they became the prototypes of the well-to-do, with private homes, securities and incomes, open and hidden, almost like the building contractors. Today not even the formidable monopoly connotation will hide the deplorable fact that a member of the Dan cooperative is, when all is said and done, no more than a bus driver. Driving is not, apparently, what it used to be, if any woman can become good at it.

Journalists in Israel enjoy a status totally out of proportion to either their talent or value. If you are a big-time Israeli journalist, all doors are open to you and all men seek your grace, if not out of respect then out of calculation. Local newspaper people, regional correspondents and departmental scribes, whether in sports or fashion, enjoy power and esteem in their particular circles, based on nothing worthier than their ability to cause trouble. This development may be due to the size of the country, where journalists can easily become, like Cabinet ministers and ministry director-generals, members of the elite cocktail sets.

Also, among Jews there is still great respect (largely unjustified) for the written word. Then again, the Israelis are avid newspaper readers to begin with.

The status of authors and poets in Israel has taken a rough tumble. There was a time when the Hebrew writers were the glory of the community, its pride, inspiration, leadership. Nowadays, the influence of the writers on what transpires in the country is nil. Those who are elderly and/or have won important awards in Israel and/or abroad will continue to have people reading their poems and buying their novels, but they are dispensable. Only Haim Hefer, Natan Alterman or Haim Guri, who have integrated poetry with journalism, still have an effect on public opinion in Israel, but they are no longer the standard-bearers. What Jewish mother in Israel would want her boy to be a poet? A writer of pop tune lyrics which everyone sings, yes! But verse, mostly unintelligible and without rhyme, is hardly a career for a young man from a good family.

Entertainers, on the other hand, have never had it so good. Character actors and the artistic exponents of the great tragedies always enjoyed good standing in the community, thanks to the Habimah National Theatre and the revival of Hebrew on the stage, but the level of singers, entertainers and comedians, even the popular ones, used to be only one step above the lawyers (a decidedly diasporic calling) and the Mandate officials (servants of the occupation forces). Today, the status of the entertainers, in song and story, anecdotes and interviews, is the peer of the Shakespearean, in days past.

A serious problem caused by the Israel schizophrenia of the desirable vs. the existential is the attitude toward service jobs. In the past, pioneering looked askance at service jobs because they are not productive; women in the *kibbutzim* were, therefore, not eager to work in the kitchen or in the laundry. However, reality tends to achieve what wishful thinking cannot, and today that's where most *kibbutz* women work, just as they did before the invention of equality. Even today, with eight per cent of the population engaged in rendering personal services, this negative attitude still crops up. Today's waiters have the same approach as did the pioneers because in essence it isn't proper that one Jew should serve another; this, at least, is how the waiters behave.

One way of circumventing the problem is by sugarcoating the service job: a flight stewardess is no more than a winged waitress, yet her status is far above her ground counterparts in the "Rebecca," "Leah" or "Rachel" Restaurant. Of course, now that a trip abroad is no longer a dream but is within reach of a good portion of the populace, and now that foreign fabrics are no longer among the primary wonders of the world, the stewardess status does not hold the fascination for our choice young ladies that it used to have. Today we are in the Age of Fashion Models.

Elsewhere in the world, service workers are attired in resplendent uniforms, with glittering buttons and miles of gold braid, as a means of bolstering their professional pride; indeed, no image tends to arouse greater respect than that of the doorman at the Plaza or the Dorchester. In Israel, the uniforms, if any, are drab, devoid of stars or gold piping. Mailmen wear khaki; waiters shuffle about in checkered shirts, sometimes clean; cabbies and chauffeurs wear what comes to mind, and are therefore indistinguishable from their fares. And if there's anything that can console the average Israeli for his having to chauffeur silly tourists around, or to wait on or shave stupid customers, it is the fact that they are stupid enough to tip him.

Tipping is another expression of the change that has taken place in the Land of the Pioneers: only fifteen years ago you hesitated to tip the hairdresser or the waiter or the cabbie, lest you offend a citizen with rights equal to yours and as proud as you are. But today you will offend him only if the tip is not commensurate with the esteem that every Israeli bears toward himself.

On Striking Out

AMONG US there are still old-timers, oddballs, *kibbutzniks,* new immigrants, academicians and housewives who never in their lives had to go out on strike, and soon they, too, will vanish, like wild flowers and rare birds and Chinese lilies. Today the strike is an integral feature of our existence. We shall have to learn to live with it, as we have learned to live with traffic tieups, air pollution, *hamsin* hot spells and migraine headaches. Of course, in the event of war, the desire to strike leaves us for many months. You don't idle a plant for a three per cent pay hike or for a revision of job rating—not when you have just finished congratulating yourself because you and your family have come out of it alive, and that your country is still in one piece. But as the threatening clouds of annihilation which hovered above Israel, in May of 1967, disappeared from view and the nation returned to normalcy, back came the strikes.

To the Israeli man-in-the-street it would seem that we hold the world's record for strikes, since everyone in this young country of ours has apparently been on one: post office porters and National Health doctors, bus drivers and sanitation workers, high school teachers and municipal employees, Kol Yisrael engineers and El Al pilots, Zim seamen and T'nuva milk distributors, miners in Timna and stevedores in Eilat and   everywhere. And yet, when we prod the statisticians for substantiation of this gloomy appraisal and the conviction that, with us, striking is as natural as breathing, we discover that our proportion of days lost in strikes compared to working days is no greater than it is in countries which serve us as models from afar, at least— Britain, France, the United States, Italy.

Because our country is so small, however, we do tend to feel the impact of strikes more forcefully. Movie ushers in Jerusalem go out on strike, and the entire country is aware of it. Perhaps this is because we are still laboring under the Utopian image of a state immersed in uninterrupted work and economic wheels spinning merrily. We have to treat strikes the way a cold is treated in a family with many children: if we find, once in a blue moon, that all the children are well, we know that the next cold is just around the first sneeze.

In one respect no statistician can deprive us of our uniqueness: more than anywhere else, here the strike no longer serves as the workingman's weapon. The strike has become a public instrument, without distinction as to class or party, living standards or the stake in socialism. We have had strikes by merchants (against the income tax), by cattle slaughterers (against the Municipality of Petach Tikvah), by purveyors of seltzer (against the Ministry of Commerce and Industry), and by academicians (against everybody).

The strike has come a long way since Creation (the expulsion of the farm hands from the Garden of Eden was a clear case of arbitrary infraction of the labor contract by the landowner), even from the time that it became the weapon of holy war of the toiling masses against the exploiting classes. Strikes as spontaneous manifestations first reared their head in England, at the end of the eighteenth century, as the protest of a semi-religious movement against the replacement of hand looms by machinery. The first organized strikes took place there, as well, first over the issue of voting rights for the workers and later over the right to organize and improvements in wage and working conditions. Striking, in nineteenth century England, France, the United States and Germany was fraught with risk and danger: clashes with the police and the legal institutions, deportation, arrest, expropriation, torture and death. One had to be on the brink of despair, ablaze with wrath or possessed of infinite faith to be part of a strike. We have seen such men in books and films: the Welsh miners, the California fruit pickers, the Lyons weavers—haggard and impoverished, but filled with fury, ready to die, marching in tight ranks against guns, the banner of labor aloft.

The big strikes which attended the rise of the labor movement in the Land of Israel also bore this aspect of courage, class con-

293

sciousness and labor solidarity. Those were the days when the issue was the elimination of cheap and unorganized Arab labor from the employment market, or the right to organize, or the amelioration of working conditions—things which today seem most elementary. There was that big strike in the Froumine Biscuit plant in Jerusalem, in protest of the employment of unorganized female labor, which moved the community to conduct a campaign to aid the 25 strikers (Kibbutz Afikim contributed $7.50, and the Afula Hospital patients refused to eat Froumine products in protest). Construction workers in Petach Tikvah struck against Jewish contractors over the right to organize the industry. In Kfar Saba orange grove workers struck against growers who employed Arab labor; their slogan was "Do not oust the Jewish worker." In all of these strikes the Jewish employers called on the British police to maintain order, and in all instances there were arrests and days of hunger for the strikers. The latter had the sympathy of the entire community, and there was complete solidarity between the leaders of the labor movement and its rank and file. That was thirty-odd years ago.

In a speech attacking the late Ze'ev Jabotinsky, the leader of the Betar-Revisionists (that movement, being opposed to class struggle in the Land of Israel, refused to acknowledge the validity of strikes by members of the Labor Federation, and Betar people were in many cases employed as scabs), David Ben Gurion listed the causes of strikes in 1931, a total of 55: thirteen over arbitrary dismissal without compensation, 13 over employers' refusal to recognize the labor organization and their employment of scabs; 12 over non-payment of wages; six over wage cuts; two over demands for an eight-hour working day; two over offending a worker, and the rest for diverse reasons.

True, nowadays no one goes on strike over the right to organize (on the contrary, members of one *moshav* went on strike for the right to employ unorganized Arab labor), nor, needless to say, do we have strikes over failure to pay compensation or to protest a wage cut; such payments are always made and wages are never cut. However, the causes of today's strikes are basically the same: demands for wage hikes and better working conditions—more economic security, in other words—only today we call it wage adjustment, change in ratings, linkage, wage differentials, augmented compensation. The causes are the same, but prices have gone up. And the reasons today somehow do not seem to be as legitimate and as convincing as they were once upon a time; the goals of yesterday's strikers appear to be self-understood.

With the establishment of Israel a new category of strikes arose—against the institutions of the very state for which we had been striving so valiantly. There were strikes against the rationing policy (furniture dealers and shoemakers struck because they weren't getting raw materials); new immigrants struck against the Jewish Agency (insufficient grants of land, no means of subsistence, transfer to other localities and for the abolition of the shanty towns); the unemployed struck for working opportunities, a reason which today seems to outweigh all others. But all of these strikes faded into oblivion. Now we cannot exactly recall just when did the big strike of the bus drivers take place, when we had to go to work on foot and consequently cried out against monopolies. Then there was the prolonged strike of the high school teachers, which shut down the schools for almost two months and forced a postponement in the date of the matriculation exams. There was the bitter 32-day strike of the engineers, in which the Government threatened to use emergency measures. And there was the worst of the lot: the seamen's strike of 1951, with its overtones of the political strikes in years gone by—fear and cruelty, helplessness and heartbreak. Haifa's Independence Boulevard looked like a battlefield, stones flew from doorways and hoses of water swept the seamen off the decks, wet to the bone, overcome, faces tight and drawn like prisoners of war.

Then, as in any major strike, another factor entered the picture: "the public" . . . the public will not stand for it . . . the public will not put up with it . . . the public is in complete accord with the demands of the strikers, but this is not the way to go about it . . . the public is losing its patience. The sequence is almost always the same, with the public coming on the scene when the strike affects the newspapermen. The public does not deny the right of the workers to strike, but in this particular instance it hurts either the national income or the national weal or the export contracts or the good name of Israel or the future of our children. Every strike hurts someone, obviously; that's its purpose. A strike which hurts no one also concerns no one, and its chances of success are nil.

295

This is why authors never strike, regardless of the straits in which they may find themselves; they can be gotten along without. As for the question of the legitimacy of a strike, it can be yes or no. If the El Al crews strike and attain their goal, obviously the strike was a legitimate one. Absolute justice is, of course, a myth these days.

No one, in our day, loses anything by going out on strike, provided that he belongs to a body that can afford to do it. Even if the demands are held to be excessive and even if the strike is "contrary to the express policy of the Histadrut" (the term "wildcat strike" is not bandied about lightly in trade union circles), and even with the newspapers joining in the hue and cry—as long as there is sufficient pressure behind it, the strike is bound to gain *something:* a few of the goals, swifter negotiations, change in rank or rating. What should the devoted father then say to his son, who wants to know: to strike or not to strike. Strike, my son, but never on Saturday.

At times the strikers seek the sympathy of the public, with declarations in the press or calls to briefing sessions. This search for solidarity indicates an overdose of naivete, since every person weighs the legitimacy of the strike on the scales of his own interests: academicians will look in vain for understanding on the part of the farmers, and no great success will attend the appeal of the carpet loom workers in Bnai Brak to the workers in the Arad chemical complex. In the age of linkage and differentials, solidarity is linked as well.

Only the seven-day strike of the mailmen, in 1962, evoked something akin to solidarity from the populace. This apparently had nothing to do with their depressed wages (the sanitation workers didn't earn any more, yet they didn't gain the support of the public). Our attitude toward mailmen is absolutely irrational. We await our mailman's advent daily, as though he were the bearer of THE glad tidings. If he doesn't stop by, life on that day seems to be devoid of meaning. The mailman brings to us our daily portion of hope; we won't haggle with him.

Every strike is bound to be a confrontation of forces. In Israel, however, it doesn't represent a clear-cut struggle between the two contenders—the employer and the employee, the laborer vs. the capitalist. Today it's a mass brawl, and the blows fall on the leftist and on the rightist. Only on rare occasions is the struggle between the worker and the employer in support of labor principles, as the textbooks have it. More often it involves the workers on one side and the employer plus the trade union on the other, or between the workers and the Histadrut in its role as employer, or between the members of a cooperative and the hired hands. At times the conflict is between the workers and the Government plus the Histadrut. The current distinction is between the wage payer and the wage earner, between those who give the orders and those who have to take them. Nor is the wrath of the striking workers any less when it is directed against a public institution than it is against a private employer.

Strikes, by all against all, point to an undermining of man's attitude toward work as the center of human experience (the slogan "To Labor Is to Live" went out with the machine), as well as to the confusion in the relationship between a laborer and his organization. But strikes also indicate how much of a common denominator the job rating has become in our lives; workers with the same job rating have an economic affinity toward one another, whether they are journalists and sewage engineers, nurses and lab technicians, kindergarten teachers and youth instructors—all are bound by the bonds of the strike.

Israel's children learn the facts of strikes early in life, from their kindergarten teachers, instructors, parents. In the lower grades they are kept out of school by a quarrel between the parent and the principal, perhaps over transfer to another school, or in protest against the second shift or against the location of the bus stop. In the rural areas and in the development towns, immigrant-parents may keep the children out of school in order to strengthen their bargaining power in matters which have no direct connection with their children's schooling: the poor financial situation and difficult housing conditions.

We of the pre-state generation tended to regard the strike as a step which should be considered most seriously, but the youngsters grow up looking at it as an acceptable technique for bolstering a claim, without any affinity to class or labor conditions. One becomes eligible for striking as soon as he attains traditional manhood, at Bar Mitzvah. "My first strike (so will go a diary circa 2000) came when I was fourteen, before my first love . . ."

The Great Day ha: dawned. Students are no longer merely drawn into strikes; they themselves are its instigators: over bad food (Mikveh Israel School) or the poor teaching level in the French Department (Bar Ilan University), a raise in tuition (Bezalel School of Art), a change in the curriculum (Technion) or the system of conferring degrees (Hebrew University). Then, one bright day, the students become the academicians.

Strikes by members of the free professions are a totally unknown phenomenon in the world, chiefly because if the members do unite, it is invariably to further their professional interests, for the promotion of knowledge but not for collective bargaining over working conditions. Secondly, unlike the working class (except in the people's republics), they do not have to fight for status. Here, the seeds of the struggle by the professionals were sown in the days of the Second Aliya, when university graduates came from the Diaspora to become manual laborers in the Land of Israel, when a laborer was worth vastly more than a lawyer and you couldn't get one lathe operator for five Herr Doctors. Today the entire nature of the struggle on the part of engineers, doctors and high school teachers, singly and collectively, is a residue from the heritage of those years and the desire to get away from it.

The categories of strikes have varied with the years, but the types of strikes have remained as limited as always. There's nothing new on the strike front. A warning strike carries hardly any weight; no one pays any attention to it—unless it happens to involve a vital service, such as the supply of electricity or public transportation. A slowdown strike is better, without piece work, without overtime, slow and easy like, but it can get on your nerves. Well, what's left? A full strike. You shut the drawers, clean the machines, and go home. You laugh and joke, like soldiers before they go into action, confident of victory but a bit worried about the enemy counterattack. The meeting's tomorrow morning. God, not at eight; let's sleep a bit longer. And now's the chance to paint the balcony. As far as I'm concerned it will be a week without problems. I have plenty to do.

Sit-down and hunger strikes no longer befit a professional struggle. The sit-down strike may be good for new immigrants, the handicapped welfare cases (against the Jewish Agency, the

Malben rehabilitation network, against social services). This is the weapon of the unaffiliated individual, of the helpless group. The person who adopts the tactic of a sit-down strike has nothing to lose, no concern over his social status. As for the hunger strike, from the viewpoint of strategy it is most untenable. Hunger has no voice. One does not know what goes on in his neighbor's stomach. A hunger striker is always suspected of having sweets in his pocket. And the success formula of the strike is to have it discomfit others, not yourself.

A Time to Age and A Time to Retire

A WELL-KNOWN figure in public life is never to be openly referred to as being "old," regardless of his age. The word should be used, in public, as a noun, never as an adjective. "The Old Man," as a nickname, denotes a man who may be advanced in years but in full command of his powers; on the other hand, prefixing "old" to the family name is considered to be a gross personal insult. Roving reporters, when interviewing a public figure or merely the man-in-the-street, invariably describe the subject as looking "young for his age," since it is unthinkable that anyone should look old for his age, unless he is a welfare client, a chronic victim of bad luck, or the fellow-traveler of low society. The journalistic cognomen is just a cliche; we shall not be able to describe the real signs of age until we have precise published standards as to how people should look at their age, as to what is the age norm of a man of sixty who looks his age: how many grey hairs, if any, he must have in his head, in this benign era of "Wella" and "Clairol," or how many wrinkles may be etched in his face. Gold in a man's teeth indicates not his age but his dentist's, who had obviously not yet acquired the enlightened methods of dental camouflage. Round lenses in metal frames, favored as the symptom of old age by painters depicting nineteenth century folksiness, are worn only by children and Mods. The field of pinpointing elderliness is wide open, and the time has come for our legislative body, which has been in personal contact with the subject for some time, to turn its attention to it.

Terminology referring to the subject is no less confusing. As far as employers and immigrant agencies are concerned, an elderly person attains that stage at fifty-five; according to the press, an elderly person is any unidentified pedestrian killed in a traffic accident. The term is not to be applied to someone you know, certainly not in his presence. No one would dream of calling Hanna Rovina "an aged actress" without inviting an outburst of public indignation. Actually, the term refers to a social status, rather than to chronological age; the elderly are always anonymous.

In Israel, "old" and "elderly" as designations of advanced age are considered to be rather crude and therefore have more genteel substitutes. The *kibbutzniks* talk about the "parents," as do the intellectuals. "Parents Residence" has replaced the traditional "Home for the Aged" and is today an institution testifying to a generation of sons which knew not how to live with its elders. The very old are mentioned in the plural only, chiefly for statistical purposes, while "sated with years" has gone completely out of style. The hunger for years is too great.

Age is a relative matter: in the Israel Defense Forces, a man of forty is considered to be on the threshold of old age, while in the Knesset he would be a pup who is not to open his mouth without permission from his elders. Basketball players are past the hoop at thirty. Politicians, on the other hand, regard seventy as being their peak-of-strength milestone. Age is also what it looks to others. To the twenty-year-olds of the Second Aliya, the 50-year-old socialist theoretician A.D. Gordon appeared quite venerable; today, at that age, he would belong to the younger generation of Kibbutz Degania.

Age as a political instrumentality came into use here only in recent years, with the impact of JFK's presidency and the advent of this peculiar mood throughout the world; with the aging of the Establishment and the impatience of the 50-year-olds, the young men, to wait until they are released from the nursery. The only bothersome obstacle is that the seventy-year-olds, having enjoyed so many years of authority, are disengaged from the helm only with the greatest reluctance on their part. What will happen later, when the youngsters now in their fifties and sixties, having spent so many years waiting, will be asked to vacate their posts? They will have to be removed from their chairs with a scraper.

More than two-thirds of the members of the Sixth Knesset are past 65, yet there are no spokesmen or lobbyists for the interests of the elderly, as there are for *moshavniks,* the Egged Bus Coopera-

301

tive or the Working Women. Apparently the elderly legislators are too busy maintaining the image of their youthfulness to come forth as champions of old age. However, since the percentage of the Israelis above sixty is rising annually, the day will dawn when the political parties will have to be cognizant of them, just as they have already become aware of the aggregate value of the academicians and of the clans in the Arab villages. Most of the parties, from the rightist religious Agudat Israel to the leftist labor Mapam, are headed by elderly men, but they are not interested in problems of old age, which do not affect them personally —neither the retirement age, nor the 120 Pounds per month social security subsistence, nor the final haven in this world, the Parents Residence.

Retirement age, equivalent to an official certification of elderliness, is currently for the most part a matter of social status. Minor clerks retire at 65, and nothing will help them, neither the Lord nor their participation in the jog around Mount Tabor. A manager or foreman may postpone the moment for a few more "good years." Laborers, when the final punch of the clock comes around, must go on pension whether they want to or not, but union officials may go on with their noble work indefinitely. The word "pension" smells of scorn among those still on the job and is reserved for old nags who no longer can carry their weight and must be treated with fatherly tolerance. The kindlier term "he has retired" at least carries with it the illusion that the surgery was performed with the patient's consent.

Retirees in Israel are also less fortunate than their counterparts abroad because they grew old in a land where labor has been a religion, a faith; because they were born to a people which, accustomed to devote its time to *avodat haboray,* the service of God, finds the purposeless passage of time repugnant; because the very thought of being no longer capable is inconsistent with the reputation of our boys for knowing how to do everything, to "put up a house and build a highway," as the song goes. But they cannot escape the injunction of the calendar and the clock, even though they try to circumvent retirement by ferreting out another job somewhere, with regular hours and schedules and no leisure time left. They simply haven't learned to accept old age, and it comes upon them while they are totally unprepared for it. Just as

302

no driver actually believes that he will ever become a traffic statistic, so does no Israeli believe, as long as he feels his strength holding out, that it will happen to him—no, he won't become senile and he won't become a cussed bother and they can't pressure *him* into retirement.

No matter how they at times wanted to escape the time clock, or how they hated the office manager or despised the clerk in the next cubicle, when the day of the farewell banquet comes around (with fine words of appreciation by the supervisor and a gift from the plant and the staff—a gold watch with an engraved inscription, if the others are sufficiently generous and no more original— followed by the vacuum of infinite and dragging time), the period of nostalgia sets in. They go back to their place of work, at first ostensibly to settle matters of compensation, pension, certification; then, later, they drop by out of sheer habit, and longing. The other employees welcome them with a clap on the back (and they're supposed to say "and-what-a-time-*you*-must-be-having"), with news about weddings, births and quarrels, then steal a glance at the watch: *we* can't waste time this way.

The retiree invariably imagines that he has left an unfillable vacuum in his place of work and will be begged to return and help out because, without him, things aren't what they used to be. Nothing is more painful than having a capable and efficient successor, regardless of the status of the position he has inherited. Of course, it would be disloyal to hope that the successor should turn out to be a complete flop (after all, this would mean that years of dedicated toil would go down the drain), but extravagant ability won't do either. A few drops of new blood, yes, but not a complete transfusion. One can even make peace with the idea of a young successor if the latter is inclined to respect the opinions of his elders.

When it comes to the working woman, setting a uniform retirement age involves a good measure of arbitrariness. As for the notion of having the female retirement age antecede the male by five years, it is quite ridiculous. The pioneers were either incorrigible romanticists at heart and, despite all social progress, continued to regard woman as the weaker sex in need of special treatment, or perhaps they were intent on proving the superiority of the male, in that he was capable of retaining his strength while

303

hers was already ebbing. It may also be that our wise legislators envisioned the tortures of the retiree, suddenly thrown into the lion's den of long hours at home, under the nagging supervision of his spouse, and therefore granted him a five-year extension. Or perhaps the 1953 Knesset legislated out of the illusion that a woman of sixty can still run around after her grandchildren, while their mother goes out to work.

However, the grandmother, as the unpaid maid and governess, is vanishing from the Israeli scene. She may still be found—the traditional figure of an indulgent old lady who tells stories as she knits socks—in the complex families where three or even four generations live under one roof, or at least in close proximity. But when the young couple wanders off to where the housing is, or when grandma puts on a semi-mini and takes a full-time job, or when the two generations are set apart, among other things, by two buses (no transfers) in each direction, and when every additional yard of living space is achieved through years of toil—the chances of having grandma around are very, very faint.

Generally, an individual with an eye to the future will not even take in a grandmother, though she may be in full possession of her faculties, because on any day she might become a bed-ridden burden. In order to circumvent this eventuality, the loving children invented the aforesaid "Parents' Residence," built at some distance from the urban centers. The appearance of the elderly makes a tolerably good impression if they are white-haired and wrinkled, somewhat stooped but in fair health and free of the maladies which shock the esthetic sensibilities. But as human scrap, as trembling skeletons impregnated with the smell of urine, how else can they be regarded by their progeny than as a terrible bother and nuisance, to be removed from the healthy members of the tribe?

Old people nevertheless like to live where life swirls all around them, to see the girls go by, the children at play, to listen to the cab drivers address each other and to hear the peddlers chanting their wares. The panorama of life is better for their inner being than trim lawns and social events organized by a professional social worker. This is why the elderly put up such a struggle against being dispatched to a "Residence," even if it is surrounded with greenery and exudes a well-managed atmosphere, because at times this means complete severance from the past, from habits of many years, from everything that was, once upon a time, a shield and barrier against the inroads of time. To the new immigrant, the Malben rehabilitation home in a way supplants the home he has left behind, but to anyone who has grown old in Israel, the transfer to a "Residence" is almost like a partial exit from life. The "Efal Home" or the "Home for the Elderly of Central European Expatriates" may be comfortable and well-appointed, but when you ask yourself: "Would *I* be happy within these walls, in a one-room-and-kitchenette-and-balcony?" everything within you rises in protest: no, this is not for me! I am going to remain active, independent! I won't have to fall back on others! I won't be a burden. People won't have to be tolerant toward me . . . Yes, happy is the man who dies in his own home, surrounded by his books, his paintings, his belongings, his final friends, who dies while he is still himself and not a spirit that brings nightmares to those still on the scene.

Mortality, in Israel, is a strange thing: the young people are much closer to death than are the oldsters. Israel Defense Forces servicemen, regulars or the reserves—and this takes in most men under 45—have learned to live with death, to feel its presence, to see their comrades fall and to know that, in another day or two, someone may be covering *them* with a blanket. Death is real and tangible; it can happen any day, any hour—and many young men in Israel have learned, very early, to accept life as a gift, conditionally. Each day the radio announces the names of soldiers who fell; the newspapers give us the photographs of their young faces, their eyes looking at a world no longer theirs; daily we sense this needless death, initiated from beyond our borders, with grief and helplessness. The Soviets decide to heat up the Suez sector—and ten fall in one day and ten pairs of parents are left to mourn the unrequited promise. And since the country is small and the life of an individual still means something, each death is felt many times over, as a personal loss. After all, how many are we, all together?

As against the almost stoic attitude toward death in battle, the grandiose mourning accorded by the old-timers to the "pillar of the people" from their own midst stands in glaring contrast. Lengthy eulogies, oral or in writing, attend the day of death, the

305

end of the prescribed seven-day period of mourning and on the thirtieth day after burial—with assemblies and memorial meetings, and especially with the unique Israeli custom of death notices, framed in mournful black borders, column upon column, hundreds of inches of costly newspaper space, so that the importance of the dear departed can be tangibly measured by the aggregate space which various organizations have taken, commensurate with their own estimate of the individual.

The old-timers are obviously capable of sensing the pleasure of the departed soul as he listens to the glowing delineation of his deeds and image, but the young ones don't know how to compose eulogies worthy of the name, nor are they capable of overruling reality and tailor the image of the departed to the expectations of the survivors, who are unwilling to arouse the ire of the spirits in the other world, if any such exist.

An outsider witnessing an Israeli funeral for the first time is likely to be jarred by the swiftness of the proceedings, by the visible lack of esthetics; the corpse being buried on a plank rather than decked out in a casket, so that the outline of the body is readily discernible beneath the black cloth draped over it. Compared with our starkly unadorned cemeteries, without lawns and statuary, with a forest of almost identical tombstones—functional, practical, unmitigated by sentiment—the old European cemeteries seem intimate and cozy, a pleasure to abide in. But whoever has witnessed an American-style funeral, with makeup, embalming, gorgeous casket lined with silk and adorned with silver handles, will readily accept the Israeli formula in death: better a burial in twenty-four hours than an infantile cult of the dead.

Some of Our Very Best Friends

WE CHERISH no self-delusion. We know that we have our short-comings—and they are numerous—but with all our eagerness to understand this human race beyond our own tiny province, we still cannot grasp it: why have so many, for so long, hated so small a people, so much? One may despise Jews, but within limits; we ourselves are not enthused about all of our brethren, wherever they may be, but within reason.

Let's look at it mathematically, Comrade Gomulka, if you please: with but twenty thousand Jews to go around for thirty-three million Poles, why, a genuine Polish anti-Semite doesn't even have enough to sink his fangs into! What's more, among these Jews are the sworn communists, the citizens devoted to the people's democracy, most of whom regarded their origin as a regrettable chromosomatic mistake and preferred to nestle in the bosom of Mother Poland when they could have emigrated to Israel, yet there they are, charged with Zionist contamination.

The World Zionist Organization should indeed send a letter of thanks to the Polish Government; at least someone in the world still ascribes formidability to the Zionist movement. We in Israel have long since buried "Zionism"; we wink whenever it is men-tioned and associate it with sterile speeches, honeyed words and political treadmilling. Yet here we see the progressive world endowing it with the attributes of invigorated youthfulness and clothing it with hidden powers that not even Dr. Nahum Gold-mann thought ever existed.

Our trouble is that we are invariably lumped together with all sorts of associates, without our preference even being asked. We, the stalwarts of progress, the disciples of Borochov and Yaari, as true to proletarian solidarity as though it just emerged fresh

307

out of the Marxist oven, we are placed aboard the same ark with imperialists, colonialists, capitalists, reactionaries, fascists and militarists. We are lucky if we even get to be included with the Stalinists, just to be with someone from the left. The Ku-Klux-Klan has us caged with the Catholics, the Negroes and the Pope, while the Germans affiliated us with the Bolsheviks and the Free-masons. The Bolsheviks identified the Jews with the Trotzkyites, the Czechs aligned them with the Germans, the French paired them with the Protestants, the Negroes grouped them with the whites, and the English attached them to the Levantines—each nation and its pet political peeve. In our innocence we hoped that the Nazis would never be bracketed with us, out of deference to the Master Race, but if Hitler would know that we are being made to share the same platform, "Nazi Zionists," his exit via suicide would be of small comfort to him.

Jewish thinking on the theme is subject to two contradictory elements: on the one hand, we are never surprised by any out-cropping of anti-Semitism because, as far as we are concerned, there is something of the anti-Semite in every Gentile, unless he has proven it to be otherwise; on the other hand, we always allow ourselves to be led afresh to believe that some decisive cure for anti-Semitism has been discovered, somewhere: equal rights or enlightenment, liberalism or socialism, the impact of the Holo-caust or sympathy with Israel. Then, as anti-Semitism rears its head again we yell loudly, for anti-Semitism is even more stubborn than the Jew. Once it was believed that anti-Semitism keeps pace with the density of the Jewish population within a given country; now we know that its physical presence is not even required Anti-Semitism, like Ole Man River, keeps rolling along, even without any Jews around.

The meticulous among us tend to differentiate between anti-Semitism and the active hatred of Jews. Anti-Semitism is allegedly the natural antipathy towards Jews, emanating from the fact that they are what they are, that there is—how does one say it?—something strange, odd or queer about them: they are loud and brash, smell of garlic or go about in furs and jewels. One can be anti-Semitic and yet have Jews among his very best friends, partic-ularly if they are as normal as everyone else. Margot Asquith, wife of former British Prime Minister Herbert Henry Asquith, illustrated this very well in her description of Lord Reading: "Rufus Isaacs is one of the best fellows that ever lived. By race a Jew, he is British to the core, neither touchy . . ." One can be anti-Semitic as a non-passing fancy, but the hatred of Jews is already a program and an ideology.

Anti-Semitism has many faces, not all of them vicious. It is the face of a surprised peasant woman, right after the end of the war in 1945: "What do you mean, the Jews are coming back? We thought that all of them had been done away with!" The charming smile of a friend: "But you are really one of us—as if you had never been a Jew." Some of our good friends were anti-Semites, despite so much to the contrary: Lord Balfour, who gave us the Balfour Declaration, a sympathizer with Zionism and a friend of Weizmann, describes, in a letter to his family, a long and tiring weekend at the Sassoon estate in Brighton: "I believe the Hebrews were in actual majority; and though I have no prejudice against the race (quite the contrary) I began to understand the point of view of those who object to alien immigration." Not everyone, however, is as frank as was Thomas Masaryk, first president of the Republic of Czechoslovakia, who came out in defense of the Jew, Hilsner, in a blood libel, and who still said, in his memoirs about his childhood (as noted by Karl Capek): "As for the Jews, I was afraid of them. I believed that Jews had to have Christian blood. You see, all my life I tried not to bring evil upon the Jews, and for this reason people said that I was on their side. But if you ask me at what point I overcame the folk anti-Semitism, I shall tell you: my friend—never, emotionally. Only rationally. After all, my mother raised me to believe the blood libel."

Why should we take exception to De Gaulle, when all he said about us was that we are "an elite people, sure of themselves and dominating" (he said worse things about the English and the Americans), when greater and more enlightened Frenchmen than he—and there have been such—were much less complimentary. Jean Jacques Rousseau said that the Jews were "the lowliest people on earth," and Voltaire declared them to be "a nation of barbarians and ignoramuses which combines lust for gain with superstition." We should not allow ourselves to be overly sensitive, really, else our blacklisting at the hands of the greats of the nations would equal the length of the Jewish exile, from Cicero to Dostoyevsky, especially when they gave vent to their opinions in public and in writing.

But where are those good old days, when one could be an anti-Semite without arousing a hue and cry on the part of Jewish organizations and the world's liberals? Ever since the close of World War II one has to possess real character to practice Jew-hating. A cultured westerner, no more anti-Semitic than may be expected, must watch his tongue, lest he be held responsible morally for the entire Holocaust. But things are getting back to normal; what kind of a world would this be, if the little man couldn't hate his little Jew?

It is not by chance that several of the Popes in the Middle Ages tried to curb the appetite of the Crusaders for Jewish lives, out of genuine concern for the existence of the Jews. To persecute—fine; to annihilate—no. Persecution substantiated the sovereignty of Jesus. From this viewpoint, the Catholic faith is much more rational than the Jewish. We blame none but ourselves for the evils that befall us. We confess our sins and regard our suffering as divine punishment. This is a sick approach, leading to neurosis. It is much healthier for the soul of the universe to blame the Jews for all the ills that visit the world, for it is they who caused Jesus to be crucified and the Kingdom of Heaven postponed until further notice.

Simple Jewish logic holds that whoever hates the Jews for their alleged role in the crucifixion of Jesus should really love them doubly, for having given him life and hailed him as the Christ. On the other hand, were it not for these accursed Jews, one could sin to his heart's content, undisturbed and spiritually unmolested. It is they, the Jews, with their Ten Commandments, who spoil *la dolce vita*. Anyone who comes up with such unrealistic suggestions as "love thy neighbor as thyself" deserves to be hated. Small wonder that some of the most virulent Jew-haters came from the Catholic priesthood! They had it the worst. Just imagine: St. Simeon Stylites spent thirty-six years on a pillar fifty feet high and allowed himself none of the pleasures of life, not even walking or lying down, yet he didn't forgo his hatred for Jews. From his lofty perch he sent a letter of protest to Emperor Julian for his defense of the Jews.

The day comes for every Jew to discover history, and then

310

nothing surprises him any more—not his being accused of wanting in loyalty to the nation among whom he abides, nor the frightened protestations of the "Jews of the Mosaic faith" and their constant declarations of undivided loyalty. This is one of the advantages enjoyed by whoever is a Jew: he can do what is not permissible to the Gentiles—he can scorn the Jew genuflecting before the authorities; he can say publicly that the best reasons for Jew-hatred have been furnished by the Jews themselves. It was Theo-bald, a converted Jew, who informed the world, back in the twelfth century, that it was a Jewish rite to suck the blood of a Christian child on the Passover. Nicholas Donin, another con-verted Jew, wrote the first diatribe against the Talmud and gave it to the Pope. The name might be Johann Pfefferkorn or Otto Weininger or Elmer Berger. Even anti-Semitism has room for Jewish brains, it seems.

Anti-Semitism seeps out of semantics, too. The British lexicon of Mandate days, of blessed memory, describes the self-respecting Arab as "proud," since he rode a noble steed, was hospitable and kept his women in their place. But the word for the self-respecting Jew was "arrogant," the difference between the adjectives being the measure of the right to self-respect that the observer is willing to acknowledge in each.

Now that the Ecumenical Council has finally decided to clear us of the charge of deicide, and now that no longer is any validity being attached to the cherished allegation that Jews are unfit for manual labor, and since it has become abundantly clear that the entire world loves gold and that the smell of garlic abides where poverty does, Semitic or Aryan, there remains only one last emergency ration of fuel to stoke the fires of anti-Semitism: the Jews control the world. In that case, seeing that we Jews control finance and the international press, world trade and science, then why the devil don't we get to reap the profits therefrom? Why do we have to knock ourselves out for every fourth-rate clerk in the Foreign Office or the State Department? Why do we have to invite here all kinds of correspondents, with free trips and kosher meals, just to convince them of the righteousness of our actions? If we do rule the world, let's get something out of it.

Epilogue

WE IN ISRAEL must be incorrigible optimists if, every few months, we can drop some of our illusions, and still have enough left to stand another disappointment in the world's attitude towards us. No matter how realistic we are and how often we repeat that we can depend on none but ourselves, deep inside hope springs eternal that we have been wrong. We simply find it difficult to reconcile ourselves to the thought that we, a mere handful, stand alone against the world.

A few carefree years went by before it finally dawned on us that we, at first 600,000, then a million, and now some 2,400,000, have to contend with seventy or a hundred million Arabs. Then, just as we discovered that this situation was not only tenable but actually not too bad, the front against us widened. The Soviet Union and the People's Republics, the lands of Islam, the Afro-Asian bloc, France, Britain, the United States—they all sit in judgment on us. At times it seems that the sole purpose of all the authority vested in the United Nations is to put us on trial, and the Security Council was created only to condemn Israel, this being the one and only action that the Council has been able to execute efficiently, unanimously and speedily; it's as though the U.N., like the Almighty himself, wants to place all the responsibility for the Commandments on the shoulders of the Chosen People. Other nations are allowed to transgress right and left—they can freely invade, conquer, oppress, subjugate, liquidate, destroy, discriminate; *they* were not charged with implementation of the kingdom of heaven on earth.

Standing in front of the grey glass edifice on the banks of the East River, you are seized with the desire to pick up the clump of bronze at the entrance and hurl it, not like David but like Goliath,

312

right through the windows: by what right, Almighty God, does the Soviet Union presume to sit in judgment on us, less than a year after her strangulation of Czechoslovakia? By what right does India come to condemn us, when the most impoverished among the refugees in Gaza live like kings, compared with millions of India's inhabitants? By what right do the Great Powers exercise moral superiority, or superior morality, if not by virtue of their size? The leviathans have always managed to get away with a morality quite different from what is required of the small fish, but never was this discrepancy so cynically camouflaged as under the emblem of the United Nations.

Only a member of a small nation can genuinely feel impotence and rebellion, in attempting to prove to everyone that being bigger does not mean being better or more in the right. The little man would like to dwell under his little figtree, and the nation would like to do the same on its little patch of soil, and they find it difficult to agree that, in reality, the biblical phrase "this one shall wax large" is mentioned only at the circumcision ceremony, and that small nations must exist as pawns on the chessboards of the big nations. From a certain standpoint, Israel's struggle is the struggle of all the small nations for the right to follow their own destiny, without the need for a permit from the Big Brothers; following Czechoslovakia's surrender, however, there aren't many contenders left to vie with Gulliver. We, too, might have preferred disarmament and the protective wings of some Great Power; it's just our luck that we are unwanted.

One needs no better example of our constant search for some sign of understanding, sympathy or friendship than the quest for quotations in the few newspapers throughout the world which in any way acknowledged the justice of Israel's action in Beirut Airport. One Turkish newspaper understood our mood; a Swiss paper declared that, under certain circumstances, Israel could have no choice but retaliation; two French newspapers went so far as to mention the casualties in Jerusalem's Mahne-Yehuda market place explosion, in which twelve died. Had we found two words of understanding of our position in some newspaper in New Guinea or Burundi we would have quoted them in detail, as well, against the torrent of press criticism in America, Canada, Sweden, Norway, Denmark, West Germany, England, France, South

America, and even Hong Kong; all of them were profoundly shocked by Israel's excessive action.

Now what kind of action, pray tell, would have been reasonable, rather than excessive—reasonable and acceptable? Should we have destroyed an Arab airliner, in some foreign airport, together with its passengers? But then, our luck being what it is, had it been we who decided to do away with plane and passengers at takeoff, the action would have been done according to plan, not partially. Our state of affairs, diplomacy-wise, would naturally have improved, had all the mines, bombs and explosives planted in Israel, during the past year, gone off according to plan and hurt those whom they were intended to hurt. In this area, our capacity to stand firm is working against us, just as it did in the Six Day War.

Lo and behold, the world was so passionately with us, following the Arab attack on the El Al plane in Athens. Fools that we were! Instead of continuing to shovel in sympathy by making it possible for a few more of our planes to be pirated and attacked, we went ahead and upset the apple cart. If we would only have agreed to sacrifice a few Zim ships as well, for good measure, the world's sympathy would have come a-gushing, and had we been even bigger-hearted and allowed a few of the time-bombs planted in movie houses and supermarkets and public places to go off, this sympathy would have overflowed all banks. But it seems that our values are all wrong: we prefer staying alive rather than gaining the commendation of the world.

Some forty states have come into existence since World War II, and none of the births was attended with so much hue and cry— and for so long—as was Israel's, with so many cradle consultants and child-rearing experts. Two Foreign Secretaries or two heads of state meet in Costa Rica or Lesotho, in the course of a world jaunt paid for by their respective taxpayers, and, instead of chatting about the weather or the quality of food in the restaurants, they issue a joint statement of their views on what's going on in the Middle East. Why is it that the whole world insists on having a say in our affairs? Is it to retaliate for our having imposed upon it the burden of One God and his proscriptions?

We would gladly join those thinkers and historians whose conclusion, as they view the progress of mankind in proper perspective, is that the whole world is gravitating toward a globe of giants—no small nations, please; *but,* we have the feeling, deep in our hearts, that it is important that the Jewish people continue to exist. And this is not because of any sense of superiority or some conviction that mankind needs Jews the way bread needs yeast or as seltzer needs carbonation, or that we are the standard-bearers and spokesmen for humanity, but because we have no choice. Now that, after two thousand years of knocking about among the nations, we've had a taste of freedom, and now that we are aware of the difference between subservience and sovereignty, we have only one course—to fight for our future in every way we possibly can.

Anyone who has not as yet acquired proper historical perspective can have it now by emulating the world, free of charge: the U.N. condemns, the Pope expresses sorrow, the Poles are brushing up on Julius Streicher's pearls of wisdom—and suddenly you realize that, except for the founding of this queer State of Israel, little has changed in the course of generations. The Jew is being placed beyond the pale of the family of nations because he is a Jew, and for no other reason, but where previously he was outside the scope of international law, today Israel is the only country against which the "morality" of international law is being directed. If any other nation had done exactly what we have been doing, neither better nor worse, some country would have come to its aid, out of a sense of kinship based on faith or race or language or political belief; someone would have called out: "Indeed, thou art our brother."

At times you get the feeling that you, too, have been clothed in the black vestments of the Eternal Jew, and the fact that you are no longer the Wandering Jew stems from the fact that you are clinging to this land tooth and nail.

The past two years have made the Israelis more Jewish, for they have come to understand that here, too, in their sovereign state, there is no escaping the burden of Judaism; here, too, they must bear the yoke of history, like blocks for the pyramids. Slowly, sooner or later, all of us come to the conclusion that an Israeli is a Jew—only more so.

At times, when the sequence of shocking news—sabotage, shelling, mining, bombing—is too frequent, and the number slain in a

315

given week is even greater than that to which we have become accustomed, after days of tension and as a matter of course, we become terribly tired: how long are we supposed to take it? Many years, apparently, if life can manage to go on as usual: an infernal machine goes off in Mahne Yehuda, and one hour later the stalls are selling tomatoes and quince; a bundle of explosives is discovered in a theatre, and the projector keeps operating—not because we are exceedingly brave or apathetically dulled, but because this casual attitude is the only one which assures some measure of emotional stability. If we wouldn't go on with this version of life-as-usual, celebrating Bar Mitzvahs and putting on fashion shows and brawling on the soccer field, we might never be able to look forward to normal life.

In none of the countries which presume to pass judgment on us and to decide our fate do citizens become accustomed to death at so early an age—and I do not mean accustomed to the death of an elderly aunt or a grandmother or to death in a traffic accident, but to the close and tangible death of classmates, teammates, the fellows in Company "A".

Death, in Israel, isn't something confined to old age. Death is known to the young, and even children are aware of its presence. One cannot live in this country without becoming a pocket-size philosopher, contemplating life and death, whence a man comes and whither he and his offspring go, the chain of life and the purpose of existence, although by nature and preference we would rather pay attention to cake molds or fishing rods, girls' legs and shades of fabrics.

Sophists though we are, we are naive enough to repeat the same mistakes: sparing the holy places in Jerusalem at the cost of our soldiers' lives—and expecting the world to applaud the fact; winning the war and expecting the Arabs to acknowledge our existence, once and for all time; making sure that, in the course of attacking a Lebanese airport, no harm should come to any living creature, and hoping that the world will acknowledge this. And even if our soldiers, in the course of the last-mentioned operation, had handed out chopped liver sandwiches or swept the runways after the blast or destroyed only two aircraft, the world would still deny the Israeli soldier any image of a gentleman, since he is efficient—and efficient soldiers are associated with tough and

316

militaristic peoples. Weak and vulnerable countries also have soldiers, but they, at least, are more moderately successful. The deficiencies in the Arab armed forces, so goes the argument, are proof in themselves that the Arabs really have no intention of annihilating Israel.

At first we believed that our achievements would speak for themselves, with no need for eludication. The nations would come (like Isaiah's End of Days vision), see our *kibbutzim,* the wastelands now fertile, the Arabs abiding peacefully in our midst, and would go away convinced of the justice of our cause. Later, as we became aware that many might not want to embarrass their prejudices by coming here, besides those who insisted on placing their country's minor interests above Israel's major needs, we decided that the way to go about gaining the world's understanding was through the dissemination of explanatory information. In every major capital we would have an Officer of Information who would write letters to the editors and appear on TV—and truth would dawn along the international horizon. Then we realized that one such Officer would not suffice; information, like warfare, is something to which every Israeli would have to lend a hand— students, tourists, experts, wherever they might be; the Ministry of Information thereupon disseminated "Know-What-to-Answer" pamphlets, wishfully thinking that knowledge of the facts would bring on the sympathy. Now that we know that the battle of information is as endless and unremitting as war with weapons, we are inclined to cry out: "The devil with it! Let the world take the noble Al-Fatah adders to its bosom! Let it bemoan the fate of the poor refugees! Let the newspapers adorn themselves with the visage of the self-styled would-be liberator of Palestine, Yasser Arafat! We need the world's sympathy like a hole in the head."

In the current family of nations portrait, the custodians of morality are seated around the banquet board, while we, like naughty children, stand in the corner. We aren't all alone there, by any means; Rhodesia and South Africa are there, too. We make strange corner-fellows, since we had already abolished human bondage when the forerunners of enlightened countries were still dwelling in caves, but we shall have to get used to the idea, abominable as it may be, that we may be more readily under-

317

stood by a regime as it becomes more rightist and less progressive.

In the eyes of the "third world"—the angry and the avant garde, the wave of the future—we simply don't fit into the scheme of things, neither as objects of sympathy nor as the dispensers of this largesse. We are too advanced technologically to qualify as a developing nation, and we are not sufficiently helpless to merit their feeling of smug self-righteousness. Our contribution to dissertations about new and revolutionary trends, the courageous Israeli soldier, the valiant *kibbutznik,* even the pretty girl soldiers grasping their weapons, are old-hat. As equal Partners-in-Progress we are too outmoded; we talk about a land of our own and the struggle for existence, things that went out of style twenty years ago.

Most significant of all, we already have a mission, while one of the principal conditions for membership in the international developing world is the *quest for a mission,* an activity responsible for all the demonstrations, all the rebellions, all tendency toward anarchy and the use of narcotics.

Our hearts bleed for the poor Israelis who yearn to join Red Danny and Professor Marcuse's disciples, to quote reams of Mao from memory and to carry around a photograph of Che Guevara —yet who cannot attain those heights because they come from "a militaristic people." We, too, would definitely love to fight against international oppression and the arms tycoons—if only we could afford the luxury.

Glossary

agora—smallest Israeli coin
aliya—immigration to Israel
alte zachen—old clothes
baclava—honey dipped Arabic strudel
blintzes—healthy crepe suzettes with cheese or other filling
challa—a twist bread glazed with egg yolk, used for sabbath and holidays
farfel—noddle bits
fedayeen—Arab infiltrators
felah(een)—Arab peasant(s)
foile shtik—shenanigans
Hatikva—"The Hope", Israel's national anthem
Hechalutz—"The Vanguard"
heder—old-fashioned Jewish primary school
hubez—bread (Arabic)
Irgun—rightist underground group in days of British Mandate
kashrut—the Jewish dietary laws
kaffiyah—Arabic head dress
kibbutz(im)—collective settlement(s)
kibbutznik—member of a collective settlement
kneidl—dumpling
knaffa—Arabic honey cake
knish—a potato filled dish
kolbiak—Russian meat pie
kugel—noodle, bread or similar pudding baked in a mold
kuskus—North African dish
labaneh—sour oriental cheese
landsmanschaft—Old World home town society
lehayim—"cheers" toast ("to life")
Lehi—extremist underground group in British Mandate days
lekker—a flatterer
lira—Israeli Pound
lokshen—noodles
mahlabia—Arabic milk pudding
matza—unleavened wafer-like bread, mandatory on the Passover
menorah—candelabrum
mititei—small meatballs, Rumanian style
mitzvah, a good deed—commandment

GLOSSARY

moshav(im)—settlement(s) of farmers, wherein each owns his land but marketing and other activities are done cooperatively

nudnik—a bore *ad nauseam*

peetah—flat pocket-forming bun, usually about 5″ in diameter

sabra—a native-born Israeli

shalom—"peace": the Jewish hail and farewell

shikseh—a Gentile girl

shnorer—a handout seeker

shvitzer—a boaster

tzaddik—a saintly person and transmitter of divine grace

tzores—troubles, specifically Jewish

ulpan—crash course in the Hebrew language

yeshiva—academy for Talmudic studies

Zahal—Israel Defense Forces

zalata—salad (Arabic)

zivda—butter (Arabic)

zuica—Rumanian plum brandy

yecki - precise person or braggat

DATE DUE